A Cadre of Experts

An LSAT Novel

By Jacob Erez

A Cadre of Experts
Copyright © 2016 by Jacob Erez. All rights reserved.
Second Edition: April 2016

ISBN-13: 978-1523272921
ISBN-10: 1523272929

Formatting: Streetlight Graphics

All rights reserved. No part of this publication may be reproduced, distributed, or transmitted in any form or by any means, including photocopying, recording, or other electronic or mechanical methods, without the prior written permission of the publisher, except in the case of brief quotations embodied in critical reviews and certain other noncommercial uses permitted by copyright law.

From the Back Cover

More than anything, Alexandra wants to conquer the LSAT and go to law school. Alexandra is an average girl: She doesn't possess any superpowers that will help her on the LSAT, nor does she come from a long line of lawyers. But with Noah, a successful attorney and former LSAT instructor at her side, along with Noah's expert friends and Alexandra's relentless tenacity and laser-focused study, this unique educational fiction tells the story of Alexandra's path to LSAT success, a path that you too can follow.

Ripe with relatable tension and a sprinkle of humor, A Cadre of Experts explains in detail many LSAT concepts and exam strategies, all told through the growing friendship between Alexandra and Noah as they travel the country to consult with various experts in preparation for the exam. We are witness to the emotional rollercoaster that Alexandra rides, sharing the emotional highs of over-confidence and the lows of discouragement—and we see who she is when her journey is over.

Join Alexandra and Noah on their LSAT journey. Meet the Cadre of Experts.

"I'm having a great time with you," he said. "On our LSAT journey."

"Me too, Noah." I wasn't sure exactly what he meant. Then Noah snapped out of his trance.

"We were starting to talk about study methods, right?" Noah asked, as if I had a choice. "I was thinking of driving back to Manhattan, but now that you want to talk about study methods, let me take you to an expert."

Some people collect stamps, coins or records. Some collect comic books, action figures or baseball cards. Some collect cars, games, or Japanese erasers. Noah? *Noah collects experts.*

www.cadreofexperts.com

Acknowledgments

Many thanks to all those whose work, research and support helped me to write this book, my own cadre of experts, especially my aunt Donna Levin, author and J.D. (*and badass mom*), for her insightful advice on the writing process, and for her unconditional love and encouragement.

Thank you to my editors, book cover designers, critics, and friends. Special thank you to my editors Alec Ross, Ellen Brock, and Quata Diann Merit, and book cover designer Tara Mayberry. Thank you to Glendon Haddix for your invaluable insights and formatting wizardry.

And most of all, thank you, my readers. Without you, this tree would fall off the bookshelf and not make a sound.

INTRODUCTION

The LSAT. The acronym—for Law School Admission Test—means a lot to a lot of people. Some people hear it and tremble with fear, or get the jitters from excitement. Others hear it and recall a horrible few months of their lives or a wonderful time where they grew intellectually. What people have in common is that the LSAT is a test they have to take to get into law school. For most people it's hard, and they have to study for it.

Everyone loves a story. And reading a story that can teach you something is an even more pleasurable pastime. The story you're about to read offers the best of both worlds. I did my best to make it a great story, with likable characters and a fun plot, one that is worthy of your time. Woven into the plot and dialog are many of the principles you'll need to know for the LSAT— logical fallacies, reading comprehension strategies, study methods, tips for the logic games, brain health tips and so much more.

But this book wouldn't be complete without addressing an integral element of studying for the LSAT: the emotional rollercoaster ride you take.

The emotional *stuff* manifests itself in a variety of ways. Some people get hyped up and decide that they'll score a perfect 180 and snag a 120% scholarship to Yale (the extra 20% comes in the form of an allowance from the law school, just to thank them for coming). Then they receive a blow after they take their first practice test and score a 125. At that point, some quit, some whine, some study harder, and some say the LSAT is just plain stupid.

Whatever emotional rollercoaster you may be riding on, I hope you find some consolation in the fact that basically everyone goes through the same *crap*. Even Alexandra.

Who is Alexandra? Alexandra is the girl taking the LSAT, taking that emotional rollercoaster, and taking you for the ride; in short, she is the protagonist of this book.

Perhaps the most important part of this book is Alexandra's transformation. The LSAT isn't just a test. *It's a transformative tool.* If you study for it with the right mindset, it will clean up your thinking, improve your reasoning and reading, and make you smarter. In fact, it's been proven to do just that.[1]

This book is full of advice, tips, wisdom, exam strategies and much more. Alexandra benefits from taking notes – and you might, too.

You are about to begin a journey—a journey that will lead you to law school, a legal career, private yachts and limos. Maybe not *your* yachts and limos, but if you're lucky, you'll have friends who have yachts and limos. Even if not, you'll be okay. The legal profession is a noble and lucrative one.

As the wise person said, "A journey of a thousand miles begins with one step." A journey to law school and a legal career begins with one test, the LSAT. And what's a better way to begin your LSAT journey, than with Alexandra and Noah, and their Cadre of Experts.

Jacob Erez
San Francisco,
April 1, 2016

---

[1] Frontiers in Neuroanatomy. August 2012

DEDICATION

This book is dedicated to my grandfather, Marvin Levin, ESQ., the smartest man I know, the head of the cadre. He is my mentor, hero, and friend. And for this, I am truly grateful.

A Cadre of Experts

By Jacob Erez

"Alexandra London!" Professor Williams yelled in a booming voice. "What are the facts in Queen v. Dudley and Stephens?"

"This case is about the morality and legal authority of taking another's life to increase one's odds of survival. In 1884, Dudley and Stephens were in a shipwreck that left them stranded at sea. Out of what they claimed was a necessity, they killed and ate Richard Parker, a 17-year-old seaman who was aboard the ship. What troubled the judges, in this case, was the question of who would be qualified to make such a decision of who would live and who would die, were the principle of taking another's life allowed as a necessity defense to murder. The judges believed that such a principle might evolve into a "legal cloak for unbridled passion and atrocious crime."

"Mr. Andrews! How did the prosecution prove jurisdiction?"

I was off the hook, at least for now. I'd been waiting for this moment—to be sitting in a law school classroom, get called on, and give an excellent answer to the Professor—for a long time. And it just happened.

I come from an average family in upstate New York. I'm the first in my family to finish college, let alone attend law school. I feel confident in my ability to succeed as a law student. My thinking has developed considerably, and I consider myself a critical and deep thinker. But I wasn't always this way. It took a long, complex and multifaceted journey to get to this point. I did it with laser-focused study and tenacity, and with the help of Noah and his cadre of experts.

Let me start from the beginning.

Chapter 1

Red and blue lights flashed through the back window. My heart stopped. Chelsea's mouth dropped open. The sirens started—loud and piercing.

"No way," Chelsea said, shaking her head. "No way, Alexandra, I wasn't even speeding."

"Everything will be okay," I responded, trying to keep her calm. "It's probably just a broken taillight."

Chelsea maneuvered the car over to the side of the road while sucking in noisy breaths. The cop pulled up behind us and the sirens stopped.

This was bad.

Chelsea rolled down the window, and the hot summer air wafted in. In the rear-view mirrors, we saw two cops walk toward the car. On the left, a tall, blond and slim, young looking officer, accompanied by his partner to the right, an older man with messed up hair. The younger officer had one hand holding a flashlight and the other hand on his gun; the older officer had his hands in his pockets.

"Step out of the car, both of you," the younger officer hollered. "Keep your hands up high, where I can see 'em."

"I don't think this is for a taillight," Chelsea said, as we unbuckled.

"Maybe they think you were drinking. Unless your latte had alcohol in it, I don't believe we have anything to worry about."

We stepped out of the car, holding our hands up, blinded by the flashlights.

"What, um, is this all about, officer?" I asked the younger officer.

"Put your hands on the car," he demanded.

The cops frisked both of us. I felt violated. I didn't understand why this was happening. The younger cop cuffed me, and the older cop, taking his time, cuffed Chelsea.

"You're under arrest for car theft. You have the right to remain silent. Anything you say can and will be …"

"What? What is this? I didn't steal this car," Chelsea cried.

"You have the right to an attorney, if you cannot afford an attorney–"

That was an understatement. Chelsea and I couldn't even afford a free attorney.

"Excuse me, officer," I said, interrupting our Miranda rights. "You see, the thing is, um, well, this isn't our car. Not that we stole it; we borrowed it." Damn, that didn't sound right. "It belongs to Chelsea's boyfriend, Randy. I'll call him and we can straighten this whole thing out."

The cops shoved Chelsea and me in their police car and slammed the door.

"Why were you driving around in a stolen vehicle?" the detective asked me after we arrived at the precinct.

"I don't know–"

"You didn't know it was stolen?"

"Um, well," I said nervously, allowing a long pause between each word. I've never been questioned by a police detective.

"Were you involved in the theft as well?"

"*What?*" I had no information for the police—and they hated that.

"For how long did you know that the car was stolen?"

My eyes started to swell. I hoped I wouldn't start crying. "I have no idea what you're talking about. This doesn't make any sense. We were coming back from my birthday party."

"How old are you?"

"I turned 21 yesterday."

"So you two went out drinking."

"No, I don't drink."

"You and your friend are looking at jail time, so you better speak up. How did the two of you end up in a stolen vehicle?"

"Look, I'm sorry about all this," I said, not knowing what else to say.

A Cadre of Experts

"You're sorry for stealing the car?"

I started to cry. Randy, Chelsea's boyfriend, came running into the police station.

"Alexandra, where's Chelsea? Is she okay? What's going on?"

"And who are you?" the detective asked Randy.

"I'm Chelsea's boyfriend. I gave her my car for the evening."

"Your car? So why was it reported stolen?"

"I didn't. Why would I do that?"

"The car they were driving tonight was reported stolen, son. Either the car they were driving isn't yours, or your car is a stolen car. Give me your license. I'll run it through the system, and if it matches the car, then the three of you are free to go."

"Well you see officer," Randy said, "the car is registered under my friend's name." We found out later that Randy registered the car in his friend's name because Randy's insurance rates were ridiculously high.

"This friend of yours must have reported it stolen," the detective said. "Why would he do that?"

"Maybe because of the tickets," Randy said, looking down at his feet. "I have a lot of unpaid parking tickets on the car and my friend was getting the bills."

"I can't believe you'd put Chelsea and me through all this, Randy. We've been arrested and put through hell because you didn't pay some stupid parking tickets."

"Get this friend down here," the detective said. "He'll have to revoke the report and claim the car. Otherwise, these two will have to stay here the night."

Three hours later Chelsea and I were released, but we still had to appear in court a month later. Now was time to look for a lawyer we could afford.

We arrived at the Manhattan Supreme Court. Standing outside and staring up at the columns—you could feel the authority. If there was a higher power that had created the earth and left the ingredients for the installment, fabrication, molding and casting of stone into artistic forms to be worshiped, humankind had certainly done a good job using that bequeathed breadth of raw earth to instill something of equal power that created it.

"Docket number 2543289 ..." the clerk called out.

We stood, as did our lawyer.

Chelsea and I had found an attorney, Naomi, who was willing to help us out for a relatively small fee. She understood our position, the mix-up, and our lack of funds. We spoke to her over the phone and met her for the first time less than an hour before the hearing. She came prepared with her notes and motions and briefcase, and she was well dressed too.

"Your honor, this case was a simple misunderstanding," she said, gazing directly into the judge's eyes. "You have the motion in front of you, your honor. Motion to dismiss for an improper criminal complaint."

"I see," the judge said. "It seems the owner of the car recanted his original report of the car theft. Still, your clients were driving the car without clear written permission from the owners. I'm dismissing the theft charges and issuing a $125 fine."

The judge sounded his gavel.

"It's a slap on the wrist," the lawyer whispered to us. "They went way out on a limb arresting you. Letting you go without at least a fine would look bad."

"We shouldn't have to pay anything," I whispered to Naomi. "We did nothing wrong."

I would have loved to get up there and argue with the judge, but with my arguing skills, the judge may have just sent us to Sing Sing.

That night in the precinct and the subsequent court hearing changed the course of my life. I had felt helpless, useless, and scared. When we met the lawyer for the first time the morning of the hearing, I saw the lawyer as the only person in the world who could help us, and she probably was. I felt gratitude towards the attorney; but there was something more.

In the days that lead up to my court hearing, I would lay awake at night and imagine how terrible my situation would be if I actually had stolen the car—or if I had been slammed with heavier charges. I felt like there had to be more people like me out there—people who were up against way more than they deserved. The system was harsh; I wanted to help people in that situation.

Without knowing anything about the law, or how it worked, I knew at that moment I needed to become a lawyer. I had no idea how the law worked, but I wanted to find out.

The next day, I went to the bookstore below my apartment and bought every book they had on one specific topic: the LSAT, which stands for "Law School Admission Test."

I was going to law school. It turned out there are no prerequisites to get into law school—all you need is a bachelor's degree, in any subject, and you have to take the LSAT. This winter I would study full time for the LSAT. I had some money saved from my waitressing job, so I'd take off work, put my last few college credits on hold, and study full time for the LSAT.

I bought books about law school admissions, law school reviews, and, of course, a pile of LSAT study guides. I even bought some brain games books. I wanted to attack this test from all directions, to make sure I'd get into a top school. If I was going to be a lawyer, I wanted to be the best lawyer possible.

Winter came, and I started to study. The books advised taking a practice test, meaning that I had to take a full five-section exam, with the same time constraints you're under on the actual test day. Out of the five sections, only four are scored. The fifth section, although it can be any of the five on the real exam, is the experimental section. On a scale of 120-180, I scored a 134.

Every day I sat at home and read my LSAT books, did practice questions, and researched law school admissions online, occasionally Googling terms such as 'LSAT tips,' or 'LSAT techniques,' or even 'LSAT secrets.' There seemed to be a great deal to it, but I expected that I'd pick up on it eventually. I looked into LSAT courses and tutors, although I didn't believe I needed that stuff. After all, I had the books. And the LSAT is a multiple-choice test; how hard could it be? Maybe a few weeks before the test I'd hire a tutor for three or four hours.

After about three weeks, I started to get bored studying at home and decided to venture out to the city and study in the library or occasionally a coffee shop. I developed a routine. At 7:00 a.m. I'd work out at the gym for an hour—mostly cardio—shower, and then hit the library.

I stopped every day at a coffee vendor on the street corner of West 60th and Broadway. The owner of the coffee stand was a nice guy named Lloyd. He had a variety of coffees, but I usually stuck to my morning latte.

About a week into this routine, I went to the gym and stopped at the coffee vendor as usual. It was a cold, rainy and windy Tuesday morning. I had on gloves and my favorite scarf, and I was wearing my toastiest coat.

Only this time, *I met Noah*.

Noah was also buying a latte. He projected confidence. He looked rugged and neat at the same time. His hair was obviously styled, but he had full stubble, shaved just the right amount to make him look amazing. He was well dressed, sporting a simple black suit and tie. I figured he was in his early thirties. The faint creases on his forehead suited him.

Noah noticed the LSAT books I was holding and nodded.

"Taking the LSAT, huh?"

"Um, yes," I answered, not sure what why he was asking. Was he going to be one of those people who told me not to waste my time with law school? Or would he say that he, too, had taken the LSAT, but decided it wasn't fair and dropped it?

"And how's it coming along?" Noah asked.

"It's alright. What's your acquaintance with this notorious exam?"

"I'm an attorney. I double majored in computers and philosophy in college. I tutored students for the LSAT for about five years. And of course, I took the LSAT myself and scored in the 99th percentile."

Noah took a sip of his coffee, careful not to spill it on his scarf. Only a lawyer would wear such a fancy scarf.

"Hey Noah, that will be $4," Lloyd said.

Noah handed Lloyd two $100 bills. "Put the change on the free coffee account."

Noah handed me his business card and pointed to his office address.

"Why don't you come to my office tomorrow morning?" he asked casually. "We can talk about the LSAT and law school."

A Cadre of Experts

He certainly had the credentials to give me some tips.

"Sure," I answered, "see you then. By the way, what is the free coffee account?"

"Oh, that. Well during the winter, I give Lloyd some money so that he can give away a few cups of hot coffee every morning to some homeless folk. It can sure get cold in the winter, so we have this little arrangement. Anyway, I'll see *you* tomorrow."

Noah's 30th-floor office in midtown Manhattan was modern and well decorated. I was greeted by the powerful scent of wood polish. Four black leather chairs sat in the center of the reception area. A leather couch was against the wall. In the center of the seating area was a small wooden coffee table with a tasteful arrangement of sweet-smelling peach roses. On the other side of a set of double doors was a meeting room with a long table that was polished to a shine.

I walked up to the secretary, feeling out of my element and severely underdressed. She greeted with a smile.

"You must be Alexandra," she stated.

The secretary told me to take a seat, and that Noah would be right out. I noticed a sign on the wall that read, "Success is the only option," with a picture of a person jumping from one cliff to the next, with the sun setting among some clouds in the background. It was signed by Brian Mullen, the famous hockey player. It seemed that Noah lived by that motto—his office was situated on prime real estate.

Noah opened the door to his office. He stood there with a big welcoming smile on his face. I followed him into his office and sat in a chair directly across from him.

I took a moment to take in my surroundings. A cozy seating area near the back of the room consisted of a brown leather sofa and chair that looked much more inviting and lived-in than the seats in the other room. Most impressive was the panoramic view of the city from the crystal-clear windows. The whole town skyline was spread before me. Noah looked out the window for a few seconds. He turned around and sat in his big leather chair.

"So, you want to be a lawyer, Alexandra? Good luck!"

I wasn't sure if Noah was being cynical. "Thank you, Noah."

"Here's the big question I'm sure you've been asked before; why do you want to be a lawyer?"

"Well, I majored in liberal arts. I started off with pre-med, but I quickly learned that I'm horrible at science. I took classed in psychology, social work, even mathematics. None turned out to be my passion."

"One second, Alexandra."

Noah asked his secretary to bring us coffee and wrote himself a quick reminder on a sticky note as he dictated to himself, to remember to call the assistant district attorney in Queens and tell her that he would stipulate to the blood alcohol levels of his client Mr. Schwab. He then tapped his pen on the sticky note about five times. He was a lefty.

"Did you consider other avenues besides law school?" Noah asked me.

"I was pre-med for a while, probably to show everyone I was just as brainy as my oldest sister. She's a physician, and she's brilliant. College didn't do much for my self-esteem, though. I still feel mediocre when it comes to intellect."

"You seem bright. Don't give yourself such a hard time."

"What sort of law do you practice?" I asked.

"I do a lot of high-profile criminal cases and some probate and estate planning as well," he said quickly, "although my passion is helping mothers get what they deserve in divorces—I take on pro bono cases now and then. Often the husband hires a fancy attorney and the wife, who doesn't want to fight, just gives in. It's not right, you know?"

No, I didn't know. I'd never tied the knot myself, and my parents divorced when I was young, so I knew nothing about the process. But if I wanted to be a lawyer, I figured, I'd better not seem ignorant. I nodded; it was the best I could do.

"What kind of law are you interested in practicing?" Noah asked me.

I frankly had no idea, but I pretended to know what I was talking about. "I'm not sure exactly, either criminal or corporate."

Noah chuckled. "Those are two different types of law. Have you ever been exposed to what a lawyer does, on a daily basis?"

I'd heard that one before. Why couldn't people give me a break?

A Cadre of Experts

"Um, no, but I thought you could help me with that," I said, kicking the ball back into his court.

"Sure, we can talk about that. How about breakfast?"

In the lobby, we noticed some movers in the entrance of the building hauling a huge couch off a truck and through the doorway.

"I think someone's moving into the vacant office below mine," Noah said.

"Judging from the size of that couch," I said, "those guys must be really strong. Or maybe the couch is just really light."

Noah stopped in his tracks. He looked straight into my eyes. I wasn't sure what I'd said to make Noah, who seemed like a rational person, stop so abruptly.

"Alexandra, if you're to deliver the goods on the LSAT, you must alter the way you think and talk. What you just said was a *logical fallacy*, and there's no room for those on the LSAT."

I'd studied some logical fallacies, but I wasn't sure which one Noah was referring to. Noah didn't leave me in suspense.

"I know that in real life, nobody would ever point this out. But as a future attorney, you can't make logical errors, however minor. What you said was that either these men are very strong, or the couch is very light. But maybe the men are not very strong, and the couch is not that heavy. There's something called the middle ground, that you left out, as one of the possibilities. And that is a *logical fallacy*, called the fallacy of the excluded middle."

"I get it," I said, putting my index finger to my temple. "If I don't train my mind to think logically all the time, studying for the LSAT will be useless. If I continue committing everyday logical fallacies, the studying won't have a big enough impact on my thinking."

"You took it a step further," Noah said, "which is where I was heading."

He seemed impressed, which was awesome. I figured I was pretty much off the hook, but *that* was just the start.

Chapter 2

Midtown Manhattan sported many little cafés, but none was quite like the LSAT Café. It had standard café-style seating: four small chairs, red cushion on black metal, all arranged around a round white table. The ceilings were higher than normal, and cream paint coated the walls. Plenty of light flooded into the café through wall-length, arched windows. Hanging from the ceiling were golden light fixtures each adorned with five spherical lights. Against the walls were the booths. They always filled up first.

The bitter aroma of coffee filled the diner and the environment was relaxing. We sat in the booth closest to the entrance.

"This is a charming café," I said, "maybe I should come here to study for the LSAT."

"Are you certain about that?" Noah asked quietly.

"What do you mean?"

"The environment here is noisy; it might not be the best choice for a place to study. Maybe try some other places that have less noise so that you can get used to deep concentration."

The waitress took our order. We both ordered coffee and eggs; mine scrambled, Noah's Benedict.

"In the coffee shop, you have loud music, the waiters asking you if you need anything every five minutes. In short, a café is not the ideal place to study. However," Noah continued, "it is a perfect place to make plans."

"Plans about what?" I blurted. Noah smiled.

"Benjamin Franklin said, 'By failing to prepare, you are preparing to fail.' Yogi Berra said, 'If you don't know where you are going, you'll end up someplace else.' And my favorite saying is from Abraham Lincoln:

'Give me six hours to chop down a tree, and I will spend the first four sharpening the ax.'

"You have to make an LSAT study plan. What books are you going to use? How many hours a day you are going to study? How often are you going to take a practice test? You'll require a weekly schedule up to and including what to do the week before the test and on the morning of."

"Now I see what you're saying."

"There is one caveat, though," Noah continued. He seemed to handle everything like a lawyer. A lawyer can't give advice without clarifying the exceptions. "Again, this is a quote, this time from President Eisenhower. 'In preparing for battle, I have always found that plans are useless, but planning is indispensable.' Plans often don't work in real life. We create a plan, but later, we may see it's not working. Then why is planning indispensable? Because we can always change our plan as we go along. But without having a plan in place, we won't recognize if we're heading in the right direction."

Noah cleared his throat. "Let me give you an example. Jets are equipped with a useful device that tells the pilot whether the jet is going up or down. In high-speed maneuvers, when the jet is twirling and spinning, the pilot can lose his sense of which way is up and which way is down.

"Your plan, be it for the LSAT, law school admissions or anything else, works in the same manner this device works for pilots. It lets you know which way is up and which way is down."

"Okay," I said.

"Okay is right, now where are my Eggs Benedict?"

Less than four seconds later the waitress arrived with our order.

"Let's get into the nitty-gritty of planning. Always focus on your end result. When you plan a road trip, for example, you start with your final destination in mind. Once you know where you're going, you can plan what to do on the way.

"Here, you know your goal is to get into law school with as much scholarship money as possible. So that's your end result. Work backward in time and accomplishments. Say you're scoring 155 on your practice exams. You've set your goal for a 168, so you need a 13-point increase.

You're taking the June exam, and it's now January. That's five months to gain 13 points. That means you need to improve 2.6 points each month, which is doable.

"Next, you need to decide where you're more likely to get those 13 points. Should you work more on the logic games? You can squeeze quite a few points out of those games, and you like the games, so it makes sense to invest a substantial portion of your time into the games. Of course this is just an example.

"A month goes by, and you take another practice test. You score a 156, a one-point gain from last time. It's disappointing, but one of two things could happen. For many LSAT students, it takes time for the LSAT takes to 'click,' at which time students see a jump in their score. If, however, three months go by and you're still scoring around 156 or 157, it's time to reevaluate your goals. You'll have to make some decisions. Do you change your studying habits? Hire a tutor? Decide to take the exam at a future time? These are all important decisions, but you'll know exactly what your situation is because of the plan. Without it, you'll be like Alice in Wonderland when she asked the Cheshire Cat which way to go."

"Enlighten me."

"When Alice asked the cat which way to go, the cat responded that it depended a great deal on where she wanted to go. Alice said she didn't care where, to which Cheshire Puss replied, 'Then it doesn't matter which way you go.' I can't name every scenario you might encounter. But I will say this: don't make plans and decisions on your own. It's always important to have a fresh set of eyes. We have mental blind spots that are hard to spot without someone else's input.

"This person doesn't have to be an LSAT tutor or a lawyer, although it would be smart to have someone with relevant experience serve as your go-to person."

I took a few bites of my eggs, thinking about what Noah had said. It made sense to make plans, and to think about the end result and working backward made sense too. I started to add sugar and milk to my coffee, not thinking Noah would have something to say about *that*.

"It's well documented that sugar affects the brain in a negative way,"

A Cadre of Experts

he said. "I'm not saying to cut sugar out completely, but do try to limit it as much as possible."

"I've read some of those studies, and I agree," I replied. "When I drink soda, my brain feels foggy. But coffee is my one guilt-free pleasure."

"For the LSAT, however, you should focus on your brain health. The rule of thumb is: Whatever foods are good for your heart are good for your brain."

"Are you sure? Nuts like pistachios are good for your brain, but they also contain cholesterol, and that can't be good for your heart."

Noah laughed. "You committed the greatest logical fallacy, *of all time*."

I wasn't sure how pistachios could be a logical fallacy.

"What I said was, whatever is good for your heart, is good for your brain. In logical terms that would be 'If A, then B.' If (A) it's good for your heart, then (B) it's good for your brain."

"Right."

"What you inferred, however, was 'If B, then A', or 'if it's good for your brain, then it's good for your heart.' It is a fallacy to infer the inverse.

"The only thing you can infer from an 'If A, then B' statement is: 'If not B, then not A.' In our case, the only thing you can infer is: If something is not healthy for your brain, then it is not healthy for your heart. And back to your inference. Pistachios are indeed full of cholesterol, so they are not healthy for your heart, but that doesn't mean they are not healthy for your brain. Saying that would be like saying 'If not A, then not B. ' If it's not healthy for your heart, then it's not healthy for your brain. Not everything that is not healthy for your heart is not healthy for your brain, but whatever is healthy for your heart *is* healthy for your brain."

I thought for a moment, trying to process all the information Noah was feeding my mind. "Let me see if I get this. Let's say 'All girls like blue.' I'm translating that to 'If A, then B.' So, if you are a girl, you must like blue."

"Go on."

"So the wrong type of inference—"

"The inverse."

"The inverse, thank you, would be 'If B, then A', if you like blue, you must be a girl. That's obviously wrong because boys too can like blue."

"Continue."

"But what you can infer is: 'If not B, then not A', if you don't like blue, then you are not a girl."

"And that is called the *contrapositive*. So important."

"But what if I'm a girl who doesn't like blue?"

"We're accepting the statement as true, so, there is no such possibility, in this little hypothetical world."

"I get it. So, what exactly *is* healthy for your brain?" I asked, eager to return to the topic.

"What I am I, a brain scientist?" Noah asked, smiling. "How about this? For homework, research online and make a list of the most important habits for brain health. Bring it here tomorrow morning at 8:00 a.m. sharp."

"Sounds like a plan."

"Oh, and for homework, translate the following into logical terms: 'If you bring the list, I'll buy you a cup of coffee.'"

"Will do."

"There's also one important tip I want to give you right off the bat. On the logical reasoning questions, always read the question stem before the stimulus."

"Why is that?"

"Do you read a manual for your phone the same way you would read a letter from a friend?"

"I haven't received any letters from friends since I was eight."

"You get the point."

"If I received a letter from a friend, I'd read it much more carefully than the manual for a cell phone."

"And not only would you read one more carefully than the other— you'd read them *differently*. You might scan a manual for important points while a letter from a friend you'd probably read word for word. And you'd read the two differently only because you knew ahead of time what they were.

"When you read the question stem first and see that you're dealing

A Cadre of Experts

with a question asking you to identify a flaw, you'll actively look for the flaw in the argument. If you're asked to find the main point, you'll look for that.

"Let's say you're dealing with a flaw question. If you don't read the question stem first, then the argument won't make sense to you because of the flaw. You'll sit there scratching your head, trying to understand the argument when in fact it's simply a bad argument to begin with."

"**When you know what kind of question it is, you know *how* to read it**, since you'll read every question type a bit differently," I said.

"Perfect. By the way, as soon as I get back to my office, I'll email you a PDF with a list of the all the logical fallacies you'll need for the LSAT."

"Sounds great."

Noah had to appear in court that morning. I couldn't imagine how he could be so calm less than an hour before a hearing. Maybe experience helps. I asked if I could come to court to hear him argue, and he agreed. Asking him was a courtesy—the courts are open to the public.

At precisely ten o'clock, the court was in session, and the judge ordered the prosecuting attorney to call his witness. Then it was Noah's turn to cross-examine the poor guy. I say poor because Noah didn't cross-examine him. He destroyed him.

"Mr. Adams, you said you were working the morning shift at the bank the morning it was robbed?"

"Yes."

"And you were able to make a facial identification?"

"Yes."

"The robbery took place at 9:30 a.m., according to the bank's cameras, correct?"

"Yes."

"But you didn't clock in until 10:00."

"Well, um ..."

"If you weren't at the bank at 9:30 when the robbery occurred, how could you have made a face identification?"

"I started my shift that morning at 9:00 a.m. I forgot to punch in when I got there, so I punched in at 10:00 a.m."

"And after the robbery, did business continue regularly at the bank? Or was the place swarming with cops? Didn't the CEO of the bank herself show up shortly after the robbery took place? Is it safe to say that the rest of the day was hectic?"

"Yes, there were police and all that. We were all in shock."

"You have a coworker, a Mrs. Miller?"

"Yes, she's the manager."

"She was quoted on the news as saying that the workers were upset that the bank has an open teller counter, and no bulletproof glass, like many other banks use. Were you one of the staff that felt that way?"

"Objection, hearsay."

"I'll allow it," the judge said. "Mr. Brill please answer the question."

"Sure, our safety is important."

"Can you tell me how, at a time when your bank is swarming with police, the CEO is present, all the workers are upset, including yourself, and somehow you all of a sudden remember you didn't punch in? Had you ever forgotten to punch in before that day?"

"Yes, a few times."

"And did you get paid for those shifts?"

"Yes, we have a manual time sheet as well."

"So it's safe to say you would have been paid for that shift anyway, and yet out of all the activities you might do after the robbery, such as call your wife or talk to the news reporters, the one thing you made sure to do was to clock in?"

"Well ..."

"Isn't it true that you were called in after the robbery that day to cover for the teller who was actually robbed?"

"Objection, assumes facts not in evidence," the prosecutor hollered.

"Sustained."

"But since that teller was too shaken up and refused to testify, the bank asked you to pretend you were there and then come today to testify against my client."

"Objection, your honor. Speculation."

"Sustained."

"No more questions, your honor. I think this witness's credibility, or lack thereof, is evident to everyone."

I was impressed, and it seemed that the jury members were too. I started to think about keeping my eyes on the prize. Right now I'm studying for the LSAT. But I'm spending all this time and effort studying for the LSAT to get into law school, and that is to get to a point where I could do what Noah was doing right now. I wasn't sure I wanted to be a criminal defense attorney, but I wanted to practice law. In a sense, all my LSAT studying wasn't for its own sake. It was an end to a means.

After court, besides seeing Noah in a different, even more dignified way, I shared my thoughts with him. We went outside and stood at the top of the courtroom stairs, observing the people walking up and down the steps.

"Of course, each part of the journey is its own entity," Noah explained, holding his hands in front of him as if he was holding onto an invisible ball of energy. "But they all lead to the same place. You have to do well at each stage, but I believe that keeping the end result in mind helps to keep you on track and stay motivated."

"I have to say, Noah, I was impressed by your performance today. That guy didn't know what hit him."

"I hope the jury agrees with you."

"I'm sure they will."

"So you still want to be a lawyer?"

"Of course. Why do you ask?"

"Many people want to go to law school without having any idea what lawyers do, except what they've seen on TV. What went on in that courtroom is only a fraction of what I do, and it's not what most attorneys do. Many attorneys never appear in court."

"What exactly *do* lawyers do?"

"A bunch of things. You know what, though? I'll scribble down a few thoughts and share them with you. I'm not going to get into the nitty-gritty of what lawyers do on a daily basis, which can be a lot of legal research and writing, depositions, client intake, negotiations and the like, rather I would like to share with you the overall goals and objectives. Let me start by giving you one idea."

I grabbed my iPhone and started typing.

What Lawyers Do #1: Know the law

"First of all," Noah began, "Lawyers know the law, and the best ones can take them to the limit by pushing them as far as possible. At the most fundamental level, lawyers apply common sense to everyday and extraordinary situations alike. A lawyer's responsibility is to use common sense in every circumstance and case. Whether it's a constitutional law issue such as human rights or a common traffic violation, lawyers need to deal with conflicts from all walks of life. Their job is to resolve issues between people and find common ground that will work for both parties. Interpreting the law, using legal principles or protecting the defenseless, they're all in the lawyer's hands."

"I'm assuming there's a lot of other work lawyers do."

"Like I said, I'll put together a list of ideas and hand them over to you, one at a time."

"Sounds like fun Noah, I can't wait."

Today, I did four logic games, reviewed them, and then did them again. I did 50 logical reasoning questions, untimed, and four reading comprehension passages, and then I reviewed them. I never move on until I completely understand why I got something wrong. Then I review those questions a few more times, so that I'll never make those mistakes again.

Chapter 3

Noah's ability to motivate people was remarkable. All right, maybe not *people*–maybe just me. I'm not sure exactly what it was about the homework assignment, but it challenged me. That night I researched brain health until the small hours of the morning.

"Good morning, Noah," I said, smiling. "Someone owes me a cup of coffee."

I had arrived early that morning at the LSAT Café to go over the list once more so that I could speak about it confidently. Noah walked into the café five minutes later, his scarf wrapped around his neck as if someone had tried to strangle him with it. He held his briefcase in one hand and his cellphone in the other. He looked eager. Was he eager to hear about my research?

Noah unwound his scarf. "Did I say I would buy you a cup of coffee?"

"Um, well you did say if I bring the list, then—"

"If I recall correctly, Alexandra, all I said was that for homework, you need to translate the sentence 'If you make the list, then I'll buy you a cup of coffee' into logical terms. I didn't actually say I would buy you a cup of coffee."

My mother warned me about lawyers.

"Alexandra, it's time you take some lessons from the LSAT and apply them to real life. Logical inferences are a part of our daily communications. I won't promise you much, but I will promise you that if you use the precepts of logic in your everyday relations with people, your life will be more comfortable, and the road will be smoother."

"I'm starting to think that **studying for the LSAT can have a much bigger impact on students than just getting into law school.**"

Noah smiled and nodded. He had a dimple on his right cheek.

"It may have sounded like I made an offer to buy you coffee, but I didn't. You know that a cup of coffee isn't the real issue here. And of course you don't need to overanalyze everything you hear. As the joke goes, two psychologists are sitting for lunch when a third psychologist walks past them and says 'Good afternoon, gentlemen.' The two psychologists at lunch look at one another, and one says 'what do you suppose he *really* meant by that?'

"But do need to listen carefully enough that you understand what people, ads, contracts, the law, or anything else, are indeed saying. Take the logic games, for example. A rule says 'A is not before B.' At first, that might sound confusing, but all it's saying is 'A is after B.' That's an easy one, right?"

"Sure."

"This comes up quite often on the logical reasoning sections too. The LSAT will present you with an argument, and ask you to spot the main point of the argument. Rest assured, the main point will be cleverly hidden, but it's there."

"I've come across those types of questions. What I noticed is that on main point questions, the main point is not necessarily the last part of the stimulus, as is the case with many arguments."

Noah nodded. "I believe that's true, but I'd be careful not to stack the rules into neat piles, as in 'main point questions are this way', and 'assumption questions are that way.' Some rules are consistent, but many are not. It may help at first to categorize, but you need to let go of that crutch."

"I get the idea," I said. "And I think that is an advanced tip for LSAT prep: **"Categorize at first, but learn to be flexible as soon as possible."**

"Well said, Alexandra. Back to the main point questions. A stimulus says 'Mayor X has impressive characteristics, including an impeccable record of being truthful. Only candidates who are truthful are worthy of becoming our town's mayor. The only other candidate for the mayoral elections is Mr. P, who has a bad reputation when it comes to telling the truth. Every voter should vote for the candidate he or she believes to be most worthy.'

"While the argument didn't explicitly say to vote for Mayor X, that is what the argument leads us to conclude. There are more advanced examples of this concept, and you'll come across some of them while studying, but meantime, let's order something to eat. I'm starving."

As if on cue, the waiter brought menus. Noah excused himself to go to the restroom, but not before ordering eggs and home fries, and a cup of coffee. He seemed obsessed with coffee.

"I'll have a stack of buttermilk pancakes," I said, "with a side of bacon."

"Anything else?" the waiter asked.

"Anything else," I sounded out leisurely, all the time looking at the menu, "Yes, there is something I want to ask you, but let's keep it between us."

"Certainly. What is it?" The waiter probably wasn't used to being asked confidential questions this early in the morning.

"Do you know Noah for some time?"

"Yes, he's been a regular here for a few years, since he opened a law firm in the building."

"And have you seen him come with other, um, women?"

"Not in the last year, ever since his wife passed."

"I'm sorry to hear that," I said. "I-I didn't know that."

"Let me get you those pancakes …" The waiter retreated into the kitchen, through those tall double doors, one for going in and one for coming out.

"Noah, I don't think I know what your marital status is," I said to Noah as he returned from the bathroom. He stared down at the table.

"I was married to Stephanie for eight years, she was a terrific woman. We met and got married in law school. About a year ago, she fell sick and passed away. So I guess that is my marital status."

The waiter brought out my order, telling Noah that his order would be out most *ricky-tick*.

"I'm so sad for your loss. I hope I didn't hurt you."

"Not at all. How are your pancakes?"

I was waiting for the waiter to bring Noah's meal before I started.

"The bacon looks good," Noah commented.

"Yeah, it does. Would you like some?"

"Oh no, I don't eat pork, I'm Jewish. No pork–and attending

synagogue on Yom Kippur–that sums up my Jewish practices. So … where's that research you promised me?"

"I did a lot of research last night. Here are the results."

Brain Health Tip #1: Exercise

"Exercise is the number one tip for brain health. Exercise does a lot for you regarding blood circulation, energy, focus, and more. Exercise seems to lock in the ideas you've learned and strengthen the connections in your brain.

"Exercise reduces stress and helps you focus. When we get nervous, our breathing shortens, which is a problem for the brain that needs oxygen to function. Strong cardiovascular health ensures that, even when we're under stress, our breathing isn't shortened. That ensures that the brain will still operate at its best."

"Exercise sounds like the Holy Grail of brain health. How much exercise do you need?"

"Forty-five minutes of cardio three times a week will strengthen your cardiovascular health."

"Sounds manageable."

"What's even more impressive, is that cardio improves your IQ by a staggering 33%. If you're studying for the LSAT, how can you *not* exercise?"

"How does it do that?" Noah asked.

"Exercise (and studying for many hours at a time) is a challenge to your brain. Your brain, in response, starts to create stress-response pathways that help your brain handle the stress. When this happens, neuro-circuits are activated, which then promote the growth of neurons and the formation and strengthening of synapses. This will enhance the ability for neurons to grow and sustain the connections between each other, thereby boosting your memory and learning ability."

"All this talk about exercise is making me hungry," Noah said.

I was beginning to think Noah had the wait staff on remote control; as soon as he spoke, the waiter brought out his plate. Now I could start my pancakes.

"Bon appétit," I said, as Noah began to dig into the eggs and home fries placed in front of him by waiter confidant.

Chapter 4

Noah had to be in court after breakfast, to file a motion to set aside a plea. My plan was to study all morning. Noah advised that I take a practice test. We decided to meet the next morning at the same time and place.

In an upbeat mood, I went to the public library, with an LSAT practice exam in hand, along with some pencils and erasers. I'd been studying for a few weeks, so I figured that the studying plus the feedback and advice I'd received from Noah would boost my score by about, I didn't know … five points?

I'd scored a 134 last time, so I should get around 140. I read and analyzed, skipped ahead, came back, set up logic games, made deductions and inferences, summarized, found flaws, assumptions, main points, strengthened, weakened, deduced, reasoned, bubbled in and double-checked my answers. Three hours and a headache later, I finished the test.

I checked my score not once, but three times. My score was 134. *It didn't make sense.* Tears ran down my face; my heart became heavier than a rock. If I went swimming, I thought, I would sink from my heavy heart.

If I couldn't improve on the LSAT, I wouldn't get into a top law school, so what was the point, anyway? I knew to some people that might sound idiotic, but getting into law school, and a good one, was about much more than being a lawyer. To me, it was about proving to the world that I was smart.

All my life, I'd heard how attractive I was. My biggest problem in high school was choosing which boy would take me to the prom out of the many that asked me. Even my 12th-grade teacher, Mrs. Gordon, hinted at it once. She told me that after I had failed miserably on a chemistry test, a test she had tutored me on.

"You're such a lovely young lady," she said sympathetically, "maybe academics just isn't your thing?"

I'd show Mrs. Gordon what my "thing" was when I got a perfect score on the LSAT. Although after today's practice test, a perfect score looked as strange as ketchup in Paris. But I thought all this time that I spent with Noah would have increased my score. How in the world had my score not gone up?

Noah emerged from the courtroom and saw me waiting on the courthouse steps.

He raised his eyebrows and spoke rapidly. "Is everything okay, Alexandra? Were we supposed to meet?"

"No, Noah, and I hate to bother you, but I'm all torn up inside after taking the practice test you told me to take." I didn't want to sound as if I was blaming him. The last thing I wanted was to lose our student-mentor relationship.

"I listened to the things you told me, and I honestly thought I'd improve by at least five points. Instead, I got the exact same score. How can that be?"

Noah set his briefcase on the ground.

"I'm not sure why you had this idea of a five-point increase or any increase for that matter. The LSAT is an aptitude test. It's not a little endeavor to improve your raw intelligence, not without an ample amount of work. But you know what? How about we visit a good friend of mine? What are you doing this afternoon?"

I just nodded. Since going swimming wouldn't have been a good idea with my heavy heart, I could go on this mysterious trip.

Noah's limo picked us up at his office at 5 o'clock.

"You look a lot better, Alexandra."

"I definitely look better than your limo's floor," I remarked half-jokingly, after noticing the messy floor. "Yeah, I relaxed after talking to you. I also got excited about meeting this friend of yours. By the way, do you have the list you prepared about what attorneys do?"

A Cadre of Experts

"Sure. I have it in my briefcase."

Noah fiddled through his unorganized mini-office, looking for his yellow legal pad.

"Here we are."

I took out my iPhone and opened the notes app.

What Lawyers Do #2: Litigate

"Lawyers have a gift for debate. They know how to win arguments and wreck their opponent's case in a courtroom. Whether they're defending someone's rights, discrediting a witness or protecting a victim from harm, lawyers must know and have all the tools and knowledge they need to make things right. In a courtroom, a lawyer must be prepared and thoroughly knowledgeable about the case. Lawyers have a unique chance to help people and make their problems go away. For some people, a lawyer is like a hero. They are there, helping you when no one else believes you have a chance."

It was dark when we reached the small town of Lawrence, on Long Island. The streetlights were little help. Less than an hour away from Manhattan everything looked like a different world. There was no need to circle the block multiple times to find a parking spot. The streets were clean and there was a natrual air freshener in the wind.

Noah's friend had an old, large brick house. It was relaxing to stand there in the quiet darkness, listening to the crickets chirp. I closed my eyes and tried to picture myself in a place like this, after I'd finished law school and worked as an attorney for a few years–and, honestly, I could see it. I closed my eyes and took a deep breath, and then opened them to let it soak in.

As we walked past the flower pots and neatly trimmed grass, the front door opened, and a man came running out to greet us. He was about Noah's age, maybe a bit younger. He and Noah shook hands, but that quickly turned into a big hug. Noah introduced me to his friend.

"Alexandra, this is Dr. Stern. Doc, this is my friend, Alexandra. Alexandra is studying for her LSATs. She wants to be a lawyer and sue doctors like you for malpractice," Noah told the doctor. I hoped Dr. Stern understood Noah's humor.

"In that case," Dr. Stern said, looking firmly at me, "I'll have to up my game and be more careful with patients."

"That's exactly the point," Noah almost yelled with excitement. I knew exactly what he meant. If tenacious lawyers are suing the pants off doctors for malpractice, doctors will indeed be much more careful. If doctors are more careful, patients benefit. If a company that makes car seats is vulnerable to lawsuits, they'll make sure their products are top notch. *Lawyers make a difference.*

Dr. Stern gestured for us to come inside.

"You're here to see my mom, Noah?" Dr. Stern asked.

"Yup," Noah replied.

"She's in the study. I believe she's preparing for a lecture next week at Columbia University. But she's expecting you, go right in."

"Noah," Dr. Stern's mother—also Dr. Stern—called out as soon as we walked in. "How the hell are you, son?"

"I'm super, Doctor. This here is Alexandra."

"Hello Alex, may I call you Alex, dear?" Dr. Stern asked.

"Sure. All my friends call me Alex," I responded. None of my friends called me Alex. The last one who called me Alex … well, let's just leave it at no one calls me Alex.

"I taught Noah in college quite a few years ago. He was my star pupil, and excellent at science. Never understood why he went to law school, but it seems to have worked out okay for him."

I couldn't help but think that we had driven here in a limo.

"Noah tells me you're taking the LSAT and going to law school, is that right?"

I nodded. I didn't mean to be rude, but I didn't know what to say.

"Noah also tells me you were expecting a vast increase in your score after a couple of weeks of study?"

"Yes, I was disappointed my score didn't go up after studying quite a few hours every day for the past couple of weeks."

"Well, darling," Dr. Stern the mom said, "I'm not sure what Noah told you about me, but I've dedicated the past 20 years of my life to brain research. The brain is so amazing; it can blow your mind."

I loved that. A highly educated doctor with a corny sense of humor. Classic.

A Cadre of Experts

"The old-school thinking about brain chemistry was that a person was born with a fixed IQ, and nothing could improve the brain's thinking or abilities. The brain could deteriorate, though, for reasons such as age, nutrition, or brain injury.

"The new school thinking is much more exact. We scientists now believe in something called 'brain elasticity,' the brain can grow and develop, even during adulthood. This can be achieved through brain exercises, but can also happen through intensive studying, primarily studying subjects such as spatial logic, deductive reasoning and, even more, by strengthening something called our 'working memory.'"

Noah was sitting quietly on a comfy sofa, his legs crossed and his ears perked up, attentive to every word the doctor was saying. He appreciated her wisdom.

"Isn't the LSAT all about spatial logic, like in the logic games?" I asked.

"True," Noah answered.

"In fact," Dr. Stern said, "there has been a good deal of research on the correlation between studying for the LSAT and the improvement of one's IQ. Turns out that studying for the LSAT will indeed increase your IQ, Alex."

"Then how is it that after studying for a couple of weeks I didn't improve by even one point?" I asked, hoping I didn't sound too desperate.

The doctor and Noah chuckled.

"A couple of weeks, dear? That's not nearly enough time to see significant improvement. You'll need at least three months, and even then, it won't necessarily come all of a sudden. Sure, you can pick up points here and there, but lasting development takes time. It's a long process, but an unbelievable journey. You should be *grateful* you have to take this test to get into law school. If it weren't for this test, when would you invest such a significant amount of time in improving your intelligence, Alex?"

"That's a good point, Dr. Stern." I wished I could have addressed her using some annoying nickname she hated.

"You're saying if I study for this test, my IQ should go up? And that should improve my LSAT score?"

"I hate to toot my own horn," the doctor said, "but a few years ago

I resolved that I wanted to join Mensa, 'the geniuses secret society.' I looked into it, and it turns out they accept an LSAT score above the 95th percentile score as 'proof of genius.' And I'll let you in on a small secret. Before going to medical school, I considered going to law school and took the LSAT, so I used my score to get into Mensa.

"Why does Mensa accept LSAT scores as proof of genius? Because the LSAT is in many ways an IQ test. Studying for the LSAT—which, as we said before, improves your IQ—will improve your LSAT score as well. Your LSAT score and IQ go hand in hand. Does that make sense?"

"But let's say someone takes a practice exam without any prior study and scores a 120. Then they open a study guide and learn how to set up logic games. By learning a few simple rules on how to set up logic games, the person's score will go up quickly, to say a 125. Did they improve their IQ in those short few hours?"

Noah decided to answer that one.

"Initial studying simply levels the field. After you learn the techniques, you will start to perform at your current full potential. Sometimes that can take a while. But when you continue studying and hacking your brain further, that's when the improvement in IQ comes. Any increase in score *after leveling the field* is an actual increase in your potential, and or IQ, in turn raising your LSAT score."

"This is incredible stuff," I said, "I don't think this is the common notion among students studying for the LSAT. I can only imagine what would happen if this type of thinking was more mainstream. I know my perspective has changed."

"That's why I brought you here, Alexandra," Noah said. "If you study for a few more weeks and your score still doesn't improve, you either haven't hit that budging point, or you might need to evaluate your study methods and habits. We can talk more about study habits on the ride back to the city."

"What do you mean by 'hitting that budging point'?" I asked.

"Did you ever see the movie 'Winnie the Pooh,' dear?" the doctor asked.

"I don't think so. I know who the character is, though."

"In one of the old movies, Winnie the Pooh gets stuck in Rabbit's house after eating all of Rabbit's honey. For days he's stuck as a result of his weight, until one morning, Rabbit leans on him and hears a simple cracking sound, indicating Winnie had budged. Rabbit gets all the others together and they yank Winnie out of the hole.

"That's what Noah and I mean by hitting the budging point. You might sit on logic games or assumptions or conditional logic for a few days, without much progress. But one day it simply budges. All the hard work you've been doing adds up and things *click*. That doesn't mean it becomes one hundred percent clear, but it becomes workable."

Dr. Stern, the son, came in and offered us some decaf coffee.

"What else can I provide you Alex that will help with your LSATs?" Dr. Stern asked rhetorically. "The fundamental problem for students is that they often disconnect from what they are studying. I have that problem sometimes, especially at the end of a long day. It can be hard to study for three or four hours. The mind can wander, and you may end up retaining only a small amount of information.

"One practice that might help you is meditation. This is a science I feel strongly about. It can help you with attention and focus. Meditation is proven to help with stress relief and chronic pain, but other studies indicate that it also improves helps you fight mental distractions."

"Distractions are my number-one enemy," I said.

Dr. Stern, the son, returned with our coffee.

"Just because we do poorly on a test doesn't mean we're stupid. It means that our working memory—the thing that helps us focus on what we're studying and later recall it—isn't working as well as it could. A great study aid is meditation. Have you heard anything about this, Alex?"

Again with the Alex. "Not really, doctor," I said politely.

"Meditation is unparalleled for calming us before studying. Fifteen minutes of meditation before and after studying is great for memory retention. If you don't want to meditate before and after studying, meditating at any time of day will also have a positive effect on your memory. Increased focus while studying leads to increased performance during tests, which means better scores. This is interesting, because meditation doesn't involve drugs or caffeine, which people sometimes use to focus. Meditation harnesses the power of the mind itself."

"Are there any specific tips you can offer?" Noah asked.

"The trick is to keep up the meditation regularly. It's like exercise; you have to work out regularly to keep the muscles strong. Meditation for a more focused mind is the same thing." "Maybe I should take it up too," Noah said. "Before we go, anything last ideas you can offer us?"

"Another thing you can do to improve your attention is to lower significantly the amount of television you watch," Dr. Stern said.

"I heard growing up that TV rots your brain," Noah said, "but is there scientific proof of that?"

"Of course Noah. Watching too much TV affects your front polar cortex area of the brain. The front polar cortex can affect your intellectual abilities. Watching TV can lower your attention span, cause sleep problems and behavior issues. It can also alter your dreams, cause ADHD, and it's even been linked with lower verbal intelligence. In short, eliminate TV as much as you can for your brain's sake."

"I'm canceling my cable as soon as I get home," I said.

"Good idea Alexandra, you won't regret it. Some TV won't hurt you, but the less TV you watch, and ideally replace with either reading or talking to family and friends, the better."

Noah and I stood. We thanked the doctor as we walked outside, back into the darkness and fresh smelling air. I could hear the crickets chirping again, reminding me that I could go back to being Alexandra.

Chapter 5

Leaving Long Island, I noticed some stunning, gigantic houses along the streets which were eerily quiet and yet inspirational.

"That was fun, wasn't it, Alexandra?" Noah asked.

"I learned a lot."

Noah didn't respond for a minute or so; he only looked out the window.

"I'm having a good time with you," he said. "*On our LSAT journey.*"

"Me too, Noah." I wasn't sure exactly what he meant. Then Noah snapped out of his trance.

"We were starting to talk about study methods, right?" Noah asked as if I had a choice. "I was thinking of getting back to Manhattan, but now that we want to talk about study methods, let me take you to an expert."

Some people collect stamps, coins or records. Some collect comic books, action figures or baseball cards. Some collect cars, games, or Japanese erasers. Noah? *Noah collects experts.*

"I didn't know you studied science in college, Noah."

"You also probably didn't know I studied the Talmud."

"The Talmud?"

"The Talmud is the ancient central text of Rabbinic Judaism. The Seleucid Empire of Greece controlled Israel and the Jewish nation during the second century BC. At that time, they took over the education in Israel. The Mishnah, the original rabbinic text, was interpreted, according to some historians, using the traditional Greek methods of logic. The Talmud is similar in its analysis to Greek logic, which is the basis of modern logic. Many of the logical terms you may have learned—such as *ad hominem* and others—are found in the Talmud.

The expert I want you to meet is somebody who has been studying the Talmud his whole life. He is quite knowledgeable about study habits, among other things."

"How long is this Talmud?"

"Pretty long." Noah turned to his driver. "Hey Sam, take us to Williamsburg, Brooklyn, please."

"Will do, Noah," Sam replied.

"His whole life?" I asked.

"I know, quite remarkable. He must be in his late 80s. But he acts like he's in his mid-80s."

I laughed. "I'm sure he'll be an interesting person. Thanks, Noah, for taking me to Dr. Stern and now to this study-habits expert."

"Rabbi Posner."

"Sorry?"

"His name is Rabbi Posner. We should be there in about 30 minutes. And you're welcome."

Noah answered an urgent phone call from a client, giving me time to ponder a bit. I watched as the cars on the other side of the highway drove passed us. This was so exciting, traveling with this flashy attorney, riding around in his limo and meeting his friends. I liked Noah. I felt for him that his wife passed because he seemed lonely at times. Was he dating?

Which law school would I go to? Should I stay in New York, near friends, near family, near… Noah? Or should I travel to, say, Los Angeles? There were supposed to be some high ranking schools over there, but other than their names and rankings I didn't know much about them. I was sure I could ask Noah some of these questions.

When should I take my next practice test? How would I do? I took Dr. Stern's advice to heart. **I wouldn't look for a quick fix with my LSAT score.** I'd give it time; like a seed you plant in the dirt. You water it, leave it out in the sun, and wait for it to grow. It is growing; it just takes time before you see it on the surface. But it also is frustrating waiting for my score to increase. If I'm using the wrong study methods, I wouldn't know it until I failed on the LSAT. I didn't want to wait until … *then.*

My mom always said good things are worth the wait. The LSAT

A Cadre of Experts

and law school, at this period in my life, are the only good things I'm waiting for. I wondered what the Rabbi would tell me. Since Noah was taking the time to drive to Brooklyn, he must offer wise advice.

I was grateful I met Noah. Everyone needs a mentor. I hoped one day I could pay the favor forward and offer expert advice to others. One day.

Noah finished his phone call right before we reached Williamsburg. I realized I was so focused on my thoughts I hadn't overheard any of Noah's conversation.

"Here we are," Noah said excitedly, with a childish look in his face. Noah learned with the Rabbi as a kid, for his Bar Mitzvah. Sometimes, when you return to a place or meet someone from your youth, you start to act as if you're that age again.

Williamsburg was a fascinating neighborhood. In places, it feels like you've entered a time-travel machine and set it for 1850. And of course there's the hipsters.

We pulled up in front of the Rabbi's home, a relatively quaint and cozy looking building. It was tall and narrow, constructed in the manner of many houses in the neighborhood, with bricks in different shades of the archetypical muted red. There was a raised platform where a small, beautiful tree with clusters of pink blooms graced the branches. Aside from the tree, the only other flora in the yard consisted of a small row of box hedges beneath the tier with the tree. The windows were like those of any other urban home, with the exception of a stained-glass window in front. A white door at the bottom of a small flight of stairs appeared to lead to the entrance.

We walked up four flights of stairs. We didn't walk up the stairs for the exercise; the building didn't have an elevator. Noah knocked on the door. A little wooden plaque nailed to the doorway had the name "Posner" on it. The door was old-fashioned wood, with a peephole and three different locks. It probably took an hour to lock, but it opened in much less time—and there was the Rabbi, standing and smiling on the threshold, gesturing for us to come in.

The home projected a feeling of warmth and family. It looked lived in, as if it had seen many joys throughout the years. We walked in behind the Rabbi and sat at the living room table. The Rabbi's wife, the

Rebbetzin, brought out some tea. She asked if there was anything else we needed, and told us to feel at home. She even offered us warm towels to wash our hands and faces, maybe old-fashioned, but nice.

The living room furniture consisted of different patterns and styles. The big, floral sofa looked inviting as the fire in the hearth crackled and popped. A wooden coffee table was in the center of the room, mismatched with several other pieces of wooden furniture.

"So, Noah, who have you defended lately?" the Rabbi asked with a glint in his eye. "Anybody interesting?"

"Oh, you know Rabbi, the usual, my regular *alleged* bank robbers, nothing too exciting. The reason for our visit tonight, Rabbi Posner, is this young lady here. She's on the road to law school, and I wanted to teach her some of the methods you taught me when I was in your Sunday Talmud class. I thought I might as well bring her to hear them directly from you."

"Ah yes, I remember the good old days when I was giving those classes. Noah never missed a class, you know. And he had a great *kop*."

"*Kop*?" I asked.

"*Kop* is the Yiddish word for 'head,'" Noah answered. "And Rabbi what do you mean '*had*'?"

"Had, has, whatever. Let's get to business. What is it you want to know, Alexandra?"

"I could use some study techniques," I said. "I have this big test coming up, the LSAT, and I want to make sure my study habits are as proficient as possible."

The Rabbi didn't hesitate. "The first rule of studying is, as it says in the Talmud: 'If you have seized a lot, you have not seized. If you have seized a little bit, you have seized.'"

I hoped the Rabbi would explain.

"When you learn something," he said, "if it's a small amount of information, you will retain it. If, however, you read a whole book in one night, even if you comprehend what you've read, chances are you won't remember much of it, and you definitely won't *know* it.

"Every 15 minutes, do a quick review of what you've learned in the past 15 minutes, and every hour, review what you learned that hour. Then, at nighttime, before you go to bed, review everything you learned that day. That will keep the information *locked in*. The purpose of this type of review is to **take those long hours of study and turn them into small, memorable chunks**. Make them bite-size chunks you can retain. Every time you review something and move on, the next section of your study is like starting something new."

"That valuable advice, Rabbi," Noah said.

"It's only good advice if you use it."

The Rebbetzin came in and brought more tea.

"The next idea," the Rabbi continued slowly, "derives from a famous Talmudic quote that says 'create signs.' If you have to memorize a list of words, take the first letter of each word and turn it into a word you can easily remember. Or you can add a mental picture to a particular subject to remember it. Let's see if I can give you a good example."

The Rabbi sipped his tea. "The tea is hot, by the way," he warned. "But you knew that, of course, since it's tea."

The Rabbi took a few more sips. "Let's say you are trying to memorize the logical fallacy *ad hominem*, or, in the language of the Talmud 'accept the truth from whoever said it.' If a smoker tells you not to smoke because it's not healthy, and you tell him he has no right to say that because he himself smokes, that would be an *ad hominem* response. Ad hominem, as it's called in Latin, means an attack on the speaker. Don't attack the person; attack the argument, if you want your argument to be logical.

"Create an emblem. Think of a friend who smokes, and imagine that person wearing a t-shirt emblazoned with the phrase '*ad hominem.*' Now add a bubble to your mental image, like in a comic, of that person saying obnoxiously 'You shouldn't smoke.'"

"The more extreme you make the picture, the more memorable it is, isn't that so, Rabbi?" Noah asked.

"*Yuh*," the Rabbi answered in Yiddish, meaning *yes*. "When you need to recall the idea, just remember that mental picture. It all comes back to you in a moment."

I liked the technique and wrote it down on my iPhone notes app.

"So to summarize, review your material periodically," the Rabbi said, heading his own advice, "and create visuals. Now let me give you the meat and potatoes of study methods. We've actually learned this worthwhile study method from the Passover holiday and the Passover Seder, where the youngest child in the family observes the different rituals performed only on Passover. The child then asks four questions, is given detailed answers, and then a final summary. This process involves four steps: observe, ask, clarify, and summarize.

"So, first, observe what is going on. If you're reading a reading comprehension passage, observe whether the passage is an argument, a summary of opinions, if the author takes a side, and more general thoughts about the topic.

"Then, ask questions. Why is the author writing about this? Is the author passionate about the topic, or critical? Why does the author start a new paragraph exactly where she did? Why did the author use a phrase such as 'Most engineers use the old approach to…'? Will the author now advocate for a new approach?"

The Rabbi paused. "So far, so good?"

"Absolutely, Rabbi," I said.

"Good. The third stage is to clarify your questions using as much detail as you can. Yes, the author is passionate about the topic because she started with a phrase: 'A promising new science that could solve the earth's water problem….' Or she seems to be critical of the lawyers because of X, Y or Z. Do your best to answer your own questions with a lot of detail until you start to understand the passage at a deeper level. The more you do this, the faster you'll get, and the more deeply you'll understand.

"Lastly, summarize. Now that you understand the passage on a deeper level, summarize the points of the passage along with your deeper grasp of its meaning. 'The author started a new paragraph here because although it was the same subject, the author transitioned to criticize the topic,' and so on. Starting to make sense?" the Rabbi asked me.

"I'm just not sure how I'd apply it to the logic games."

"I can try to answer that," Noah offered. "**Observe** what kind of game it is. Then **ask** questions like 'what's unique about this game? What rules create two different options, such as 'Charlie is either first or last' and the like? **Clarify**: if Charlie is first, then Dani is third, and so on. **Summarize:** set up some options."

"Even though it all makes sense, Noah, I can't imagine having enough time to do this on the exam."

"This isn't a strategy you use during the exam, but practicing this method will help you better understand what you're learning. With practice, it will become engrained in your thought process," Noah answered.

"That's right, Noah," the Rabbi said. "After a while, your subconscious will do all the work for you – sometimes all four stages in a split second. Well, Noah, as always, it was a pleasure. Please don't be a stranger. You too, Alexandra."

Noah and I stood. "Thank you, the pleasure was all ours," Noah responded.

"Thanks for the advice Rabbi, and thanks for the tea," I said, as we headed back down the four flights of stairs.

Today, I did twenty logic games in a row. There's something about doing so many games in a row that helps me understand logic games better. Maybe doing this helps me see the many variations of game types, rule types, and the many different possible inferences. I started to notice which games and which rule types I find tricky, so I can focus more on those. After doing all twenty games and reviewing them intensely, I repeated them and focused on improving my speed.

Chapter 6

"Noah, I have an issue I wanted to ask you about," I said, sitting down at our regular booth at the LSAT Café. "I have a problem with my short-term memory. I read a passage or diagram a rule, but sometimes, just a few seconds later, I can forget what I read or what rule I had diagrammed. Any thoughts?"

"We *just* spoke about this problem a few minutes ago. Don't you remember?"

"Very funny Noah. But seriously, how can I improve my memory?"

"I have a friend Josh who's a memory expert. He can remember numbers, names, whole books, just about anything he ever hears or reads. But his wife says that even with his incredible memory, he still forgets their anniversary. I think he can help though."

Where does he live?"

"Josh lives in Park Slope, Brooklyn. I'll call Sam. And I'm glad you asked about short-term memory, because short-term memory is one of the **most important elements of intelligence** and thus LSAT success. Improving your short term memory will not just help for short term recall such as with logic game rules, author opinions in reading comprehension passages and the like; it also will strengthen your overall IQ."

"Sounds great. I'll try to remember that."

"I bought some multivitamins," I said, as I sat in the limo. "The brain needs a lot of vitamins to function properly."

"That's a smart idea. Did you get a recommendation about which brand to buy?"

A Cadre of Experts

"I saw a commercial for this brand. The ad said they're the first company to be accredited by an independent agency. So I figured they must be the best brand," I said.

"I hate to break it to you, but that would be a logical fallacy."

"A logical fallacy about multivitamins? I have to hear this one."

"The real fallacy is simply an assumption. You're assuming that because they were the *first* to be accredited they're therefore *better* than the other companies."

"Oh, I see."

"Let's try this hypothetical. Cell phone company X tells you they have better service than company Y. Company Y says that they give 1% of their profits to charity, and that company X exploits their employees and pays them minimum wage. What fallacy would that be?"

"It sounds wrong, but I'm not sure."

"This fallacy is called the 'Straw Man' fallacy. Mark asserts a claim against Joe, who responds by addressing a similar, but still different claim, that doesn't actually refute or challenge Mark's claim. Company Y may have a good point, but in addressing the service issue, they committed the Straw Man fallacy."

"How does that apply to my vitamins?"

"Well, let's just assume that another vitamin company claimed that they're better than the one you bought. Your statement that you should buy this brand because it was the first to be accredited is like saying that the other company's claim to superiority isn't true because this one was accredited *first*. What does being accredited first have to do with quality? Couldn't the company that was accredited third or fourth or fifth be the best one? Therefore, that claim is strawmanning."

"I would have never thought of that while watching the commercial."

"You will now."

I wrote down the flaw on my iPhone notes, took out my water bottle and swallowed a multivitamin, hoping that the quality was indeed good.

"Hello Mr. Levy," Josh said to Noah, as we walked into his cozy apartment.

"When's the last time we met, Josh?"

"That would be last April. April 22, to be exact. At 6:30 p.m."

"I told you he has an incredible memory, Alexandra," Noah said, still looking at Josh.

"I remember it because it was my son's wedding," Josh said. "And the wedding was on his birthday."

"So, how can I help you two?"

"I'm studying for the LSAT, and I asked Noah how I can improve my memory. He told me you're the expert."

"So you want some exercises?" Josh asked.

"I would love that."

"Why did you ask Noah about your memory, to begin with?"

"Because I don't think I have a good memory."

"That's your first problem," Josh almost shouted.

"But that's why we're here," Noah said.

"No, you don't understand. *Saying* you don't have a good memory is the problem. Your mind believes whatever you tell it. If you say you don't have a good memory, the mind says 'OK,' and next thing you know you can't find your car keys, you forgot to refill your medication, and you can't go to the pharmacy to pick up a new bottle because you can't find your car keys."

"In that case, where does the first episode of forgetfulness come from?" I asked.

"Ah, I can see the lawyer in you Alexandra. Well, once upon a time you forgot something. No big deal. Even the strongest and deepest minds in the world forget things once in a while. But you're hard on yourself about that one episode, *and the saga begins*. First of all, you must break the habit of giving yourself a hard time when you forget something. I'll give you two exercises. But before I do, why don't you tell me about your day?"

"I woke up in the morning, had a cup of coffee ..." I said.

"What kind of coffee?"

"Um, instant coffee."

"Was it decaf or regular?"

"Regular."

"And was it a new jar of coffee?"

"No, I opened it the other day."

"Which day? What time?"

"I think Tuesday …"

"You think?"

"No, Tuesday for sure. I remember because it was raining."

"Aha. What kind of spoon did you use? Plastic or metal?"

"Metal. I only use metal for hot drinks."

"I see where you're going with this, Josh," Noah chimed in.

"Yeah, so do I," I said.

"So this is the first exercise. At night, before you go to bed, say out loud all the things you did during the day, and go into a lot of detail of one or two activities. The memory is a muscle, and simple recall exercises can strengthen it. When you made yourself that cup of coffee today, you weren't trying to commit all the details to memory. You probably weren't paying much attention to the details. That means the event is still in your memory bank, but not at the top of the pile; it's more likely at the bottom. Recalling a memory at the bottom of the stack requires more effort, so it will strengthen your memory even more."

"That's awesome," I said. "Do you do this exercise yourself?"

"Absolutely. In fact, I do a lot of mini exercises throughout the day."

"What do you mean?" I asked.

"I try to recall a lot of small details from my daily experiences. For example, if I meet somebody, I try to recall what they were wearing, from their clothes to their eye color to their jewelry. But that's only if I didn't notice what they were wearing while I was speaking to them. Otherwise, it's too easy.

"If I get a number while standing in line, like at the DMV, after I leave I'll try to recall the number on the ticket. Stuff like that. When you do a lot of these mini exercises, it adds up."

"What other things do you do for these short exercises?" I asked.

"If I'm about to call someone on my cellphone, first I try to remember when was the last time I spoke to that person, and for how long. Then I look at my phone and find out if I was right—if my phone still has a record of it—or by how much I was off.

"Try to recall details that you didn't pay attention to at the time. What kind of car was I parked in front of? When was the last time I ate a carrot? When was the last time I had a hearing test? Random stuff. But it works the memory muscles like crazy."

"That's fantastic stuff, Josh," I said, "what's the second exercise?"

"So let's see, Alexandra, it's not as much an exercise as it is a useful tip. Where do you usually study?"

"Sometimes in the library in mid-Manhattan, sometimes at a coffee shop, or in my apartment."

"What else do you do while studying?"

"I listen to music."

"I think we've found the culprit," Josh said.

"But music helps me concentrate."

"Actually, the opposite is true. I know it may *seem* like music helps you concentrate, but by definition, concentration means you block everything else out. If you have a concentrated liquid, and you add water, you are diluting the liquid. **Anything you add to your awareness is diluting your concentration.** I know it might be hard, but try not to study at coffee shops. It might be okay if you have some light reading to do. But if you're trying to commit things to memory, don't burden your brain with the extra noise. And when you're at home, save the music as a reward after studying. You can also try reading out loud, as a way to improve your comprehension and retention."

"Giving up my study music might be tough, Josh."

"Try it for a few days. I'm going to guess that the benefit will become so apparent you won't understand how you ever were able to study while listening to music. And this is something you should probably get used to now before you start law school. It will be an excellent asset to know how to study more efficiently."

Noah got a phone call. We had to call it a day.

"Josh, it's good to see you again. Thank you for helping us. I learned an important lesson here myself, too," Noah said.

"Of course. Stop by anytime."

"And Josh, one more thing," Noah said. "November 12th, 1981."

"What about that? You say it like it should mean something, but I can't put my finger on it."

"Josh. That's your anniversary."

"I *knew* it rang a bell."

A Cadre of Experts

I met Noah the next morning at the LSAT Café. It was raining heavily, and the wind messed up my hair. Luckily the subway station was close to the café.

I shook the rain off my umbrella and entered the café. A man was exiting and held the door open. Noah was waiting at the table and reading the *Wall Street Journal*. His suit jacket hung on a chair, probably to dry from the rain. He wore his black tie and white button-down shirt.

"I was speaking to a friend this morning about the LSAT," Noah began, "and he told me many students are concerned that the reading comprehension has increased in difficulty. Is that something you struggle with?"

"Noah, the reading comprehension section is by far my worst section. It's so abstract, and I miss a lot of questions. On the logical reasoning and logic games, I miss some questions, but I look at them again, and I understand why I got them wrong. But with reading comprehension, I read it again and again and I still don't get it. So it's fair to say I struggle with the section, like your friend said."

"Alexandra, I'm not interested in problems, I'm interested in solutions. This friend of mine might be able to help."

Noah loves his experts.

"This friend of mine, Brian, is a real reading expert. He'd better be—he's a judge. He was one of my professors in law school, and he took a judgeship down in Austin, Texas a few years ago.

"Originally he graduated as a social worker, but then he went to law school. In fact, he was still studying social work while in law school. He's extremely smart."

I hope we're not going to drive there, I thought to myself. Noah seemed to have read my mind.

"It would be impractical to drive there, but if you're up for the trip, we can take a flight. It's only about four hours."

"I can imagine Brian has a lot to offer, being a judge and all."

"He sure does. Let me call Chris my assistant and have him book us two tickets to Austin."

With Noah still on the phone, Chris bought two tickets right there and then. We would fly out at 10:00 a.m. the next day.

"Meanwhile," Noah offered, "we can talk about the subject a bit. Wait a minute; we didn't order anything to eat."

Noah waved politely to the waiter to come over. It was good old waiter confidant. Noah ordered his usual eggs and hash browns. I got eggs, sunny side up. Of course, Noah ordered coffee for us both.

As the waiter went to the back through those tall doors to hand over the order to the cook, Noah returned to our topic.

"You know Alexandra, reading comprehension—not the section, but the skill—is incredibly important not only on the LSAT but in law school and in life. The fact that you may be struggling with it at the moment is not a horrible thing; rather it's an opportunity to improve. Just as Dr. Stern said about the LSAT's intelligence component, when else would you dedicate time and energy to improve your reading skills? I see it as a blessing."

The waiter brought our coffee.

"Reading is essential to every aspect of the LSAT, law school, and the legal profession," Noah said.

"I understand the importance of reading," I said, "although I'm not sure I understand the importance of improving my reading skills. I read, and I understand. What is there to improve, exactly? I'm not doing well on the reading comprehension section because the questions are hard."

"That's a real question, Alexandra, and it's not easy to explain. It's one of those skills you have to improve on to see the difference. Once you develop your reading skills, you'll realize how important it is. When you comprehend more, you won't understand how you used to read.

"If a third-grader and a twelfth-grader both read the same book, you can assume the older kid will get more out of the book than the younger one. And honestly, the difference between my reading comprehension before the LSAT and law school, and my reading comprehension today is as big a difference as between a third-grader and a twelfth-grader."

Noah gave me a minute to think about what he'd said. If it was true—that one could improve their reading that much—it would be incredible.

Noah took a sip from his coffee.

"Cool stuff," I said, "so how can I improve my comprehension level to that extent?"

"How the heck am I supposed to know?" Noah answered with a smile. "Do you think I bought two tickets to Austin for fun?"

I just realized. Noah had bought us two tickets. *Us*. I didn't know how I felt about his paying for it. After all, the trip was for me. Sure, Noah had the financial means, and I was still in college. Was he doing it all as a friend, or was he expecting to take the relationship further? I was also curious about what this Judge Brian would tell me. Why couldn't Noah just tell me and save us the trip?

The waiter brought our food.

"Noah, if you know what Brian will tell me, wouldn't it be more time-efficient if you told me yourself or if we phoned him?"

"He never answers the phone."

Well that's convenient.

"The more energy you invest in something, the more impact it will have on you. If you go to the bookstore and buy a new book, take it home, make a cup of tea, sit in your favorite rocking chair and read it, taking notes and highlighting words and ideas as you read, that will have a greater impact than if you read the same material summed up on a blog post. Does that make sense? Taking the flight to Texas will subconsciously have a better outcome than if I just tell you the ideas here at the café. You will feel more obligated to use his method and do the exercises. You don't need to get on an airplane every time you want to learn something new, but I think this occasion warrants it. Besides, I don't know what Brian will tell you."

That made more sense than the first answer.

"Especially since reading is so important," I said, "it's worth the time and effort to make the trip. I feel bad I don't have money to pay you for the tickets."

"Pay me back when you're a lawyer. Or better yet, pass on the ideas I'm teaching you to another student in your situation in the future."

"That's what I'm planning to do," I said. "Is that why you're teaching me this stuff? Did you have a mentor?"

Noah didn't pause. "Every successful person has a mentor or two...

or three. Fisch taught me the LSAT; Professor Levine mentored me in law school. I would love for you to meet both of them."

"Sounds like a plan," I said.

We had almost finished our breakfast when Noah suddenly recalled my list of brain-health tips. "Weren't we up to number two?" he asked.

I opened up my iPhone notes app.

Brain Health Tip #2: Go easy on the sugar

"The worst food for your brain, and body, is sugar. That sweet, innocent-looking, everyday household item is awful for you. If there's one dietary change you can make to maximize your brain health, it would be to remove as much sugar as possible from your diet."

"That is an awesome tip. Maybe not easy to adopt, but an important one for sure. Would you recommend one of those sweeteners? You know, the sugar-free sweeteners they offer instead of good ol' sugar?"

"Those can be just as bad as or even worse for your brain than sugar. In short, for optimal brain health, cut out all sweeteners. Over the last few weeks, I've tried to reduce the amount of sugar I consume in my daily foods like coffee, tea, and the occasional cake I bake at home. It's not a piece of cake—no pun intended—but I'm starting to notice that I slowly crave less sugar less."

"Would you recommend quitting sugar completely?" Noah asked.

"Sure, either go for it or don't. If someone wants to quit sugar, they might as well quit completely. Otherwise, what's the point?"

"Hmm ..." Noah hummed. "That reminds me of a ... logical fallacy. Care to hear about this one?"

"Sure, why not?"

"There is something called the *false dilemma,* which means it is a flaw to assume there are only two sides to a situation. You've heard the famous quote 'you're either with us or against us,' right? That's precisely the flaw I'm talking about."

"How is 'you're either with us or against us' flawed?"

"The phrase assumes there are only two possibilities. In reality, there could be a third side, such as someone who is neutral."

"Could there be only two sides?"

A Cadre of Experts

"Of course. But it is a flaw to *assume* there are only two sides without exploring the other options."

"So if you want to lower your sugar intake, you don't have to either quit completely or not quit at all. There can be a middle ground. You could cut down half, or two-thirds."

"Exactly, Alexandra."

I was happy Noah remembered my list. I'd worked hard on it and wanted to share it with him. I also think that maybe Noah purposely asked me to bring them up one at a time. If you read a list of tips in one shot, chances are you won't apply many of them. If you study them one at a time and use them, you'll have a better chance of changing your lifestyle.

"That reminds me, Noah, what about your list of what lawyers do?"

"Yes, we're due for one of those."

What Lawyers Do #3: Help children have the best chances

"Lawyers offer the best opportunity for children caught in the middle of a divorce or who suffer from educational or societal disadvantages. Defending children often gives them an opportunity for a better future and better circumstances. After all, children are our future leaders; they need the right to get there."

"That's awesome, Noah. Give me a minute to get everything down on my iPhone. Tell me more about your friend, Brian."

Noah waited until I finished typing. I've noticed that he never talks when I'm on my phone. I don't know if it's out of courtesy, or maybe he just doesn't talk to people who aren't listening.

"Brian has done a lot of research on reading comprehension. A nephew of his had struggled with reading comprehension, and Brian wanted to help. He got some help from his interns as well. He devoted a lot of work to exploring reading comprehension and how one can develop it. Exciting stuff. His nephew eventually went to Harvard law school. The point isn't to get into Harvard or any specific law school. The point is to improve your reading.

"Brian's a good person and a valuable friend. Always eager to help. Alexandra, you should make sure you have a good support team in place to help you maximize your test-taking abilities."

I had no idea what Noah was talking about, but by now I'd learned he always explains himself.

"A support team isn't as scary as it sounds. It just means to think about the people around you. They know you're taking the LSAT and fully support you. And if they don't support you, make sure they don't know you're taking the test. Always surround yourself with people who encourage you. You know who they are. They're the friends and family who care about you and praise you for studying and reassure you over and over that you'll do great and be great. They worry about you and your future.

"Then there are the *schmucks* that give you a hard time. They ask you stupid questions like 'do you really want to be a lawyer? Why don't you finish college and go traveling or something?' Why don't *they* go traveling and leave you alone?"

I'd never seen Noah get agitated. He must have encountered people like this when he was studying for the LSAT. I didn't blame him for getting upset. He'd decided to pursue the career he wanted. And look at him today. If he had listened to those people, who knows where he would have ended up? Noah wasn't finished, but he calmed down a bit.

Noah and I simultaneously took a sip of our coffee. I was still getting used to coffee without almost any sugar. Noah continued his spiel.

"Avoid them like a witch avoids water. People like that are usually jealous of you or have a low self-image. Always, but always, **listen to those who encourage you to go for your dreams**. I don't care if your dream is to become an acrobat in outer space or a gumologist. If you don't go for your dreams, you'll never be happy with yourself."

"I totally get where you're coming from," I said. "My sister Lorraine is exactly the type you described—not very encouraging, so I know the feeling."

"Sorry if I got a little carried away. I knew a woman in college who kept telling me that I shouldn't become a lawyer."

I knew this was coming.

"She tried to convince me that I'm not the 'lawyer type,' as if she were a lawyer herself."

Noah *hated* when people expressed opinions about subjects they weren't experts in. And that's why he loves his experts—the people to

A Cadre of Experts

ask about their respective expertise. Heck, Noah was about to fly us both all the way to Texas to get expert advice about reading. I started to appreciate his passion for experts. Why waste time with somebody who thinks they know something about something, when they don't?

Chapter 7

Noah was ready the next morning at his office with a small carry-on; I had a carry-on and another full suitcase. We were only going for one day, but we'd be spending the night in Austin, so I'd brought an extra change of clothes. Okay, so I brought three changes of clothes, but who's counting? One needs to be prepared. What if there was an earthquake? I don't know whether extra clothes would be a vital part of my survival plan, but they wouldn't hurt. Noah seemed to notice.

"Good morning Alexandra, you know we'll only be in Austin for a day. Personally, I like to travel light."

"Good morning, Noah. Yes, I know we'll only be there for a day," I said, meaning, 'Don't ask questions.'

Chris, Noah's assistant, notified us that the limo was outside. I was a bit antsy, curious about what Judge Brian would teach me about reading comprehension.

"While learning about reading comprehension, I realized that I have to brush up on my vocabulary," I asked Noah, on the way to the airport. "I keep coming across words I don't recognize."

"That's a common problem. I'll give you three steps to improving your vocabulary. First, **list the unfamiliar words you come across**. Look them up and write down their definitions. Learning even 30 common LSAT words can have a noticeable impact.

"Second, you need to **start using these words in everyday conversation**. It can be intimidating to use a word if you aren't sure how to use it, but using new words in actual conversation is the best way to expand your vocabulary. A friend of mine in high school took French, but he could hardly speak more than a few sentences. That summer, he went to France. Can you guess what happened when he came back?"

A Cadre of Experts

"He learned how to make French toast?"

"That too. But he also came back fluent in French. Using new words in conversation is the best way to master them."

"What's the third step?"

"The third step is the most important. Next time you see a word you don't know, don't look it up. Instead, **read the sentences before and after it**, even a few times if needed, **until you get a sense of what the word *might* mean**. I'll give you an example. Let's say you read a sentence that says 'The woman's advice began to intenerate her husband's heart.' Do you know what *intenerate* means?"

"Nope."

"Well, what if the following sentences described how the husband began to change for the better? Would that give you a clue?"

"Sounds like *intenerate* might mean *to penetrate*."

"Not exactly, but close. The exact definition is a bit different, but you've understood the gist of the sentence. If this passage were on the LSAT, you'd probably be able to understand enough of the passage to ultimately answer the questions correctly."

"So what does *intenerate* mean?"

"The precise definition is *to soften*."

"Got it."

"From now on, **use this technique as an exercise**. Whenever you come across a word you don't recognize, don't look it up right away. First try to figure out its meaning by analyzing the context. You'll get better and faster at it. On the actual exam, you can't use a dictionary, so this skill is more important than memorizing a bunch of words. And since there's no official list of LSAT vocabulary words, this technique will actually be more helpful."

We landed in Austin four hours later. We'd missed breakfast in New York, and there wasn't any good food on the plane. After getting my suitcase, we spotted a small pizza restaurant in the airport. We walked up to the pizzeria and saw the following sign on the windowpane of the store:

"At this pizzeria, we do things differently than at the big chains. Come in and we'll prove it to you."

"It must be good pizza," I said, "at least according to their sign."

Noah disagreed. "All it says is that they do things differently than the big chains. That doesn't mean they do things better, just differently. That's what's called an assumption. You are assuming that *different* means *better*. I agree the owners meant that their pizza is indeed better—why else would they hang that sign? But, logically speaking, we cannot conclude from the sign that their pizza, even according to them, is better than the big chain's pizzas.

"Assumptions are huge on the LSAT, Alexandra. Let me give you another example. I'm sure you hear all the time about global warming. Some deniers have argued that since the earth has had climate change in the past without any dire consequences, therefore, this time around there also won't be any dire consequences. There are at least two logical fallacies in this argument, and yet it gets repeated in the media. First of all, there is an assumption here that the former climate changes were at least similar to this one, and that the fact that this one comes after multiple climate changes in the past doesn't matter."

"How does the media get away with such a bogus argument?"

"Most people don't watch the news with such a critical eye, and most people aren't lawyers. The second fallacy is-"

"Wait a second, Noah, what was the first one?"

"Didn't we just mention the huge assumptions they are making?" Noah replied, worried, as if I was losing my mind.

"That was an assumption, not a flaw," I responded.

"Alexandra, have you ever thought of getting a tattoo?" Noah asked hypothetically, not waiting for an answer. "Well, if you do, tattoo this onto your writing hand:

"It is a flaw to assume."

"If the argument needs an assumption to work, the argument is fallacious. The conclusion could be 'true' in the real world, but it's still a bad argument.

"An argument must have a premise, and conclusion, in either order, and the conclusion needs to follow smoothly from the premise. All boys love pizza; therefore, Sam loves pizza. What is the assumption here Alexandra?"

A Cadre of Experts

"The assumption here is that Sam is a boy. That is a fallacious argument because I have to assume something—in this case, that Sam is a boy—for it to work."

"Perfect. To make the *argument* logically sound, you must state in the argument the fact that Sam is a boy. It would sound like this: All boys like pizza; Sam is a boy, so Sam likes pizza. Is this starting to make sense, Alexandra?"

"What I'm not used to, is noticing real-life examples, like this one about the pizza sign. I would understand it to mean that their pizza is better. I wouldn't, at least until now, have thought about it that way."

"In my younger days, I took a lot of voice lessons. I wanted to be an opera singer. Don't ask what happened. I bounced around between a few different voice teachers. My voice was getting better, but not very rapidly. It wasn't until I found this one voice teacher, Dani, and he taught me something incredibly important. And it applies to the LSAT as well."

I was curious as to how anything from voice lessons might apply to the LSAT.

"Dani taught me that I can do all the voice exercises in the world, but the exercises will only impact my singing voice if I develop and practice my speaking voice. The speaking voice and the singing voice are not two separate entities; they're the same voice. I had to learn how to talk with the same qualities I use to sing, resonance, clarity, a full tone and the like. As soon as I started paying attention to my speaking voice—the voice I use in everyday conversation—my singing voice took off."

Noah indeed had a resonant speaking voice, clear, crisp, and commanding.

"The analogy to the LSAT is as follows: Logic is one of the main two skills you need on the LSAT. (The other one is the ability to read.) As with the less frequent use of your singing voice and the more common use of your speaking voice, you have your less frequent use of logic, which is on the exam, and the much more common use, which is everyday conversations or just plain thinking."

"That makes a lot of sense."

"Good, and I'll get back to that in a moment. The second logical fallacy of that argument about climate change is the fallacy of time; it is a flaw to say that whatever happened in the past will happen in the future. It does tie in with the first assumption a bit, but it's a separate fallacy. Of course on the LSAT, if an argument has two fallacies, they won't offer the two as separate answer choices. There is always only one correct answer."

"Not like in life I suppose," I said.

Noah pulled a yellow legal pad and a silver pen from his briefcase. On it, Noah had scribbled a bunch of illegible words, some with bubbles around them, some underlined impulsively. Noah tapped his pen on the pad. He was excited to share and decipher his scribbles.

"Alexandra, as you know, I taught the LSAT for five years. Two years before law school, and during school. But it wasn't until I met you that I was inspired to compose my top tips for LSAT success."

Noah's top LSAT tips—sounded interesting. I wondered how many he had.

"Seven," Noah said, as if he could read my mind. "My seven tips really encompass my whole study theory."

Noah's Top LSAT Tips #1
"You must practice logic in everyday situations."

"The more I practice my logic," I said, "the more natural it will feel. Then when I have to use it on the LSAT, it will be second nature?"

"Exactly. That's how the principles will become ingrained in your mind."

"Wow," I said, "that is profound."

Noah and I ordered pizza and sat at a high counter on matching high chairs. Noah brought us two bottles of spring water.

"Where are you up to on the list of logical fallacies?" Noah inquired.

"I didn't have a chance to start it yet," I answered, a bit embarrassed.

"The flaws are super-important. I would even memorize them. But don't memorize them like you remember the list of states and their capitals. Instead, use the method Rabbi Posner taught you. For every flaw, find an example you can use to easily remember that particular flaw."

A Cadre of Experts

"I'll get to it as soon as we get back to New York. I'll match them with some memorable ideas like you're suggesting."

We started our pizzas. They actually were different than the large chain pizza stores, *and* they were probably better.

Chapter 8

I looked out of the window from the 15th floor of the Marriott Hotel in Austin, Texas, at the incredible view of the city. I unpacked all my outfits and hung them neatly in the closet. I lay on the bed to rest for a while. Things were going so fast. I was learning important ideas from Noah and his cadre of experts, and taking notes so as not to forget anything. It was mind-boggling how one little encounter at a coffee stand in Manhattan has changed my life so much.

I was in a comfortable hotel with a few spare hours, so I decided to take a practice test. Maybe I wouldn't do the fifth section, just the first four. I texted Noah that I would be doing a practice test, and I would be busy for the next two and a half hours. He wished me luck, texting me "*Bonam Fortunam,*" (I had to Google it too).

Three hours later, I texted Noah, "Do I need to bring anything?"

"Maybe a pen and paper to take some notes," he responded, not remembering I take notes on my iPhone.

We met downstairs in the lobby. I had finished the test, taken a shower, changed my clothes, brushed my teeth, combed my hair, and sprayed on a touch of perfume. Noah hadn't even brushed his hair.

Noah ordered an Uber. We were on our way to see Judge Brian! The view on the ride there was breathtaking. Austin's scenery is fantastic. I'd never been there before—except when I was on a flight to Colorado that stopped over in Austin, so technically I had been here—but I hadn't ventured out.

Noah asked me how I'd done on the test. I'd scored 138. Not bad, compared to my last 134. As Noah said, as long as there is an upward trend, all is well.

I recalled Noah's list of what lawyers do and asked him about it.

A Cadre of Experts

What Lawyers Do #4: Fight for justice

"Upon passing the bar, a lawyer takes an oath to abide by the law and see that justice is carried out. Once you hire an attorney, it's their job to give you the best representation they can. You cannot truly appreciate a lawyer until you're facing injustice from a system or another person. Whether you're innocent of a crime or not, a significant factor in the outcome is the skill of your lawyer. In times like these, you want a lawyer on your side who will defend you to the bitter end. When no one else believes in your innocence, your lawyer will."

Twenty minutes later, we arrived at an impressive mansion. They sure treat their judges well here in Texas. We stopped at the gate, and a security guard came out from a little booth and approached the car window.

"We have an appointment with Judge Barnes," Noah said, before the guard had a chance to ask anything.

"Are you Mr. Levy?" the guard asked slowly, with a heavy Southern accent. The guard returned to his booth and opened the electronic gate.

"The court probably supplies the judge with security," Noah said.

"What a fabulous accent the guard has. Does Brian talk the same way?"

"Brian is from New York, so probably not. But you never know. Accents can change when people move. But that's more common among younger people, especially students."

"Why especially students?"

"I think it's because students are continually learning and thus are open to change. When you look up to a Professor, you might emulate her, even speak like her. Brian is a judge here; most people look up to him. My guess is his accent hasn't changed at all, but we'll see."

We pulled up to the judge's house. The place dripped with opulence, with its lush, perfectly manicured lawns and hedges and French doors. The windows were spotless. It was as if the house was brand new, despite its air of stately Southern elegance of a bygone era. Like all the greenery, it was meticulous. Its tasteful stone columns and graceful arcs were classically beautiful.

"Welcome, Noah, how in the world are you? Marvelous to see you," the judge exclaimed.

Judge Brian stood in the entrance of his house, smoking a cigar. He was tall, about six-two. He had brown hair—with a few white ones here and there–parted to the right, and a short, neatly trimmed brown beard. He wore a white button-down shirt and a blue tie, and black pants with dark blue suspenders. He was well built. His bearing commanded respect. You could tell he stood for justice.

"Alexandra, right?" Judge Brian asked.

"Yes, your honor," I said uncomfortably. I'd never met a judge before and had never used the term, "Your honor."

Judge Brian laughed. "Call me Brian. We're out of the courtroom, for heaven's sake. Besides, Noah's friends are my friends. Why don't you join me in my study?"

I walked into the living room, awed by its lavish furnishings. Sumptuous leather sofas adorned with throw pillows of brocade and damask swirls. Walls lined in rich mahogany, with bookshelves holding dozens upon dozens of books, some bound in leather, others with vibrant covers. Heavy curtains with golden *fleur de lis* accenting a wine-colored background. Windows stretched from the floor to the ceiling, making the second-floor halls clearly visible from the first.

In the center of the room sat a stately wooden desk. Surely this was where the judge spent a lot of his time. He seemed to be a man who loved his work.

Noah and I followed the judge into his study. It was large, and its walls were lined with books, almost as many as in the public library where I sometimes studied for the LSAT. Brian sat at his desk in a tall-backed leather chair with fancy arm rests. He crossed his legs and gestured for us to sit in the two chairs opposite the desk.

Noah started the conversation.

"Alexandra is studying for the LSAT but is having some trouble with the reading comprehension section. I know you've done extensive research on the topic, so we thought you could shed some light on it for us."

"Extensive?" the Judge said, placing his two hands on his desk. "How about exhaustive, eye-bleeding, sleep-depriving, back-breaking, prescription-for-migraines research?" Brian proclaimed in a booming and resonant voice. His accent was not at all Southern.

"You did the research, Brian; I'll let you describe it any way you want. I'm sure you're not exaggerating even one bit," Noah said with a grin.

"Okay, maybe I'm tooting my own horn a little. That research yielded some significant returns, though. My interns and I may have *cracked the code*."

That sounded interesting. It was as if somebody had told me they had the gossip of the year, no, of a lifetime. He had my attention.

"Alexandra, do you know what a gaggle-gadget-maximus is?" Brian asked. "Take your time."

I had no clue, and it showed on my face. I glanced at Noah. He just sat there, smiling.

Brian continued his cruel questioning. "How about this—when I say that word, gaggle-gadget-maximus, what comes to mind? What images or pictures?"

"Images? Nothing at all, Brian. I have no idea what that means, and no images or pictures come to mind."

"Then how do you expect to understand what it means?" Brian continued to toy with me. "Now if I say 'hotel room,' what comes to mind?"

"My room at the Marriott."

"Exactly," Brian said. "When you have a clear image of something in your head, that image surfaces from the subconscious to the conscious whenever you hear or read that word. If no image comes to mind, you cannot understand what it means.

"We read and understand in pictures, not words. Words are only a way to represent their meaning. When I asked you what the gaggle-gadget-maximus is, no image came to mind, because you don't have an image you can pull up."

I got the idea, but I wasn't sure I understood how it related to reading comprehension.

"As they say here in Texas, 'Let me give you the bacon without the sizzle.' When you read a paragraph or a passage and don't fully understand it, it's because you didn't pull up enough images, from your subconscious, as you read it."

"But if I do know the vocabulary in the passages I'm reading," I said, "why would I not understand the passage?"

"Simple, Alexandra. It's because; while you know the words, even when you know the meaning, you're not allowing yourself to imagine the story being told with images surfacing in your conscious mind. You have to deliberately think of those images as you read. **You have to create a movie.** You don't need to think about every single word; just the words that create the movie in your head."

"I am eager to see how it works," I said. "Can I try it on an actual book?"

"Sure, why don't you grab the one on the coffee table?"

I picked up the book and opened it to a random page. It was a legal text on Texas's appellate court rulings. I started to read out loud. "*The defendant, Mr. Delacruz, caused physical damage to the landlord's property using a baseball bat.*"

"Ok," Brian interrupted, "what do you see?"

"Nothing yet, Brian," I replied.

"Read it again. This time, focus on the images. Actually, a better way would be to *allow* the images to rise to your conscious."

I tried it again. This time, I focused on images of what I was reading.

"Okay, so I see this guy; it's Mr. Delacruz, and he's holding a bat; he's also sweating after having gone nuts with the bat on a building owned by the landlord."

"Spectacular," the Judge proclaimed. "You did a splendid job."

Noah jumped in. "I could really see the scene Alexandra was describing. Thinking about it in the form of a story made the sentence come alive."

"Precisely, Noah. Alexandra, would you like to continue another sentence?"

"The plaintiff, Mr. Smith, brought suit against Mr. Delacruz, for $14,800 for damages and $12,000 for mental anguish, as Mr. Smith inherited the property from his late mother."

Judge Brian rubbed his hands together. "Now, what did you see? Spare no detail, Alexandra."

A Cadre of Experts

"I see Mr. Delacruz being served a summons to court, and he opens the claim to see he is being sued for $26,800. What a look on his face. I see Mr. Smith, an older gentleman, frowning because of his mental anguish. He's standing next to a picture of his mother, who gave him the property before she died. He's holding a hammer, as he is starting to repair the property. That's about it."

"Bravo," Noah and Brian said together, as if they were a duet.

"I saw the images, like you said, in a story form. This method makes everything more realistic. Amazing."

"Brian," Noah said, "how can Alexandra make this a habit and incorporate it into her reading comprehension on the LSAT?"

"You won't have time during the exam to use this method, at least not in the way you just did," Brian said. "But practicing this method will make you more conscious of it, and it will come more naturally.

"I recommend practicing this method on one passage a day. Don't rush through it. Make the reading come alive, as if you're watching a movie. Take your time and turn it into an experience. Ideally, do the process out loud, as if you were explaining it to someone."

"Should I use a reading comprehension passage?"

"Not necessarily. An article in *The Economist* would work fine when it comes to strengthening your imagery. Besides, you don't want to use up too many LSAT passages; which brings me to another point.

"**Using real LSAT questions**, when practicing for the LSAT, **is vital** to your success. The LSAC (Law School Admission Council) spends a lot of money to develop questions, and those people are excellent at what they do. I've seen some of the fake questions people write in their spare time. They're not even close. When it comes to the exercise I gave you, though, it doesn't matter."

"Besides, Alexandra," Noah added, "There are so many LSATs out there. Why bother using fake ones?"

"Back to the exercise," the Judge ruled. "Work through one article every day. Let the images flow and describe them in detail. Then, close the magazine or whatever you're reading, and without looking inside, repeat the entire article aloud to yourself, again using all the details, the colors, the sizes, the feelings, the contrast, the mood."

I took out my iPhone and started writing down the steps Brian was dictating.

Brian pushed himself back in the chair to indicate that not only was he finished, but that he was proud of himself. And why not? Most people go through life like fish in a stream. They don't try to see what happens if they swim against the tide. Brian wasn't like that. When his nephew was struggling with reading, he didn't just tell him to shut up and practice. He took it upon himself to help him. He dedicated time and effort. That was something to be proud of.

"Brian, I can't tell you how much we appreciate this," Noah said.

"Well before you go, let me give you another exercise. This one is quite straightforward. All you have to do is listen to a text being read out loud and read along in the actual text. You can do this with audiobooks for example, or with some online newspapers that have audio readings of the articles. Simply listen to the audio, and read silently inside. This strengthens the connection between what you read and what your brain hears, as often there can be a disconnect. When that disconnect occurs, it's what they call 'passive reading,' reading without really hearing or absorbing what you read."

"Sounds fascinating," Noah said.

"I would recommend trying it for an hour or so, and if you feel the connection beginning to occur, keep at it."

"Wow, thank you so much Brian," I said, "this has been a lot of fun."

"Noah, Alexandra, the pleasure was all mine. Well, as we say here in Texas, 'That's all she wrote.'"

Chapter 9

Back at the hotel, we retired to our rooms to rest and shower. We were going to dinner and then to the airport to fly back to New York.

Two hours later I met Noah downstairs in the lobby. He was talking to the front-desk receptionist, asking him if he knew any good places to eat dinner. I wasn't sure, but thought I overheard the phrase "someplace romantic."

We got into a cab and Noah gave the driver the address. On the way there, I asked Noah for his next thought about what lawyers do.

What Lawyers Do #5: Help Businesses

"Lawyers work with companies to protect their legal rights in business dealings and direct them on what a business can do within the guidelines of corporate law. Lawyers can save companies and clients a lifetime of work."

We pulled up to a cozy restaurant in a hilly area near Austin. It was getting dark, and I was getting hungry. Maybe I'd have a salad with chicken and croutons. And dessert.

The waiter brought us two menus, along with ice water and bread and olive oil. Our silverware was already on the table, wrapped in fancy purple napkins.

"I love a good hamburger," I told Noah, "but I only eat them well-done. Whenever I order hamburgers at restaurants, they never cook them fully. I don't want to waste our time."

"Does that premise support your conclusion?" Noah asked. "From the fact that some restaurants don't cook hamburgers thoroughly, can you reach a broad, sweeping conclusion that all restaurants won't cook your hamburger thoroughly?"

Here we go.

"There's a common flaw tested on the LSAT called overgeneralization. This happens in an arguement when the evidence isn't strong enough to support the conclusion.

"Think about it like a triangle. You have two points on the bottom and a third one on the top. The bottom represents a broad spectrum, and the top represents a narrower spectrum. Anything that has enough proof to be supported by the bottom two points can be proven true in the top point. Does that make sense?"

"Sort of."

"If you say that all baseball players are tall, you can conclude that Joe, who is a baseball player, is tall. So 'all baseball players' is a broad statement, a premise, belonging to the bottom of the triangle. 'Joe' is a much narrower example, the conclusion, belonging on the top of the triangle."

"I'm only guessing," I said, "but if it was the opposite, Joe is tall, therefore all baseball players are tall, it would be wrong."

"Exactly," Noah said happily. "But can you tell me how that applies to the triangle?"

"I think … that Joe being tall is an example that would be on the top, but that can't prove the bottom points, or the broader idea."

"Perfect, Alexandra. And this illustrates the ultimate triangle rule: **The triangle can only work from the bottom to the top, not from the top to bottom.**

"You can only take something from the bottom two points, something that is broad, to prove something that is on the top, the narrower example."

"Now it makes sense," I said.

"I would say your example of the few restaurants that served you raw meat isn't enough to prove all restaurants do that. The example is too small. That example would be situated on which part of the triangle?"

"At the top."

"Right. That can't be used as support for the bottom. It would have to be that 'all restaurants don't fully cook their hamburgers, so this restaurant won't fully cook the hamburger.' Make sense? Now let's order some food."

Here too, Noah had the waiters on remote control, as the waiter came within three seconds.

"I'll have the wild mushroom polenta," Noah said. "And the skirt steak San Pedro."

"Splendid choice," the waiter said. I hate when they say that. Would they ever say you'd made a *bad* choice?

"I'll have the chicken salad with balsamic dressing," I said. "Oh, and do you have a wine list?"

"On the back, ma'am," the waiter answered in a heavy Texas drawl. I flipped the menu over. "I'll have a glass of Pinot Noir."

"Excellent choice," the waiter said again. "That'll go fine with the chicken."

Okay, this time he gave his reason.

"And you, sir? Any wine for you?"

"I'll have a glass of Cabernet Sauvignon."

Noah passed our menus to the waiter. "I see my spiel didn't convince you. You know, about the hamburger."

"I actually decided to get the chicken before we arrived here. But I do understand your point about overgeneralizations."

"The truth is, in real life we don't always have to act one hundred percent within the boundaries of logic. We're not Vulcans. Especially in personal matters, such as what to eat. If you want chicken instead of hamburger because restaurants don't cook meat to your taste, as my cousin says, 'go nuts.'

"Life defies logic. Look at people who perform crazy stunts, just for the adrenaline or to become the next YouTube star. That's not logical, to say the least. It doesn't make sense to risk your life for something so unimportant, but people do it. They'll say, 'I know, maybe it's illogical, but I'm doing it anyway.' What can you say to that?"

"Sometimes life doesn't make sense."

"That said, it's always good to evaluate and take the time to think things through. So how did you enjoy Judge Brian's company?"

"He's an inspiring guy, and his house is impressive. I'm eager to try his reading comprehension techniques. I'll practice when we get back to New York tonight."

"Oh, right, about that," Noah said with a grin. "We're, um, not going back to New York tonight. You remember my mentor from Berkeley, California? I booked us tickets to San Francisco—that is, if you still want to meet him."

"Professor Levine, right?"

"I also have other friends I would like to see if we're out there. There's Donna, Graham ..."

"Sure, I'll go. Sounds fun." I knew I'd been smart to pack extra clothes. Call it a girl's intuition.

"Okay, wonderful," Noah said, "our flight is at 9:00 p.m."

The waiter brought our wine and set it on the table. We each lifted our glasses. Noah paused. "Cheers and L'chaim, to your success on the LSAT and in law school."

"Thanks." I paused for a moment. "And to your fascinating friends and your law firm."

We clinked our glasses.

"Speaking of meat, Noah, I usually prefer chicken, because whenever I eat red meat I feel tired."

"So you're saying red meat causes you to become tired? Could it be that when you're tired, you crave meat?"

I chuckled. "What do you mean?"

"Although I doubt that it's true, logically speaking when one event follows another, it doesn't necessarily imply the first one caused the second one. In this case, just because you get tired after eating red meat, doesn't mean that meat caused the fatigue. It might be the case that when your body is tired, it craves protein. I'm pretty sure that this is not actually true, but using logic, we can't prove causation from a correlation.

"I'll give you another example. They say that when ice cream sales go up, drowning, in pools or in the ocean, goes up as well. Does that mean the increase of ice-cream sales causes the increase in drowning?"

"No, maybe the fact ice-cream sales go up in the summer season has to do with it."

"Go on," Noah encouraged. "Why do the sales go up in the summer?"

"Because of the heat." I paused, wondering if I was on the right track. "And in the summer more people go swimming, hence the higher rate of drowning," I said quickly, excited at having figured it out. Or had I?

Noah picked up his glass. "Bravo, Alexandra, that's exactly right."
So I did get it.

"As you said, Alexandra, it's not that ice-cream sales caused the drowning. There is a third factor that caused both of the events to happen. While there is a correlation between the two outcomes, there is no causation; one didn't cause the other.

"Just because two events occur one after the other, doesn't prove that the first one caused the second one. Maybe when you're about to be tired, you crave red meat?"

"Now I get it. And this stuff is on the LSAT?" I asked. I learned not to be embarrassed to ask Noah questions.

Noah answered with a question. "Is Texas big? Sure, it's all over the LSAT."

The waiter brought our food. It smelled delicious. Noah took a bite of his steak and I poured balsamic dressing on my salad.

Still chewing, Noah wanted to add another point. "There's one more thing with the correlation and causation idea. After that, no more LSAT stuff until after dinner."

I was okay with that.

"The third option-"

"Wait, what were the first two?" I asked, typing.

"The first option is that a third factor caused both events. The second option is that instead of A causing B, it was actually B that caused A. Got it?"

"Yes."

"The third option is that there could simply be no connection at all. Yesterday it rained in Manhattan more than usual for the season, and there was an explosion at a factory in Nevada. Does that mean one caused the other? Probably not. It's also probably not the case that a third element caused both of these events. Not everything that happens at the same time or in concession has to have a connection."

Noah lived up to his promise. There was no more LSAT talk for the rest of the evening. We enjoyed talking about life, the food, our personal histories. I learned Noah had a comfortable childhood with his parents and two siblings. They lived in Upper East Side of Manhattan. He attended private schools, and never had to worry about money in college. Quite the opposite of my story.

"That sounds like a beautiful childhood," I said to Noah. "I never had the privileges of private schools or tutors. I actually had a pretty unstable childhood."

"You still turned out awesome."

"I'm just trying to focus on the whole law school ordeal. Thanks to you, I might have a chance."

"I'm glad to help Alexandra. Just remember this: **Don't let the LSAT or law school determine your self-worth.**"

"I know, but I've always had this need to prove to everybody how smart I am. The LSAT puts you in a percentile with other test-takers, so you get a sense of how you compare with other people."

"Well since you brought it up, it's true the LSAT gives you a percentile among LSAT takers, but LSAT takers are a smart bunch to begin with. It's not comparing you to the general population. Regardless, a person's IQ doesn't define them. It doesn't add to or subtract from their worth, in my opinion."

"Well then," I said, "what does?"

"How they live their life," Noah responded, "how they treat other people, *what people say about them after they die.*"

"I never thought of it that way. This is deep stuff for a lawyer who can see half of Manhattan from his office window."

"Did I tell you I'm writing my own eulogy?" Noah asked, jokingly, I hoped.

"No, you did not tell me that."

"I only have the first couple of sentences. I figure I have a while to complete it. I do have a deadline, no pun intended, although I don't know when it is."

"Can I hear it, Noah?"

Noah cleared his throat and recited from memory: "'Noah was a brilliant man with a high credit score. Actually, he had quite a crappy credit score, and he was average brilliant.' That's all I have."

I laughed out loud. "That was incredible."

"It's good to see you smile Alexandra. You deserve it."

We took the last sips of our wine and wiped our hands on the fancy purple napkins. Noah paid the bill, and left the waiter a massive tip.

Chapter 10

We slid our carry-ons into the storage above our first class seats. I stared out the window as the plane took off. Looking out into the infinite blue sky, there was a weightlessness that pushed us mentally towards every goal and dream that we had ever wished. Far below, beneath the cakey white clouds that dotted the deep, wide blue, houses and little buildings curled and stacked atop each other like little blocks sandwiched between blue streaks of water that trickled in and around the hullabaloo of houses and constructions of the industrial complex. Far to the left and fading away were roads, highways and train tracks that carried people to and from this magnificent spectacle of humanity—as we flew up and away. The captain announced that we reached the full 30,000 feet altitude.

"I guess we're in God's hands now," I said, looking out the window.

"Since you brought it up Alexandra, do you believe in God?"

"Never met her."

"Well what does that prove?" he asked.

"I don't know if there is or isn't a God. Nobody has been able to prove that there is one."

"If I understand you correctly, you're saying that since there is no proof God exists, he therefore doesn't? Sounds like a logical fallacy to me."

"Which fallacy would that be?"

"The flaw I'm referring is that 'a lack of evidence is not evidence.' If you cannot prove something exists, that doesn't prove that it doesn't exist. If you cannot prove that God exists, that doesn't prove he doesn't. Make sense?"

The flight attendant offered us drinks. We asked for water. It's important to stay hydrated on flights.

"I understand the idea, Noah. Lack of evidence. I'll remember that. But what about world hunger, suffering, disease? Doesn't that prove there is no God?"

"Does it?"

"I would think so. They teach that God is compassionate."

"I hear your point, Alexandra, but you're making two assumptions here. Do you know what they are?"

If I knew what they were, I wouldn't have said it. But true to my word, I would try to apply LSAT logic in my daily life.

"I'm assuming that what they teach about God is true," I said.

"Good. And the second assumption?"

"I'm not sure."

"You're assuming that if God is good, bad can never happen. Isn't the law good, even though people are wrongfully convicted? And who said God is causing the hunger? Maybe he's letting humankind run their own lives."

"So you're saying he does exist?"

"That's another assumption, Alexandra. Now you're assuming if I challenge your belief in something, I must believe in the opposite."

"So what *do* you believe?" I asked impatiently.

"I have no idea."

Great.

"Speaking of God and logical fallacies," Noah continued, "I've heard an argument that said something like this: 'The Bible is the Word of God because God tells us it is... in the Bible.' Did you catch the flaw in that argument?"

"It *sounds* wrong, but I don't know whether I can name the flaw."

"That's what's called 'circular logic.' It presupposes what it sets out to prove. It simply states as its conclusion, one of the premises. And that is something that comes up on the LSAT."

It was crazy how Noah could plug in LSAT stuff in almost everything he said, but it was working, and I was starting to get it.

"Noah, tell me a bit more about your mentor, I can't wait to meet him."

"Professor Levine, my mentor, is the smartest man I know. He won the California Chess Tournament when he was 14. And, he did it *blindfolded*."

"That sounds hard."

"Hard?" Noah asked, almost insulted. "That's not hard, it's genius. He went on to become a CPA, was enlisted in the Navy, and then enrolled in law school. He earned his Master's and a Ph.D. in business. Not that he's stopped reading since. He reads about two books a week. His father told him that college students become dumb after college because they stop reading. He made sure that didn't happen to him.

"I met Professor Levine in law school. He taught me contracts. Talk about the Socratic Method. We've stayed in touch. He even helped me find my first job out of law school."

"That is impressive," I said. "Is there anything you want to ask him specifically? Like we asked Judge Brian about reading and your Rabbi about learning habits. What is his expertise?"

"He's an expert in a lot of areas, but I want to ask him about perspective. He's been around the block a few times. He has a higher perspective on life, you'll see."

"You said there are some other friends you want to visit while we're there."

"There's a few, depending on our time, of course. You must meet Graham—he's a baseball coach for the Oakland A's. He's the best there is in training for endurance, speed, stuff like that. There are a few others, but like I said, it depends on the time."

Before we knew it, the captain announced the landing. I usually sleep on flights, but then again, I usually don't sit next to such an interesting conversationalist.

"Where do you usually meet Professor Levine?"

"I usually meet him in his office at Boalt."

"So I suppose that's where we'll meet him."

"Alexandra, the plane is about to land, so we don't have much time to talk about this, but that's called the 'fallacy of time.'"

Wow, four flaws in one flight; lack of evidence, two assumptions, circular logic, and the fallacy of time.

"It is fallacious to assume because something has happened in the past it will undoubtedly happen in the future. True, I usually meet

Professor Levine at his office, but that doesn't prove that we'll meet him there this time. In what LSAT students will refer to as 'real life,' nobody would call you out on such a flaw, but in the 'LSAT world,' that is a flaw. Don't take this the wrong way, Alexandra. I'm just trying to teach you by example so that it will stick better.

"Remember what Rabbi Posner said: use signs to remember ideas. Next time you come across the fallacy of time, you'll remember this example. It will be much less abstract now that you've used it in real life."

"I honestly love these small, real-life illustrations of flaws," I said. "It makes them feel more real. Of course I'm not offended, Noah. Hey, hand me my carry-on, will you?"

Chapter 11

I rolled down the passenger side window of our rental car. On our way from the Olive Tree Hotel in San Francisco to the famous UC Berkeley Boalt law school, I figured it would be appropriate to ask Noah for the next idea on what lawyers do.

What Lawyers Do #6: A Wide Variety

"As you know, our society, the way we live, and a large part of what we do every day are all bound by rules we call 'laws.' It is the job of lawyers to understand these rules and help people live their lives more meaningfully. Lawyers help people in distress. They advocate in areas that personally motivated them, such as women's rights or the protection of refugees, for example. There are many different fields of law: corporate law, criminal law, property law, copyright law, family law, maritime law, contract law, constitutional law, and so on. There are also a few dozen specialties, and you should look into them. You might discover types of law you never knew existed that might interest you. Lawyers work out of law firms, in private practice, in boardrooms, in a prosecutor's or defender's office, Congress, as social activists, and in academia. Here, too, the list goes on. Lawyers are often referred to as 'social engineers' because they can change laws that affect our lives every day."

"Hello, Noah," Professor Levine's secretary said, as she stood and spread her arms in a grand gesture. Her face had soft features, and her voice was warm.

"Hello, Judy. Long time no see," Noah said, smiling widely.

"Go right in, the Professor is waiting for you."

Professor Levine's office was calming. The lamps cast a light shadow over the place, allowing me to take a breath and relax. My hands rested on the velvety arms of my chair, and the feeling of the power in the room gave me a sense of urgency and pride about going to law school next year.

Professor Levine was on the phone. "Two friends of mine from New York just walked in, I have to go," he said to whoever was on the other end.

He was a noble man in his early eighties. He had strong white hair. His desk was a bit messy, and his look stern. I felt he was reading us like a clairvoyant. He had beautiful paintings on the walls, along with bookshelves containing volumes of law, history and philosophy. On his desk, framed pictures of his three daughters were displayed.

"Noah," he proclaimed loudly, "sit down, please. How have you been? And how are you, dear …?"

"Alexandra," I said. "I'm fine sir, how are you?"

"Call me sir again and I'll give you ten pushups," Professor Levine said with a grin. I was about to say, "Yes, sir," but I caught myself.

"No problem, um, Professor Levine."

"I'm fantastic," Noah said, as he sat down and rested one arm on the back of my chair. "So glad to see you, Professor."

It seemed that the Professor was a guy who liked to cut to the chase.

"I know you didn't make this trip all the way from New York just to say hello. What's on your minds?"

"We actually came from Austin, but you're right—we didn't come here just to say hello. Alexandra is studying for the LSAT, and she was wondering if you have any LSAT secrets to give her.

Professor Levine, sitting in his office chair, put on a serious look. "Well, let's see here. You came all the way here, let me make sure what I tell you is worth your first-class tickets." I guess he knew Noah pretty well.

"Back in my chess-playing days, I must have played over ten thousand games. You know what happens after that many games? Do you know what changes?"

"I'm sure you win more games," Noah commented.

"That's true, but what changes?"

"Your understanding of the game?" I said, trying my luck.

"I'm looking for something more specific. What changes, my New Yorker friends, is your *perspective.* Imagine the difference between an ant's perspective of a field it's in, and an eagle's view of that same field. The ant can see what's going on in its immediate surroundings. The eagle can see the field, the farmers, and the tractors.

"Your intention—and that's something I'll talk about in a moment—during studying should be to improve your understanding of logic, your mastery of the English language, and your analytical skills. It's not a matter of learning some tricks about formal logic or how to use the process of elimination. It's about developing a keener eye, a deeper understanding of what you're reading."

Professor Levine's secretary's voice came through over the intercom. She told him that the dean was on the phone. The Professor said he'd call him back. I guess when you have tenure, even the dean can wait.

"If you've ever seen those Disney movies," he continued, "and I've seen plenty of those with my grandkids, you'll notice that there are always jokes that are meant for the adults. Those jokes fly way over the kid's heads, but Disney knows that kids don't go to movies by themselves, so they make the movie enjoyable for the parents too.

"A parent and a child watch the same movie, but they see different things, get different messages, and hear different jokes, because they have different perspectives.

"The LSAT, or reading and logic in general, can also be understood on many levels. Your goal should be to develop a higher perspective of understanding the underlying concepts—like I mentioned, the English, the logic, and the analytical skills."

Professor Levine took a sip from his water bottle. Noah and I sat attentively, waiting for more words of wisdom.

"So, how is this done? How do you develop a higher perspective? I believe that your intention is tremendously important. When you engage in an activity, *state your intention.* Before you play a game of basketball with your friends, state your purpose. 'My intention is to have a good time with my friends, to get some stress-relieving exercise, to show off some of my basketball tricks, and to win the game.' Stating your intentions before you begin an activity sends a clear message to your subconscious to let it know the desired outcome. Your subconscious does its best to guide you to that outcome.

"If you sit with your banker and talk to her about the weather, chances are you won't get a loan. If you ask for a loan, your chances increase considerably.

"Before you study, tell yourself that your intention is to develop a better understanding of the concepts. State that you need to attain a higher perspective. Remember the ant and the eagle, and the vast difference between their views. Tell your subconscious you need to go from *an ant to an eagle*. That's your goal."

That was definitely insightful. I slipped my hand into my pocket to pull out my iPhone, opened up the Notes app, and wrote everything down. Noah, who had been quiet the whole time, spoke up.

"Professor Levine, do you use this method yourself? When teaching, for example?"

"I sure do. Before class, I state my intentions. 'My intention for this class is to provide students with a deep understanding of contracts, provoke their minds to promote independent thinking, worthy of the attorneys they aspire to be. I will help them understand the fundamentals, and teach them how to ask the right questions.' That's what I've been saying before classes for 40 years. Just a few weeks ago I started reciting it from memory."

Noah laughed. Professor Levine had a good sense of humor, too.

"That's awesome," I said, "and if I understand correctly, the best way to improve on the LSAT is to develop a higher perspective, and the way to do that is to study with that intention?"

"Yes," Professor Levine answered. "Well said. So, should we head for the café? I could use some lunch." Professor Levine said.

The three of us stood.

"Tell the dean I'll call him back later," the Professor told his secretary on our way out, winking at Noah.

We followed Professor Levine to the café. Noah and the Professor caught up while we walked. Noah talked about some interesting lawsuits he'd had. Professor Levine listened. The campus was filled with students. Hearing all the chatter of the students and seeing them carry their heavy textbooks excited me for the following year, when I'd finally start law school.

As I was walking on the campus alongside the two lawyers, I felt somewhat out of place. Young minds walked the grounds, their thoughts imparted with the knowledge that bound them to rules that created power, and empowered them to change that power once it suited their needs. Yes, I'd be going to law school eventually, but now I was a liberal arts major. I just couldn't wait.

Over the past year, I'd associated my self-worth with becoming an attorney. When you ask somebody what he or she is, they will answer an accountant, a lawyer, a doctor, a fireman, as if their profession is who they are. I know this is not true, but I fall for the delusion every time. Am I a liberal arts major? Is that *who* I am? I want to be something more, something more prestigious: an attorney. But not just any attorney. I made up my mind. I was going to Boalt. If I could get in, of course.

We reached the café and ordered a Mediterranean brunch, hard-boiled eggs, fried eggplant, tahini sauce and Turkish coffee.

"Alexandra, have you started shopping around for law schools?" Professor Levine asked.

"Not yet," I lied. I knew I was applying to Boalt, but with my current LSAT scores, I didn't feel comfortable telling the truth. "Probably a few schools in New York, maybe one or two out here. You know, to try my luck."

"That sounds like a strategy you got from YouTube or some blog. You should put more thought into your planning."

Noah spoke up. "Professor Levine, maybe you could give Alexandra some pointers."

"My number-one tip for any aspiring lawyer," the Professor said without hesitation, "would be *to go to law school.*"

"And?" I asked.

"And that's it. Do you think there's another way?"

"No, it just seems like very basic advice, that's all," I said, hoping I didn't sound rude.

"The simplest advice is usually the best, in my opinion. I know you were probably waiting to hear some deep analysis about how to compare school rankings, job statistics and faculty publications to produce some magical number that would determine the best option for you. I don't believe in that. A law school is a school of law. They teach law, and the law is taught the same wherever you go."

The Professor took a sip of his Turkish coffee. "If you go to a law school 'ranked' number one, in the first-year criminal law class they will teach you the definition of first-degree murder as 'an intentional murder that is willful and premeditated with malice aforethought.' If you go to a law school ranked 100, they'll teach you the definition of first-degree murder as 'an intentional murder that is willful and premeditated with malice aforethought.' A legal education is a legal education. Everyone has to pass the bar. If one school has a lower bar passage rate, it's because the students may not be studying as hard. Besides, there are plenty of law school deans, famous judges and other legal scholars who passed the bar on their second or third try.

"The real questions are: Which school can get you the best job? How much debt will you be left with? And where will you feel most comfortable? That's what matters. The top-ranked schools are not necessarily the top-ranked for finding jobs, or for debt, or for mental health. Plenty of smaller, local schools have faculty who will strive to help students find jobs, and may be less competitive in nature.

"There's also a better chance of landing a scholarship at one of the smaller or 'lower- ranked' schools. You have to understand that debt will cripple you. This might be simple advice, but *the less debt, the better.*"

"Are you saying it doesn't matter at all which law school I go to?" I asked, almost upset at the simplicity of the Professor's explanation.

Professor Levine made a face I'm sure he made often when a student got something completely wrong in his class. "I didn't say it doesn't matter. It matters to an extent—in terms of jobs, debt, physical location, and specific programs a student may want, but not much more than that. Some schools have classes in certain types of law that other schools don't have, like ERISA or privacy law or environmental law.

"My colleagues' kids and grandkids often call me, asking me if they should go to law school X or Y, X having a ranking of 35 and offering a 90% scholarship while Y has a ranking of 33 and is offering a 10% scholarship. And my favorites are those who ask if they should go at all

A Cadre of Experts

since they didn't get into a top three school." Professor Levine paused for a second, "You know what? They probably shouldn't go."

"What do you mean, Professor?" Noah asked, "You always encourage people to pursue an education."

"I do. However, a student who won't go to law school unless it's ranked in the 'top three,' doesn't honestly want to be a lawyer. They wish to go to a top three school for its own sake. If that student wanted to become an attorney, they would go to any law school they could get into. If someone's goal is to become an attorney, as long as they pass their State Bar, it doesn't matter one iota which school they went to."

"Now I see what you're saying, Professor Levine," Noah said.

"**Don't choose a law school because it's 'ranking**.' Even for those who care about the rankings, the U.S. News rankings change every year, from what I hear, not that I waste time reading the rankings magazine.

"Who ranks them, anyway? If it were God's Official Rankings, then maybe. But they're obviously not. They're just incompetent people judging educational institutions hiding behind the name of a magazine. Are they legal scholars? If they were, they would find a better job. The rankings do much more harm than good. **They make students believe that the 'rankings' are the only thing in the *world* students should consider** when deciding which law schools to apply to; steering students in the wrong direction and causing them more mental anguish than they deserve. Don't be a *sheep* and follow the golden-*calf* rankings."

"What if I can find a more legitimate system of law school rankings?" I asked, hopeful.

"Alexandra, the idea that all value can be measured on a generic scale of quality is ridiculous. I see value as subjective, dynamic, and contextual. The hegemony of the U.S. News rankings makes little sense to those who want to see innovation in pedagogy, the creation of knowledge, and a robust set of educational options for the many students who are seeking them. The idea of ranking schools is *flawed at its core*."

"But don't law firms care about the law school rankings?"

"No, they don't. Do you think the hiring partners or government lawyers with 20 or 30 years' experience feel a need to consult with a magazine? They know better than that.

"When I was in my second year of law school, I went to a networking event. There I met an attorney by the name of Jason. We spoke for about 30 minutes, mainly about *his* firm, the work *he* did, and *his* current cases. He didn't really care who I was, what school I was in, or my grades or class ranking. As Jason started to leave, I offered to do some free research for him, on weekends. He snapped his fingers and remembered that he indeed had some research that needed tending to. I gave him my phone number and address –there was no email back then—and a few days later I got a letter from him with a research request. The lawyer didn't even know what school I was in. And that has always been the case. Attorneys don't care which school you went to; they just care that you can get the job done. Oh, and after law school, Jason hired me. I worked there for five years. And until my last day there, he never knew which law school I had attended."

"Do the rankings have no significance?" I asked, feeling challenged by the Professor's assertions.

"We human beings have an remarkable talent. We make things up, *and then give those things importance*. Awards, rankings, social status and so on. We make up – literally, invent something out of thin air – and then give it importance. Like driving expensive cars that are actually less efficient than cheaper cars; it's just a made-up symbol of social status. And so are the dumb rankings."

This was a lot of new information and a much different viewpoint than I'd had until today. Still, I felt the *need* to argue with this genius who's been teaching law longer than I've been alive, to confirm my preexisting ideas I'd picked up from all the blogs I'd read.

"But don't a lot of employers only hire from the top-ranked schools?" I asked.

"Very few do, and plenty of employers prefer to hire from their alma mater. Any school that's been around for a while has about 20,000 living alumni who may prefer to hire students from their own law school. Besides, there's a strong local preference for hiring. Very few schools have national reach. You know who do say rankings have value, Alexandra? *The law schools ranked the highest.*

"Many of the country's best attorneys went to third or fourth-tier schools. And many graduates of the most prestigious schools never made it big. *It's about the student, not the school,* to be totally frank. Take O.J. Simpson's dream team; most of them didn't attend Ivy League law schools; they went to Loyola, Boston, San Diego, and so on. None of those are Ivy League, but are obviously good schools. One of Michael Jackson's main attorneys went to UC Hastings. In a more recent case, Dominique Strauss-Kahn hired Ben Brafman, one of the best criminal defense attorneys in the country. Brafman went to Ohio Northern University law school."

The Professor called his secretary. "Judy, can you tell me what ONU law school's ranking is?"

"Sure Professor, one moment... The most recent ranking is 145."

"I rest my case."

"And is the education really the same across the schools?"

"Of course. I could give you hundreds of other attorneys, all top of their fields and extremely successful, who didn't go to top ranked schools. I've met attorneys who've complained that at their top-ranked law school, the school hired student teacher assistants to teach classes, because the school didn't have to worry about their reputation. A younger colleague went to a law school ranked 22 the year she applied, but 40 the year she matriculated. That turned out to be the best thing that ever happened to the school. Because of that drop, they hired many new distinguished professors, opened an academic support program and more. When they were content with their ranking, they didn't feel the need to invest as much in their students. Like I said, the rankings cause more harm than good. A lot more harm."

"That makes sense."

"Sure, some students will still care, and you can't change everyone's mind, but you can decide for yourself what really matters to you."

We continued to talk as we strolled back to the Professor's office. Professor Levine turned to Noah.

"You know what I've found fascinating? Students follow the U.S. News rankings *like a religion*. I don't think that the U.S. News rankings deserve this level of reverence. They're worthy of being challenged if they're worthy of anything. Students follow the rankings to such an extent that it can affect their mental health, because tens of thousands of students are all following the *same* system and trying to get into the *same* schools.

"Imagine a ranking system for laptops. I, for one, know nothing about computers. If it weren't for the kind salespeople at Best Buy, I would just purchase the laptop based on its price, or even its look. What the salespeople do is ask me what I need, what I use a laptop for, and what I am looking to spend. They ask me for example if I need to play DVDs, which I don't. Based on all the information I provide, they help me choose the best option. But if there was some ranking system for laptops, I might just buy the highest ranked laptop I could afford. Do you see the problem with that Alexandra?"

"I do. If the top ten laptops on the list all have DVD players and cost more because of that, you might waste your money and not get the best laptop for your needs."

"Thank you. And the same thing goes for law schools; no list suits every student, or even most. There are a lot of factors you need to research about a law school[2] to find your best-match, which really isn't the same for everyone.

"The U.S. News doesn't reveal the exact formula for their rankings, so you can't use their rankings to determine anything. Once they rank Yale, Harvard, and Stanford as one, two, and three, respectively, anything after that seems legitimate. Most people agree that those three schools are the top three. Once you agree with someone on two or three things, they're more likely to accept other ideas you offer."

"Professor, don't the rankings at least provide information about employment statistics?" Noah asked.

"All that's done is caused schools to alter their employment statistics, such as by hiring their students post-law school for a brief few months. As I mentioned, the rankings do more harm than good. They make everyone run after the same schools, it's just silly. Besides, there are websites you can go to look up those raw numbers, without being persuaded to follow a one-number-fits-all approach."

"Professor," Noah said, "have you heard about the study about law school rankings? They gave a list of 20 law schools to a group of people

---

2 See Appendix

and asked them to rank them. The list included names of law schools that don't exist, such as Princeton and Brown. Many ranked Princeton and Brown in the top three."

"That's a great point, Noah. There are so many things wrong with this whole ranking business. I don't know a single attorney who cares about rankings.

"And here's another point. The top ten law schools for employment are not the same schools or in the same order as the ones in the U.S. News. What does that tell you, Alexandra?"

"That employers don't care about the rankings?"

"Exactly. If they cared, they would follow the rankings system exactly. Furthermore, the ABA has consistently refused to take part in this charade. That's probably because, *inter alia*, the ABA recognizes that a prospective law student's choice of which law school to apply to is personal; one list cannot take into consideration all the factors an individual student needs to ruminate."

"But what about prestigious jobs, like clerking for a judge or working for a large firm?" I asked, feeling like I was fighting an uphill battle – and losing.

"Remember Justice Thomas's words about the clerks he hires and where they went to law school. He said: *'I never look at those rankings. I don't even know where they are. I thought U.S. News and the World Report went out of business. There are smart kids everywhere… I look at the kid that shows up. Is this a kid that could work for me?'* He also called students' obsession with the rankings 'somewhat perverse.' He said that while he doesn't completely avoid hiring from Ivy League schools, he prefers to hire lawyers who went to lower-ranked schools. I suspect that plenty of law firms and other employers are following Justice Thomas's example, and that this trend will continue until things even out.

"And then there's this: one study compared students who went to the 'top ten' undergraduate schools with students who attended other schools. When evaluated for communication skills, creative thinking, decision-making, leadership, strategic thinking, and other valuable skills, those who went to the 'top ten' schools were rated only average or slightly above. I haven't seen similar studies about law-school graduates, but I suspect it's the same."

"Oh I have," Noah said. "A study in Nevada proved that when randomly assigned cases, it didn't matter which law school the attorneys went to; they all had the same success rate. The only thing that changed the results was how much experience each attorney had."

"See Alexandra?"

"I don't know, Professor," I said. "A friend of mine who went to law school told me that the big firms only hire from top-ranked schools."

"That must be one of my favorite arguments," the Professor countered. "One person tells me something, therefore it's true across the board. Sure, some firms will only hire from 'top' schools, but other firms will only hire from local schools. If you told me you spoke to a hundred hiring partners at a hundred different firms in New York and they all said that they care about rankings ... well, maybe. But much of what you hear are rumors. They spread among students through blogs and forums like a virus. Most of these rumors have no factual basis. They are simply not true. Once you research it enough, Alexandra, you'll realize that the whole U.S. News 'rankings' system is just a fleece."

I reflected on the professor's opinions. His eyes stared back with such confidence. His answers had felt naive, hard to accept, and true. Indeed, the man was a revered educator. He was 84, had over sixty years of life experience on students my age. Afterall, we were the ones handing over our brains to the U.S. News rankings. Of course, I didn't want to simply give deference to the man because of his age and expertise; I wanted to think it through and come to my own conclusions. However, there also was a factual matter at hand. I accepted the facts that most attorneys don't care about the rankings, and since that's true, neither should I. I felt I had put up a fair argument, although no matter how hard I tired, Professor Levine seemed always to be one step ahead of me. But he spoke the truth—and he won.

I turned to Noah. "Noah, I want to thank you for bringing me here. This has been a true eye-opener."

"Go ahead," Noah said.

"Go ahead what?"

"You said that you want to thank me."

"Good luck, Alexandra," Professor Levine said, as we were leaving. "Keep me in the loop."

We were just out the door, when the Professor made his closing argument.

"Alexandra, don't forget this about the U.S. News and World Report law school rankings: it's a *magazine!*"

Chapter 12

"Graham is an old-timer baseball coach. He's coached many teams over the years. He was recently hired by the Oakland A's. Graham has even coached coaches. He studied philosophy and psychology, and he uses his training in his coaching."

"Are we meeting Graham to speak about the LSAT?" I asked Noah.

"Many skills cross over from almost any kind of training, be it physical or mental, to the LSAT. The rules that apply to the art of training are the same for most sports. Graham will teach you *how* to train."

We parked in the Oakland A's stadium parking lot. There was no game that day. The thirty or forty cars there probably belonged to the regular staff, maintenance, security and the like—and, of course, people from New York who came to learn about the LSAT from the coach.

"This lot is probably full when they are playing a game. If we came then, we wouldn't be able to find a spot," I said.

"That's interesting, Alexandra."

"It is?"

"You committed a little logical fallacy. Not one that anyone would call you out on, but one that the LSAT surely would."

I racked my brain trying to figure out what fallacy I had committed. Noah didn't let me keep pondering.

"Remember the triangle? There are the bottom two points and the top one point. What you said was that this parking lot is *probably* full when the A's are playing a game. A 'probably' would qualify as the top point because it doesn't have much support. Then you said that therefore, we would not be able, *for sure*, to find a parking spot. That would be the bottom two points, a wider, sweeping conclusion. You can only go from the bottom points to the top point, not from the top to bottom.

"The actual name for that flaw would be 'probable to definite.' You went from probably not having a parking spot to definitely not having one."

"That makes sense, but I didn't say we *definitely* wouldn't find a spot, just that we wouldn't find a spot."

"What's the difference? Your exact words were 'we wouldn't be able to find a spot.' Right? I hear what you're saying—that you didn't use the word 'definitely' or 'absolutely.' But that doesn't matter. If I tell you 'the sky is blue' or 'the sky is absolutely blue,' logically, they're the same."

"I'll rephrase," I said. "During a game the lot is probably full, so we probably wouldn't be able to find a spot. So what can you tell me about this Graham fellow?"

"Graham is a funny guy, but he means business. He spent many years in the army, training soldiers at all levels. I represented him in a case in New York. He was visiting as a tourist, and his wallet, along with all his ID, was stolen. Without his ID, they wouldn't let him on the plane back to California. As a veteran, he got all defensive that they wouldn't let him on the plane. Eventually the airline called the cops, and he was placed under arrest as a 'suspect illegal alien.'"

"What happened in the end?" I asked.

"I convinced the assistant district attorney to drop the bogus charges. Then we sued the airline for humiliating a senior citizen who lost his wallet. Is that how you treat someone who was a victim of a crime? The jury agreed with me, and they required the airline to pay Graham a substantial sum."

"Justice, I love it." *That's why I want to be a lawyer.*

The first thing that hit me was the view from the stadium's wide window: a sea of vacant seats. There wasn't a game on, so one could truly appreciate the beauty of the empty field. Instead of the roaring crowd, silence greeted me, along with the thousands of empty metal benches where the spectators watched the game. The grounds of the baseball stadium looked immaculate, like no one had ever played a game of baseball there. The city's skyline filled the background of this image, but no building was too tall to overshadow the simplicity of the diamond.

"So I know you said you were in the area anyway," Graham said to Noah, "but knowing you, I'm sure you didn't come all this way to enjoy the view."

I shook hands with Graham. He had a firm grip, but gentle eyes. The man took care of himself.

"I was telling Alexandra about your training in the army, as well as your studies in philosophy and psychology, and how you incorporate all that into your training of athletes. She wanted to ask you about using your techniques to study for the LSAT."

"The first rule of training is that the training needs to be harder than whatever it is you're training for. I'll give you an example."

Graham picked up a bat that was hanging on the wall and held it with awe. "This bat belonged to the legendary Rollie Fingers." He put it back on the wall cleats. "When a baseball player wants to improve in strength, he takes a few bats and swings them together. If you can swing three or four bats with ease, one bat becomes a piece of cake."

"I think I get it," I said. "**The practice should be harder than the real thing.** So how would I do that on the LSAT?"

"For starters," Noah said, "practice answering questions in less time than is allotted per question. For logical reasoning, practice doing questions at maybe 30 or 45 seconds each. Do logic games and reading comprehension passages in four minutes each. You might not get everything right, but the process will speed you up. Then, when you have the full one minute and twenty seconds for each logical reasoning question, or the full 8:45 for logic games and the reading com, they'll seem easy.

"Or," Noah continued, **you can practice doing logic games without writing any notes or diagrams**. Do the whole thing in your head, which will be quite a challenge. Then using notes and diagrams will make the process seem much easier."

"That is a very good idea," I said.

"How long is the LSAT?" Graham asked.

"It's five sections, including the experimental section."

"So you can also practice this technique, of making the practice harder than the real thing, by practicing with seven sections, or even eight or nine. I mean, *how badly do you want success?*"

"Thanks for that advice."

"You betcha, kid," Graham said, as if the conversation was over.

"Uhum," Noah pretended to clear his throat. "I'm sure that you've accumulated a few more techniques."

"I've got a few more tricks up my sleeves. But after that, I'll have to charge you Noah," Graham answered.

"Send my secretary the bill. We'll pay it by the end of the century."

"I can live with that. Another important technique is to practice slowly. It can make practicing just as hard as doing everything really fast, and there are many benefits. In reality, we always learn by doing things slowly and then speeding up. But when you take this approach deliberately and practice so slowly that it annoys you, it's much easier to then make the process faster. **The slower you go at first, the faster you'll be at the end.**"

"Now that's something interesting, Graham," Noah said, "I've never heard that one."

"A lot of famous athletes use this technique. They swing a bat, a golf club, practice karate moves, whatever the sport may be, and do it in slow motion. I mean *slow* motion. Do you think that is something you can apply to the LSAT?" Graham asked me.

"I can take my time on the logic games, writing out the rules and the setups very slowly. Or read the reading passages and answer choices word for word. I can see how that would break down the process and make things more digestible. Do you agree, Noah?"

"Absolutely."

"I'll give you one more trick, guys. Do you like chocolate?"

"Of course," I answered. I was curious about this one. If chocolate was involved, so was I.

"Buy yourself some M&M's®. When you practice any of the sections and get an answer right, reward yourself with an M&M®. Don't go nuts. The chocolate can have nuts, but don't *you* go nuts."

Very funny.

"You'll learn to associate correct answers as something sweet. Animal trainers use this technique all the time. We of course are just primates."

"Graham," Noah said, "don't we already associate correct answers as something good?"

"That is a good question, Noah. Not everybody associates good grades and correct answers as something positive. And here's where I'll put on my psychology hat. You see, as kids, some of us are better in school and get better grades than others. But not all kids are rewarded for better grades. Some kids will be ridiculed by other students. Some get called a *nerd* for getting better grades. You don't even need this to happen to yourself. It's enough if it happens to someone you know, or even if you see it on a TV program. They're called TV programs for a reason—they *program* us. In fact, I believe everybody has at least a little bit of resentment toward being right. Some mothers tell their kids, 'you don't have to be right all the time.' Or, 'you think you know it all, don't you?'"

"But if this stuff happened to us as kids," I asked, "will a handful of M&M®'s fix that between now and when I sit for my test?"

"You'd be surprised at how fast the brain can make associations. I'm sure you've heard about people who are traumatized by a car accident. The event itself was maybe less than a minute long. Change can happen very quickly."

He had a point.

"Perhaps you've heard that repetition is the mother of skill. Well, the father of skill is praise. **Every time you're praised, even when you praise yourself for a job well done, the skill is reinforced**. An M&M® will do just that. But do it consciously. Say out loud: 'This chocolate is to reward myself for getting better at the LSAT.'"

"That reminds me of what Professor Levine taught me about stating intentions," I said to Noah.

"Graham, thanks a lot," Noah said, "it's been less boring than I thought it would be."

"Thanks Noah, and you weren't as arrogant as you usually are."

"Thanks a lot," I said –unlike Noah and Graham—without adding anything sarcastic.

Chapter 13

I HAD ACCUMULATED A lot of information. I was eager to return home and apply all that I'd learned to actual LSAT study. This was an insightful and enjoyable journey, but I was getting antsy. How would I do on my LSAT? Where would I go to law school? Would I be a good attorney?

Noah wanted to take me to one more place before we headed back to New York—to his Aunt Donna's, in San Francisco. She was an author and psychologist. During the hour-long drive from Oakland to Noah's aunt's home, we spoke about what we'd learned over the last few days.

Noah loved the A's stadium. I'd been inspired by Berkeley's campus. The world was so full of wisdom, there was much to learn. Meeting and learning from Noah's friends had been a humbling experience. The more I learned, the more realized that I didn't know that much after all.

"One thing I've learned about the LSAT, Noah, is that each part, by itself, isn't hard. So perhaps all in all, the test isn't that hard."

Noah put on the face he wore when he was about to give me a lecture. I'd come to appreciate those moments. And I was right, too.

"Actually, Alexandra, that was a logical flaw right there—the 'part-to-whole' flaw. Just because each part of the whole has a certain characteristic doesn't mean that the whole will share the same characteristic.

"Let's say that each cookie, in a box of 30 cookies, has less than 10 calories. Could you say that therefore the whole box of cookies also has less than 10 calories?"

"Of course not."

"So if each question on the LSAT is easy, as you said, is the whole test also easy? Maybe each question is easy, but the fact that there are 100 or 101 questions makes it hard."

"And that is considered a flaw?"

"Yes, and a common one, too. It is also fallacious to say the opposite: that since the box of cookies has 200 calories in it, then each cookie also has 200 calories in it, or if the LSAT is a hard test, therefore each question in it is hard.

"One caveat, though. There are cases where factually, part-to-whole does work, if you're dealing with weight, for example. If each person in an elevator weighs over 100 pounds, it is true that the entire group weighs more than 100 pounds. You have to think about it factually sometimes."

"If you say the plane is headed for Dallas," I said, "therefore, each passenger is heading for Dallas. That would be factually correct, correct?"

"Correct, indeed."

"What do you think Donna will talk to us about?"

"I'm not sure, what do you want to ask her?"

"Something within her expertise I suppose."

"That makes sense. But that reminds me of another flaw."

"What did I say now?" I asked.

"Nothing, nothing," Noah spoke hurriedly as if to defend himself. "I said that you'd *reminded* me of a flaw. This one is called 'an improper appeal to authority.'

"A medical doctor tells me I should vote for so-and-so as the next president, and he reminds me that he is a doctor and, therefore, he knows what he's talking about. While it might be true that he knows what he's talking about, it's not because he's a doctor; he is therefore asking me to rely on an improper authority. If he tells me to take some vitamins or something else health related, *then* it would be appropriate to remind me of his medical training.

"Like you said, Alexandra, it's better to ask someone within their expertise. It's also a flaw to misuse your expertise to sound like an expert in a different field."

"Can you use the triangle to explain this one as well?" I asked.

Noah smiled. "I see you like the triangle method. I'm glad. I came up with it during my years teaching the LSAT. So let's see ... the doctor using her professional expertise is coming from the bottom two points. She is a doctor, so her medical knowledge is wide, like the lower part of the triangle. Her advice goes upward; to the top point. She's a doctor, or bottom two points, and her prescription—the one point—follows logically.

"But if the same doctor starts talking about plumbing-"

"Assuming she has no plumbing expertise," I said.

"Very true, and good catch. So as the doctor is lecturing me about plumbing, she is now coming from the top one point. She doesn't have much knowledge in that area. She gives plumbing advice, but not just any advice—advice that she is trying to bolster with her bottom two points, by saying 'You should listen to my plumbing advice because hey, I'm a doctor.' That doesn't work.

"The same idea applies if you rely on an opinion to prove a fact. The top one point is an opinion. For example, if someone says that in their opinion, more people buy decaf coffee than regular coffee and therefore, you should accept as a fact that more people buy decaf. You went from the top one point, an opinion, to a fact, the bottom two points. Not good. You can only go upwards, not downwards."

"What about beliefs? Are beliefs at the top point of the triangle?"

"What do you think?"

"I think that going from a belief to a fact would be going from top to bottom. But could you go from a belief to belief? Let's say my friends believes that more people buy decaf than regular; therefore, some people believe that decaf is bought more often than regular. Does that work?"

"Absolutely. Also, did you know that **'some' can mean 'all'**?"

"No," I replied, "really?"

"*Some* just infers a part of the whole. If all phones are gray, isn't it true that some of the phones are gray? They are, because all phones are gray. That doesn't mean that the rest of the phones aren't gray. It's not how we use it in everyday language, but logically it's accurate. And of course *some* can also just mean *some*."

"And is it important to remember these terms? I mean, do they test this on the LSAT?"

A car started honking at us. We were driving too slowly.

"It's tested all the time on the LSAT. They won't ask you for definitions, but you need to know these definitions to understand certain arguments or answer choices. I would absolutely think that they're worthy of making it into your iPhone notes. And while we're on the subject, let's finish up quickly. 'All' is simple: all means all. You have 'most' or 'majority', which means 51% or more. But, as with 'some,' this can mean 'all' as well. And then you have 'several,' which means 3 or more."

"Okay, I got that."

"Good, then let's cover one more thing. If I say that I visit the library on Monday, what can you infer from that?" Noah asked.

"That you don't visit the library the other days?"

"That's exactly the wrong answer, but that's a very common mistake. If I say I visit the library on Monday, that doesn't mean I don't visit the library on other days; it only means what I said, that I visit the library on Mondays, but nothing more. Unless I excluded the other days by either saying 'only Monday,' you can't infer that I don't visit the library on the other days. I agree that it sounds as if I'm excluding the other days, but I haven't. It's similar to the idea that *some* can mean *all*. It would serve you well to formally study logic, Alexandra. These things come up all the time on the LSAT and a good, deep understanding of the principles will certainly come in handy."

"Some of that makes sense."

"Should I explain it-"

"No Noah, *some* in this case meant *all*."

"Funny, Alexandra. Hey—look at the sign: 'Welcome to San Francisco.'"

Chapter 14

Donna's house was charming. A single shade of light brown paint covered the majority of the house. The only other color on the exterior was a clean white, reserved for windowsills and trimmings. Blinds covered the attic window and the main window on the second floor. Subtle greenery filled a few small planters on either side of the narrow driveway and there were plants below the bay window.

The air was cold and damp; I hugged my jacket closer to my body. The San Francisco fog hung in the air as I looked around and yawned a little.

Donna was an elegant woman who looked at least 20 years younger than her chronological age. She brewed us some coffee she'd bought on a trip to Peru, and set out a plate of homemade cookies. She fixed herself a cup of tea and joined us at the table.

"So, how can I help you two? I hope it's not with directions because my GPS broke and I hate MapQuest. That reminds me of a time when ... oh, look at me, starting already with my stories. Why don't you speak, Noah?"

Noah smiled. "I can do that. Alexandra here is studying for the LSAT and is looking for some guidance."

Donna looked at me. "Do you like to write?" she asked.

"I'm not an author or anything, but I do like to write short stories."

"Beautiful. And do you like to get into your characters' minds? Do you ask yourself 'what would the character do just about now? What would they do in real life?'"

"Sometimes."

"After you write about your character for a bit, you get to know them. You know how they act, what they say, what grinds their gears, right? That happens after writing about them for a few weeks or so. But what if you write about them for 20 years? Wouldn't you know every small detail about them?"

Noah whispered: "I told you this would be interesting."

"How about yourself? You know yourself for 20 plus years. Noah has known himself for what, 30 years? I've known myself for almost 40 years." She winked at Noah.

"If you've known yourself for so long, you should know how you will act during the test. Will you be anxious? Will you rush, or go too slowly? Ask yourself these questions and write down your answers. Visualize yourself as you go through the whole process and ask yourself, as you would of a character in your short stories, 'What does Alexandra need to succeed? What will she experience during the test, and how can become a better test-taker?'"

"I can imagine that I'll experience some test anxiety. I'm not sure how exactly I would approach the problem, though."

Donna took a sip of tea, holding the cup with both hands. "**Trust your training**. That's all there is to test anxiety."

Trust your training. I like that.

"Test anxiety can be a real issue, and it's sometimes so severe that it needs the attention of a doctor. But for someone who it affects only to a limited extent, I would offer that advice—trust your training."

Noah sat up straight. "That does sound like brilliant advice, Donna. I knew that we wouldn't leave here empty-handed."

"Even so, you can take some cookies."

"That's okay, Donna, but thanks. What else can you tell us about test-taking?"

"Let's see here. Do you know the number one cause of writer's block? It's self-editing. I'm talking about that little voice in your head that tells you, 'You forgot a comma' or, 'You can't start a sentence with 'and' and the like. But it's not *your* voice—it's your high school English teacher's voice. As you write, that voice blabbers on and on, interfering with your writing and creativity. What I do, is first write out everything I want to say, and later come back and edit it."

"What does this have to do with test taking?" Noah asked.

Donna looked at me. "He never was very patient." Then she looked at Noah, "I'll get to the point." Despite her promise she paused to take a few sips of her tea.

"When you're taking a test, you have that same little voice in your head. It's saying, 'I hope that answer was right' or, 'that one took you too long—hurry up, dummy.' It's not until you learn to shut off that little voice in your head that you will ever be free. Free to work and trust your intuition, and, of course, trust your training.

"Even if you do trust your training, that voice will create doubt during the test. Tell your little voice that she needs to be quiet and that if you need her, you will call on her, not the other way around."

I have that voice on high volume all the time. She's always telling me that I'm not smart enough, or that I won't ever do well on the LSAT, that I won't get into my top choice for law school—or into any law school. But you know what? I'd never realized that I could simply ask this condescending voice to *shut up*. Still, I wasn't sure how to go about it.

"Donna, I know how powerful and annoying this little voice really is. But how do I silence her?"

Noah's cell phone rang. He picked up.

"Oh, hi, Chris." Long pause. "Okay, give me a second." Noah turned to us. "I'd love to hear the answer, Donna, but this is an urgent call from the office. I'll be right back."

Noah stood and walked out to the backyard.

"Sure, Noah. We'll just have some lady's talk. Take as much time as you need. Would you care for more coffee or tea, Alexandra?"

"I'm all right, Donna. I am definitely enjoying myself. Thank you for your hospitality."

"So how is it going between you and Noah?"

"Oh, we're not dating or anything. We're friends. You could say mentor and student, or something like that."

"It's just the chemistry between you two. It seemed obvious that you're dating, or at least that you like each other. Noah is very successful, you know. Why don't you want to date him?"

"I didn't say I don't want to, I said that we're not actually dating."

Listen to me; catching little words and building buildings on top of them, how lawyerly, but probably annoying for the potential listener.

"Do you like him?"

Donna would probably be the best person to talk to about it. I sighed.

"I do like him. He hasn't officially asked me out or anything. But he is a lot of fun to be around, and he's a lawyer, so we do have a lot in common."

"Do you know about his late wife?"

"Yes, he's told me."

"You can imagine that he's careful not to get his heart broken again. I think it's extremely hard for him to ask anybody out, so take that into consideration."

"Are you saying that I should ask him out?"

"That might not be a bad idea, but if you're uncomfortable with that, maybe just make it a bit easier for him. You know, laugh a little louder at his corny jokes, and flirt a little more. Make him more confident."

When Noah came back inside, he was visually upset.

"What happened, dear?" Donna asked.

"I have to get back to the office as soon as possible. An old client of ours passed away before finishing his will, and there is a ton of work to do. This could cost us a lot of money if I don't get back and take care of it."

We had already checked out of our hotel, and our bags were in the car. All we needed to do was drive to the airport, return the rental, and catch the next flight to NYC.

"Donna, thanks so much for having us," Noah said. "I'm sorry we have to leave like this, but business before everything, you know."

I wasn't happy to hear that.

"I understand, Noah," Donna said. "Alexandra, before you go, jot down your email so I can send you my advice about hushing your inner critic."

"Sure thing. Thank you, Donna. We'll be in touch."

"Think about what we talked about, and let me know."

We rushed to the San Francisco airport. Noah was quiet at the beginning of the drive. He was a bit pale. He was trying to keep his eyes on the road and get to the airport quickly without getting into an accident. But I hoped he wasn't mad at me. I didn't cause his client to die, but I was the reason we were in California.

"Excuse me if I'm a bit preoccupied, Alexandra. It's just that this was totally unexpected. I met with this client last week, and he seemed fine."

"Yeah, most people don't die so suddenly."

"This guy did. The same thing happened to another person I know, so I'm not sure your rule applies to 'most people.'"

"Is a sample of two people enough to refute my claim?"

"Actually, no. *Mea culpa*," Noah said. The blood was coming back to his cheeks. "You caught me on a flaw known as 'improperly refuting a probabilistic conclusion.' You gave me a piece of information: 'most people don't die suddenly.' We'd have to check that statement for argument's sake, but for now, let's assume it's true. I gave you two examples of people who did. Two! That's hardly enough to refute a claim that starts with 'most people.'"

"In fact," I said confidently, "it doesn't disprove it one bit."

"Absolutely correct. Did we talk about that flaw before?"

"No, but I did read about it in that PDF of logical flaws you sent me."

It was fulfilling to catch Noah on a flaw, as it was usually the other way around. Not that I enjoyed catching people's flaws, just Noah's.

"I'm sorry I got upset. Don't take it personally, Alexandra."

"I totally understand your frustration. What I didn't understand, and I'm frank with you, is when you mentioned that business comes before everything else. Do you actually feel that way?"

I was taking Donna's advice. Testing the waters. Noah looked a bit uncomfortable.

"Right now ... well, yes. I'm not married, as you know, and I don't have kids. What else would be my first priority?"

"But if you *were* married, your relationship would come first?" I asked.

"Of course."

"Oh, well that's a relief; you're not 100% lawyer. You're still part human."

"Yes, Alexandra, I've still got some human in me. That said, there was something I wanted to ask you. I hope you don't mind that I'm driving."

Noah hesitated, and took a deep breath. "So what law school are you going to apply to?"

Huh? That's what he wanted to ask me? For that I was supposed to care that he was driving? I didn't think so. I remembered what Donna said, and understood that Noah was hesitant to start a new relationship. I decided to give him some help.

"I was thinking of applying to Berkeley, but I'd rather apply to a school somewhere in New York. You know, near you."

"Who said that I'll stay in New York?" Noah blurted out.

"Are you a Bar member of any other state?"

"Good point," he said. "You're right. I probably won't leave New York. Assuming I continue my legal work, of course. But why is my location important? You'll be done with the LSAT in no time."

"Well, I'd love to stay in touch, Noah, even after the LSAT. Wouldn't you?"

"Stay in touch?"

"Come on Noah," I said, "say what you want to say."

Noah was watching the road, but I could see his frustration. He wasn't used to being on the defense. Nor was I used to being on the offense.

"When we get back to New York, can I take you out on a date?" Noah uttered, probably in less than a second. He must have broken some sort of record for speed talking and nervously asking a girl out. For a man who argues cases in front of judges and juries—and wins – he sounded quite nervous.

"Sure, why not?" I said. "I'd love to." I didn't want it to seem like I was taking it too lightly, but I didn't want to add to the tension. I *was* happy he'd asked me out in fact, as happy as the sun at noon.

We stopped at a red light. Noah looked at me.

"In that case," Noah said, as he leaned over and gave me a small kiss on my left cheek.

Chapter 15

Noah pulled out his yellow legal pad, the one with the scribbles. "Remember what Graham told us in Oakland, about learning slowly?" Noah asked, after getting comfortable in our first-class seats. "Over the next few weeks or so, I'll share the rest of my tips with you, one at a time. That'll give you time to process and apply them."

"Sounds good, Noah. Let's hear the second tip."

Noah's Top LSAT Tips #2

"**Be humble and assume a beginner's mindset**. When students start studying for the LSAT, they tend to overestimate their abilities and shoot for a perfect 180. Nothing wrong with aiming for a perfect score, but if at the same time overestimate your current aptitude, you're bound for disappointment."

"I have fallen victim to that. I thought I'd get at least in the lower 170s after a few weeks of study. How dumb."

"No, Alexandra, not dumb, just ambitious. How would you have known what you'd score? And that's why **students need to take a diagnostic test** at the beginning of their LSAT journey to get a sense of where they stand. Don't overestimate your skills and think that you can improve 20 points in two weeks. It's just not realistic."

"How long does it take to improve?"

"Isn't that the million-dollar question?"

"What's the million-dollar answer?" I asked.

"As lawyers love to say, *it depends*. It depends on where someone starts, how many hours they study, how many distractions they have and many other variables. Each student is different."

"So you're saying to be humble when assessing your score and how much you want to improve?"

"That's only a tenth of it, actually. Sure, be humble when making assessments and the like, but the main thing is: **be humble when you're studying and learning new material**. Most students start with little knowledge of logic, understanding dense texts, spatial logic, or working under time pressure. When your heart is humble and you understand that you have much to learn, your brain is more receptive. If you think you already know everything, it's harder for you to accept criticism and process new information. Think of soil. If soil is hard, rigid, or rocky, it won't be much good for growing anything. If the soil is soft, tender, and pure, a small seed can eventually grow into a huge tree. The brain is the same."

"How did you come up with this idea?"

"Mostly by observing my students. The ones who were humble were able to understand that when they chose the wrong answer, it was because of *their* misunderstanding."

"Who else is there?"

"The arrogant ones were sure that the LSAT was wrong, inconsistent, or just plain dumb. That type of thinking makes your thought process crooked. I've seen students explain why their wrong answer was actually correct, and *how the right answer was actually wrong*. It's one thing to think that two answers are right, but to take a correct answer and twist it so much that it comes out incorrect, is another thing. **That's training your brain to think in the wrong way**."

"I see why that's one of your top tips."

Noah bought two glasses of champagne. I wondered what else was written on that yellow legal pad. Meanwhile I had this one to think about. Try to be humble. It sounded easy enough.

"To your success on the LSAT, in law school, finding a job and paying back your loans." Noah and I clinked glasses to his toast. I liked the part about paying back my loans. I hadn't thought much about that.

Professor Levine had told me that the less debt, the better. That was one reason why I was trying so hard to ace the LSAT. They say the higher your LSAT score, the better your chances are of landing a scholarship. I'd be okay. I'd take a few more practice tests, and by then my scores would be high enough.

Wait—am not being humble? Was this exactly what Noah had spoken about? Was this what he meant?

"Wouldn't it be hard to get a good LSAT score if you didn't believe in yourself?" I asked Noah.

"Nobody said anything about not believing in yourself, Alexandra. You can be humble *and* believe in yourself. Being humble means you believe you can get a 180 on the LSAT and be in the top 3% of your law school class, but knowing that it will take a lot of hard work, and then some more. You absolutely must believe in your capabilities, in your talents, in your success. You must also accept that it won't happen overnight, not without putting in a crazy number of hours. And, you must not think you know everything."

"Now I see what you're saying Noah."

"Furthermore, without humility, you are unable to learn. Intellectual humility is acknowledging the limited nature of one's aptitude and respecting others' intellect. Because caring about looking smart —even to one's self—can sabotage intellectual growth, students higher in intellectual humility have a more open mind; a substantial advantage where one is likely to come across concepts they don't understand. Intellectually humble students are also more motivated to learn because they know they don't know everything. Intellectual humility enhances achievement by promoting a more constant motivation to learn. Therefore, embracing intellectual humility is a smart move for anyone studying for the LSAT, as well as for future or current law students, as will not just make you a better student but also motivate you to put in a hell lot of study hours."

"I know that I need to put a lot of work into my studying, and I try to. It's just that I often get distracted."

"Distracted by what?" Noah asked, as if he was unfamiliar with Facebook and YouTube.

"Sometimes I need to catch up on my shows," I said, "stuff like that."

"Use your show as a reward after you study. Tell yourself that if you study for two or three hours, you will reward yourself by watching TV.

That gives you an incentive to study, makes your pleasure time guilt-free, and makes you associate studying with something positive."

"Is that tip number three?" I asked, like a detective who thinks he found a clue in a high-profile murder case.

"No, but maybe it will be tip number eight."

"But it also ties in with the tip about being humble," I told him.

"How is that?"

"If you're humble, and you realize that you have a lot of work to do, you'd be more likely to push aside other distractions and get to work."

"Very true. I love how you tied the two ideas together. How lawyerly of you."

The metaphorical hair on my arms stood up. *That's all I want to be. A lawyer.* And to be lawyerly is a good start, in my *humble* opinion. I added to my notes 'Be humble.' I also added the flaw about improperly refuting a probabilistic conclusion.

"Speaking of tips, where were we at with your top tips for brain health?" Noah asked.

The plane hit some turbulence. I hate when that happens, but it didn't go on for more than ten seconds.

"I think we're at tip number three, but let me check my phone."

Brain Health Tip #3: Drink Water

"Shaping memories requires physical growth and reshaping of networks of brain cells. Finding meaning, making associations, and solving problems are learning tasks that need lightning-fast electrical impulses between areas of the brain. When you feel that you've understood something and yell, "I get it," that is nothing more than a neurochemical process. By nourishing the brain with water, you optimize your inner atmosphere, allowing yourself to truly comprehend what you are learning and to achieve your full potential. There are different opinions as to how much water is ideal, but it's usually based on one's body weight. Drinking water is essential for brain health."

The next time the flight attendant was giving out drinks, we both asked for water. I'm sure our brains were happy.

The plane landed at JFK, where the temperature was 30 degrees lower than it was in California. That was a bit depressing, but it was good to be back.

Today I focused on reading comprehension. I tried to understand where in the passage, exactly, the correct answers came from. Then I highlighted those sentences, read the question again, read the highlighted sentences, and read the correct answer. And repeated this for every question. This helped me tremendously, and I started to understand the passages in an entirely different way.

Chapter 16

I decided to take another practice test. After all, I had learned a tremendous amount on our trip. I took out five sections and my kitchen timer, set it for 35 minutes, and let the fun begin. Halfway into section two, sweat appeared on my forehead, and my fingers felt like they were about to fall off.

Be humble, I thought, be humble. When I got to a question whose answer I was certain of, I made sure to double check it. I think it paid off.

I was so tired after my test I didn't have the mental or physical strength to check my score. I felt confident about this one. I probably scored around a 162. I went to bed with that. What a fabulous feeling.

Five minutes after lying in bed, my curiosity got the best of me. I jumped out of bed, turned on my desk light and started to check my test. I answered a few wrong here and there, at least in the first section, a few more in the second section, and even more in the third and fourth. Damn. I added up the points. I felt like someone gave me a smack in the face. I couldn't believe it—I wouldn't believe it—I checked my score a second time. Then a third time.

My score: 136.

I started to cry. How much work can you put into something without getting anything in return? How much could I take? Where was all my studying and practicing going? What was the point? If I'd done all this work without raising my score, maybe I couldn't raise my score at all. Maybe I'd start looking into third or fourth tier schools—they weren't exactly my dream schools, but they would have to do. No, I wouldn't settle for that. Should I just not go to law school?

At first, I was upset, and then mad. Mad at myself, mad at the

LSAT, and especially mad at Noah. He took me to all these places and teachers and friends of his. Had that just given me false confidence in my abilities? And after all that, he asked me out. Was it all a trick? I decided to stop seeing or talking to him. I wasn't going to meet up with that obnoxious, self-serving lawyer anymore. I'd be too busy with everything else, basically everything unrelated to the LSAT or law school. I was sick of hearing about the stupid flaws that I'd 'committed.' To hell with it all.

I heard once that a person has a destiny, and that we need to find out what that is. I still wasn't sure what mine was, but I knew what it wasn't. I was not going to be a lawyer. I wasn't smart enough, like my chemistry teacher told me back in the twelfth grade, so I would stop trying. That thought only brought up more terrible memories of kids in my class making fun of me—telling me I was stupid, which apparently I was, and am. I started crying again. Chelsea came in.

"What's going on, Alexandra?" Chelsea asked.

"I can't stand this *damn* LSAT anymore. Noah asked me out yesterday. I mean, I think I like him."

Chelsea came over and sat on my bed. She was a good friend, and she usually had smart things to say. But she hadn't taken the LSAT, so I wasn't sure whether she had any idea what I was going through. But friends are friends, and she was trying to help.

"You like this guy; what does that have to do with the LSAT being difficult, or not wanting to deal with the LSAT? Are you doing the whole thing *for him*?" Chelsea asked.

"I've come to treat the LSAT and Noah as the same thing. It's just that I'm fed up with the LSAT. Even if I do want to go out with Noah, I can't tell him that I'm not studying for the LSAT anymore. He invested a lot of time and effort. I can't give up on it like that. Does that make sense?"

"But if this guy cares about you, your law school plans shouldn't make a difference. If he likes you, it's because he's seen how beautiful you are, inside and out, and that has nothing to do with the SAT."

"L-SAT."

"Isn't that what I said?"

I laughed.

"If you like him, the LSAT shouldn't factor into the equation, Alexandra."

"You're right, Chelsea. But it's also the time and money he spent on our trips. How can I tell him I gave up the whole law school plan?"

"If a relationship isn't worth a little bit of embarrassment, the relationship isn't that important to you. I don't know, Alexandra, you're upset now. Maybe go to sleep, and in the morning you'll have better judgment. **Never make important decisions on an empty tank of sleep**. Actually, they say before you make an important decision, make sure you're well rested, have eaten a meal within the last 6 hours, and have spoken to someone who cares about you, so you won't make a stupid decision you can't change later. I'll be right back."

Chelsea got up and went to her room, returning with her iPad.

"I saw this article," Chelsea said, fidgeting with her iPad. "Ah here it is; four questions to ask yourself before making an important decision."

I wasn't really in the mood but Chelsea was trying to help.

"Number 1, what advice would I give to someone I love? Number 2, am I being motivated by love or fear? Number 3, am I upset? Number 4, can I put off making the decision for another 24 hours, while my mind has time to play with the options? Wait until tomorrow Alexandra. Right now you're as pessimistic as the witch in Snow White." Chelsea's simile made me smile.

The next morning, I woke up in a good mood to the cozy sound of rain. I love rain. As a child, when it would rain, I remember my aunt saying "Oh, it's raining; everything gets a drink and a bath." I stood and stretched, and while I spread my arms, I noticed the mess on my desk, with the LSAT books and the answer sheet with the big fat 136 on the top. I was more rested now so I could make a more responsible decision. I decided to shower and make that decision as soon as I was finished. I wasn't really thinking about Chelsea's four questions, but I'd learned that decisions need deadlines; otherwise making them can drag on for needless weeks or months.

After the shower, I made up my mind. I'd break up with Noah and quit studying for the LSAT.

I wasn't going to law school.

A Cadre of Experts

The rain continued nonstop for the next week. Meanwhile, I got nine phone calls, eleven text messages and four emails from Noah over the next three days. I didn't answer any of them. I didn't want to tell Noah the whole story, about my low LSAT score, about my frustration and my loss of interest in law school. I wanted him to understand that I wasn't going to answer. But Noah was persistent, and he kept calling. And texting. And emailing. Finally, he came to my apartment and knocked loudly on my door.

I opened it and saw him standing there, holding a bouquet of flowers. I wanted to close the door, but he was soaking wet from the rain.

"Would you care to come in?" I asked.

"I wanted to check and see that you're okay. When you didn't answer, I worried, but after three days I had to come over and see you. What's going on?"

Noah walked in and placed the flowers on the table.

"I'm fine, Noah, how are you?" I answered impatiently.

"If you're fine, why are you not answering any of my calls? Are you mad at me?"

So he'd finally figured it out.

I didn't think Noah understood what I was mad at. He caused me all kinds of tears and anxieties, but he had no idea.

"Noah, the truth is that yes, I am mad at you. You gave me false hope that I could score high on the LSAT and get into a top law school. I enjoyed our time together and I appreciate everything you did for me, but the bottom line is that I took another practice test: Do you know what I scored Noah? 136. That's only two points higher than the score I had got *before* we met. And two points lower than my last practice test. How can it be that after everything I still got the same score? I'm sorry, Noah, but I gave up on this whole LSAT and law school thing. Running after a perfect LSAT score is just a wild goose chase."

"So what does this mean for ... us?"

"I don't know," I replied, even though I did.

"What does that mean, Alexandra?"

Noah checked his watch.

"I think it means that we're through, Noah," I said, staring him in the eyes. "Look, I'm sorry for the sudden switcheroo. Maybe you're late for something. I think it's best if you leave."

Noah looked up at me. His eyes were wet, and not from the rain. I never saw him like that. I didn't know that he could possibly cry. He was more vulnerable than I thought. He barely could say goodbye as he walked out of the apartment and down the stairs. I hoped that would be the last time I saw him, that way I could forget about this whole LSAT business, stop being something I'm not, and go back to being me.

Chapter 17

Saturday morning, I woke up to my cell phone's ringtone—the Rocky theme song. It was Noah. I didn't want to answer, but I must have been too drowsy to think, and I answered my phone out of habit. "Hello?" I said in a groggy voice.

"Remember me?"

"What's going on?" It was nice to hear Noah's voice. Not that I was planning on getting back together.

"Alexandra, I know that you might still be mad at me, and I don't blame you, but if we could meet for coffee, just for ten minutes, there's something important I want to tell you. Can you come to the LSAT Café in 30 minutes?"

"We can do that."

I wasn't *that* mad anymore, and he sounded sincere. I was responsible for ending our relationship so abruptly; I owed him at least a ten-minute coffee.

The waiter brought us coffee. Noah poured, careful not to spill any on his tie or on his famous yellow legal pad that was on the table.

"I promised ten minutes, so I'll get started. I've put some serious thought into what went wrong, Alexandra. I think I might have figured it out."

Noah stashed away his legal pad and took a deep breath. "Do you remember telling me in the car when we were in San Francisco that I'm not all lawyer, and that I'm also part human?"

I nodded.

"I think that revealed some of your subconscious beliefs. I think, deep down, you don't see lawyers as being good, decent people. Deep down you don't see lawyers as something positive. Here, try this. What's the first word that comes to your mind when I say the word 'lawyer'?"

"Liar. Liar is the word that comes to my mind if I'm being honest. But I don't think that lawyers are necessarily liars."

"Then why was it the first word you associate with lawyers? Maybe deep down you believe it to be true. And I know you don't want to be a liar yourself, or any type of an evil person, so subconsciously you sabotage yourself. You either study the LSAT in a way that is insufficient or when you take a practice test your mind wanders and you're not able to concentrate.

"It's not that I want to persuade you to be a lawyer at any cost. There are plenty of other respectable professions. The reason I asked to meet with you and explain this idea is because I believe that you actually want to be an attorney for the right reasons, to help people. I think that what a person wishes to be in life is their true calling. Not everyone wants to be the same thing. That would not only be boring, but society wouldn't be able to function. If everyone wanted to be a doctor, who would represent doctors in malpractice lawsuits? Who would dry-clean their suits; who would dig for oil to fuel their cars? Over the years, I've had many clients who had many different professions, and they were all just as passionate about their work as I am about mine. That passion comes from somewhere, Alexandra.

"You should be a lawyer because it's the profession you chose. If you hadn't chosen it, you wouldn't have put in all the work. You wouldn't have spent the money on the books, and you wouldn't have put in the time to take those practice tests. Alexandra, you should be a lawyer because you *want* to be a lawyer."

I thought about what Noah was saying, and it made sense. It rang true when he termed it a "calling," because at times, I wanted so badly to become an attorney, without any rational reason. If my father had a famous and prosperous law firm, where even the youngest lawyers were driving around in BMWs and Mercedes, and I was promised a position as a partner, then that want would make *rational* sense. But I didn't have all of that, or any of that, on the table, so it made sense that this inner desire was due to something higher, like Noah said.

"I understand what you mean, Noah, but I need to think about it.

If I do decide to start studying again for the LSAT, I want to make sure that it's coming from the right place, so I don't go back on my decision again."

"I think that's a much more mature way to go about it, Alexandra. Look, our ten minutes are almost up. Promise that you'll think about it. If you want, you can let me know what you decide."

It was nice of Noah to stay true to his word and not take more than ten minutes. Although at this point, I didn't really care about the time.

"I'll think it over. And I'll let you know what conclusion I come to."

Noah stood, laid a ten-dollar bill on the table for the coffee, and walked out. And I burst into tears.

Chapter 18

Was it true that subconscious beliefs can hold you back that much? I decided to email Noah's aunt Donna, the psychologist, to ask her opinion.

I'm not sure what Noah told you, but he and I are taking a little break, you know, from each other. Meanwhile, I also took a little break from the LSAT. Noah says my subconscious beliefs are sabotaging my LSAT performance. That I deep down believe that lawyers aren't good people and therefore I'm having a hard time letting myself take this path successfully. Is there truth to that? If I do have these ideas floating in the back of my head, could they actually cause me to do poorly on the LSAT? Thanks for your help, Alexandra.

Donna replied within the hour.

I am sorry to hear that you two are not together at the moment, and no, Noah didn't tell me a thing.

What I do is help people discover what is stopping them from success in all kinds of areas. More times than not, it goes back to one's childhood. Could there have been a time when you were, say, six or seven, that something happened, somebody said something, maybe you saw a certain event on the news or heard a remark from a teacher or someone that you admired, that could have caused you to think not highly of lawyers?

I recently had a client, a man in his 50's, who struggled with quitting smoking. This guy has been smoking for 30 years. We discovered that when he was seven years old, he saw his father, who was an EMT at the time, perform CPR on someone who had collapsed. His father was not able to revive the man, and he died. Immediately after the ambulance came and took away the body, my client's father took out a pack of cigarettes and chain-smoked three cigarettes, his hand shaking the whole time. Now, can

A Cadre of Experts

you blame my client for treating smoking as a way to deal with stress? And if that's the case, why would he even want to quit something that relieves his anxieties?

After allowing this memory to surface, my client was able to realize that it was just a memory, a belief, but not necessarily true. So I ask you, Alexandra, ask yourself if there is any reason why you would have any bad associations with lawyers. Let me know what comes up, and we'll talk. Yours, Donna.

Okay, so Donna was as crazy as her nephew. What a surprise. But I couldn't help asking myself if there were any such memories. I went about my day, looking at tour-guide schools and social work programs, and it hit me. It hit me like Babe Ruth hit a baseball, at least .342 of the time.

When I was a child, my mother had owned a small clothing store. It wasn't big, but it paid the bills, as my mom would say. One day my mom came home crying, her tears flowing like Niagara Falls. She phoned her sister and read her a letter she took from her purse. The letter was soaked. She wouldn't tell me what was going on—all I was able to understand was something about a letter from a lawyer, and how she would have to close the store.

A few days later, I got the full picture. She was being sued for using a name for her store that was already trademarked. There was another clothing store with the same name in a nearby town. The plaintiff claimed that he spent thousands of dollars on TV ads, but because our store had the same name customers were coming to us instead. She was being sued for $60,000. At the time, we were living month to month, and there was no extra cash lying around the house or in the bank. My mother had to hire an attorney to help with the lawsuit, and she was paying this lawyer all the money she had, to a point where she couldn't afford to pay rent on the store.

Within a few months, she was so far behind on rent and everything else, that she was forced to close the store. She ended up working at someone else's clothes store. Since she started making much less than she had made at her own store, we had to move into a smaller apartment and cut back on a lot of expenses, and I had to change schools, losing all the friends I had at the time.

Maybe, deep inside, I felt that the letter from the lawyer had caused us all these problems, and that lawyers were so expensive that they just caused more harm than good. I thought I might be onto something. I emailed Donna about my discovery. The next morning, I awoke and saw Donna's email.

Congratulations Alexandra, I think you are on to something. Now the question is, is this belief true? Is it a universal truth, such as all people die, or that people can't fly, or that only women can bear children? Or is it a personal belief, such as fax machines never work, or that it only rains when I don't have an umbrella with me, or that I'll never be rich? If it is indeed a universal truth, there is not much you can do. **But if it is only a personal belief, why hold on to it, if it's hurting you?** *You must release it if you want to manifest your true desires and wishes.*

But how could I release it? Donna didn't exactly say. I emailed Donna again. Her response came quickly.

Alexandra, I purposely didn't tell you how to do that, because I wanted to let you think about the first part for a bit. But now that you've read my response, I will certainly share this part with you as well. While there are many ways to go about releasing something, I find this method helpful, especially for people with academic backgrounds like yours. Imagine that you are preparing for a debate. You draw straws, and you get the side that has to defend the proposition that lawyers are not just good and decent people, but that they are the best people that you can find ... By the way, you can use this process for any belief (say, if you believe that you won't do well on the LSAT or do well in law school).

Next, write a 3-5-page report that you will base your debate on. Make sure that you articulate good arguments, bring out all the relevant and important facts, and detail how you will refute any arguments from the other debater.

This process will have a tremendous impact on your beliefs. Read the report a few times, until you have convinced yourself of its truth. Believe me, it works wonders. Yours, always, Donna.

Hmm. That did sound exciting, and as a matter of fact, as I was reading the email, some thoughts came to mind as to why my belief was in fact not a *universal* one. I opened my laptop and wrote the debate that I needed to have with myself. I felt it sinking in. I was in tears by the time I finished it, as memories of that childhood experience came to mind more and more vividly. What was remarkable, was that this time, my tears felt more like a relief, rather than something sad. I felt much better, but decided to wait until the end of the day before making any hasty decisions. I printed out my five-page debate and took it to the Starbucks on the corner.

I ordered a *medium* latte, as I refuse to speak Starbucks, and a French croissant, put on my headphones and some good jazz, and I read. I had to learn what it said. My fingers had typed the report faster than I had ever typed before, inspiration flowing through them. I actually had to read my words to remember what I'd written.

It took me about 20 minutes to get through it the first time. I was reading every word and making marginal notes. I read it a second time, and a third, and a fourth. An hour passed. I finished my latte and croissant. And I made up my mind. I would buy another cup of coffee.

By the end of the second cup, I made another, more important decision. I would take another stab at the LSAT, and if Noah didn't mind my *meshugaas*—a word Noah likes to use—we could get back together.

I was going to law school!

Chapter 19

I HAD TO FIGURE out what to say to Noah. Maybe I was being immature. Noah cared about me; he wanted to see me do well on the LSAT and in law school. And I cared about him. His sarcastic, corny jokes. His confidence, good looks, style. The way he twisted his lips to the right and stared straight ahead when he wanted to convey the idea that you were being an idiot.

"I'm back in the game, Noah," I said to him over the phone. I wanted to see if he would ask about—us. He didn't hesitate.

"You know, Alexandra," Noah's voice came through my phone's speaker, "I had to gather a lot of courage to ask you out in San Francisco. I don't know if I can gather it again."

"Noah, I'm so happy you said that. I know this might sound clichéd, but it wasn't you, it was me. I'd be more than happy if you want to continue dating."

"In that case, can I pick you up at eight o'clock for dinner?"

"I'll be ready."

I was happy to be back with Noah. Now I just had to get it together so that I wouldn't lose it again. I couldn't imagine what would happen if I got another 136. I took what Noah said to heart. If my true calling was to be a lawyer, that's what I should be. It didn't matter which law school I went to, as Professor Levine said. But I wasn't disallowed from wanting to go to a top-ranked school. It meant that if I ended up going to a lower ranked school, it would be totally fine.

Chelsea overheard my conversation with Noah. She did that sometimes, but it was my fault for bellowing. She came to my room and gave me that look.

"You probably heard that I'm getting back with Atticus Finch. You

A Cadre of Experts

were right, Chelsea. I was looking at it all wrong. There's no connection between Noah and my going to law school. I can date Noah and not go to law school, or go to law school and not date Noah. But I think I'm doing both."

"Good for you, Alexandra. I'm proud of you. From what I heard—not that I was eavesdropping or anything—he sounds like a sincere guy. That's not easy to come by."

"And he's cute," I added.

"And he's cute," Chelsea repeated in agreement.

Eight o'clock came, and so did Noah. He brought flowers. We got into his limo, which was messy as always, and drove to one of the city's top restaurants.

"Since you're starting up with the LSAT again, should we continue where we left off?"

"Where did we leave off?"

"You were up to number four on your list of brain health tips, and I was up to tip number three as well on my list of the top seven LSAT tips. Should I dive into my tip?" Noah asked.

"Shoot."

"I don't have my yellow pad here, but I remember the next tip. Let me tell you a quick story. I went to the post office the other day with a package I was sending to Canada. I already had the box sealed and I had paid for shipping. I just needed to drop it off in the international outgoing mailbox. So far so good. I came up to the wall where there were two slots to put packages into. One said 'New York only' and the other one said 'all other mail.' Where should I have put the package?"

"Into the 'all other mail' slot," I said. "But since you're asking, I know the answer won't be so simple."

"No, Alexandra, actually you're one hundred percent right. I was the one being all analytical and making assumptions. I thought the slot for New York mail was there to distinguish it from all other *U.S.* mail, not international mail. I asked an employee at the post office. 'Sweetheart, all other mail means all other mail,' she said. 'Your package to Canada falls into that category of all other mail.' I was a bit upset at myself, at least at my LSAT self, if you will. She was right. 'All other mail' means exactly that."

"I see what you mean, Noah, but what does this have to do with the LSAT?" I asked, wanting him to get to the point.

Noah's Top LSAT Tips #3

"**Stay true to the words of the text**. Don't scratch your left ear with your right hand, if you've heard that expression. All other mail is all other mail. Don't overanalyze something that's not intended to be analyzed at all."

"I get the idea, but maybe you could explain how that idea manifests itself in LSAT terms."

"If an argument says that John is taller than George, one might imagine John at 5'2 and George at 6'2. But that is not staying true to the text. Taller means taller. Even one hundredth of an inch taller would qualify.

"Or if you're asked to find an inference, even the simplest inference would be correct. If the statement says that to be healthy you need to take vitamin C, and that every person should try to stay healthy, a proper inference would say that every person should take vitamin C. Some people skip that answer, because it just seems too simple, but if you're staying true to the words of the text, you'll know to pick that answer."

The waiter approached, a young guy with very dark hair and a heavy New Jersey accent. We placed our orders and got back to business.

"You know those people," I asked, "if you ask them if they have the time, will just say 'yes'? They have the time of day all right, but you didn't ask for it yet, so they didn't give it you."

"I know what you're talking about, Alexandra. My little brother did that all the time to people when we were kids. And that, too, is an example of using this approach, albeit not in the best way, or at least not in a way that will earn you many friends. But on the LSAT, it's the way you need to look at things. This tip also has to do with not changing the degree of a statement. For example, not getting mixed up between 'always' and 'sometimes,' or between 'best' and 'only.' There's a lot of these we could cover, but I'll let your study guides offer you a more systematic approach. But now when you learn those things you can categorize them under this tip."

A Cadre of Experts

The waiter brought our food to the table. Noah had ordered an Australian rack of lamb and asparagus with sea salt. I had the wasabi mashed potatoes and a prime beef filet mignon. The waiter poured us red wine, and Noah made a toast. "To your consistent improvement—*in small increments.*"

I lifted my glass. "To your law firm's success with many more not-guilty clients. L'chaim."

Noah smiled. "Indeed, L'chaim."

Today I focused a lot on logical reasoning. Knowing the question types and how they work really makes a difference. As Noah said, knowing the question types means knowing your task for that kind of question, which makes you read it differently. I did about 100 questions, untimed. Then I reviewed them and took care to understand the ones I got wrong; why my incorrect answers were incorrect. Then I did two logical reasoning sections in a row, timed.

Chapter 20

The next few weeks went by quickly. Noah was working on a huge case. No trips. I hauled my books and my butt to the library every afternoon. I studied for two or three hours, took a dinner break and studied for another two hours, and took practice tests on weekends. I only scored the test on the following Monday so that I wouldn't ruin my weekend and so I could calmly review my answers and learn from my mistakes.

I was seeing improvements—the ones Noah had toasted to—in small increments. I started to score between 137 and 140. I remembered things I was taught, for example, from Graham the baseball coach, and from Judge Brian.

I kept at it. Hours and hours and hours and hours of studying, practicing, reviewing, practice exams, disappointments, encouragements, more practice tests.

I practiced logic games without diagramming anything, and I did eight various sections in a row. More and more hours, relentlessly. Laser sharp focus. There was no other way. I sure wished there was a magic pill. Maybe I would discover it one day.

My score started to hit the mid-140s.

But I knew I could do better. A lot better.

I spoke with Noah almost every day, asking him about various topics that I was struggling with. And of course, Noah kept calling me out on my own logical fallacies.

"You know, Noah, making law school two years long instead of three is a good idea. I hear they're talking about it. It would be a third cheaper that way, and it would cut student debt by about five billion dollars a year."

"And?" Noah asked.

"There would be an enormous advantage to the economy if there was less student debt."

"Alexandra, that's what's called the fallacy of 'failing to consider disadvantages of a course of action.' When making an argument, you have to nod to the other side and offer a possible refutation of the other side's argument.

"The other side of this argument is that cutting law school by a year wouldn't allow time for enough elective classes. If that's something you think lawyers can do without, make an argument as to why. But simply leaving it out and not *considering* a possible disadvantage, that there will be any sort of consequence to cutting law school to two years, would be a flaw."

"Does it work with the triangle method as well?"

"The top of the triangle, the one point, represents just one side of the argument, that there would be an advantage to cutting law school to two years. It's just one advantage that you mentioned. Then, in conclusion, you jump downward to the two points at the base of the triangle. So that doesn't work. If you come from the bottom, however, and present a wide argument, such as the advantages of your side, and why the disadvantages of your side aren't that bad after all, then, in conclusion, you can go upwards to the one point and make a specific conclusion."

We also talked about law schools in general, and about the big case that Noah was working on. Things were starting to get better, LSAT-wise, and I felt it might be time to actually register for the test. I registered for the February exam. *The anxiety.* I printed out the ticket when it was ready and hung it on my wall. I marked the date—February 12—on my calendar, and the countdown began. Less than a month away ...

Today I did something different. Many times I've noticed that the first 10 questions on the logical reasoning sections are relatively easy, and the last five are somewhat hard. Assuming that the last five questions would always be hard didn't serve me well. I made copies of the section and scribbled over the number of the questions with a black marker. Then I mixed up the pages. This helped me to just focus on the questions, not on whether they would be easy or hard. Latest practice exam: 148.

I started to increase my study time even more, in accordance with my stress level. By the way, that was another flaw that Noah had once pointed out. I found this one to be quite interesting. When two themes are correlated, such as car accidents and bad weather, I naturally assumed that the worse the weather, the greater the number of car accidents. But it would be a flaw to assume that. If two things are in fact correlated, it doesn't mean that the *directions* on the graph are correlated as well. One can go up and one down, and *that* is the correlation. It could also be the case that when the weather is worse, fewer people drive, and therefore there would be fewer accidents. A correlation doesn't have to mean that the arrows on the graph move in the same direction.

Another few weeks passed, and I was only a few days away from the test. I was so nervous the night before. I wasn't ready. But I had already registered and didn't want to lose the money it cost to register. Besides, I wanted to become a professional attorney, *not a professional LSAT student.*

On the other hand, I didn't feel fully ready. Maybe I should have postponed it. I debated with myself for the next few hours, only stopping to think about how crazy this whole LSAT thing had made me. Seriously. I figured that if I postponed the test, I could take the June LSAT and apply to law school for the following year. I canceled the exam. I called up Noah and told him. He wasn't upset. He said that I had to do what I had to do.

I went back to my four-hour regimen. Meanwhile, Noah finished his big case. He was defending a white-collar criminal case for a client, who had somehow stolen millions of dollars from his job as a head broker at a large stock trading firm. Noah got him acquitted from most of the charges, and the client only had to pay a few minimal fines, and, of course, the lawyers.

I started to notice that when I take full exams, I have a hard time switching my focus from one section to the next. When I do a logic games section, it takes me a while to switch gears, if you will, to a logical reasoning section. So, I decided to practice mini-LSATs. I do ten logical reasoning questions, then one logic game, then one reading comprehension passage, and so on. This helps me learn to switch tasks more quickly, without needing to refocus. Latest practice exam: 150.

A Cadre of Experts

The night that Noah finished his case, he offered to meet the next morning at the LSAT Café. It was comforting to have Noah back. We met in the morning at the café at our usual spot. Noah was already sitting there when I walked in.

"So how's it going Al?" Noah asked cheerfully. He'd never called me Al before.

"Ok, Noah. Yourself?"

"Considering that this case is over, I'm going to take a week or so off. How's the LSAT? Since last night, that is, when you told me it was getting better?"

"Not that much different from last night. I got 150 on my latest practice test."

"That's much better than 134. By the way, how long are you taking to do each section, Alexandra?"

"Thirty-five minutes. That's the correct time, right?"

"That's the amount of time that they give you on test day, but they also give you something extra."

"What's that?" I asked.

"They give you a large dose of anxiety. You can't mimic it at home, so for many students it can cause real performance issues. But there's a way to get around it."

"What is it?"

"We can talk about test anxiety in more detail another time, but right now I'll advise you to do only 30-minute sections. No more 35 minutes. That will add stress and prepare you better for the actual test. Actually, Alexandra, have you met Yenta?"

I'm sure I would remember if I met a person named Yenta.

"No."

"I'm taking her to Brooklyn. Let's go pick her up. You'll love her."

"Where does, um, Yenta live?"

"With me, in my apartment. I never told you about Yenta? I'm sure I brought her up once. Maybe not."

I had no idea who this girl was, but Noah's face seemed to light up when talking about her.

"What's in Brooklyn?" I asked, trying to figure out what the hell was going on.

"Dr. Lisa. My cat's vet." I laughed. I had been getting jealous over a cat.

"You have a cat, Noah? I'd never have guessed. I love cats. Sure, I'd love to meet her."   I was finally going to meet one of Noah's friends without getting a lecture. But who knows? Maybe the cat would lecture me about landing on my feet. Or maybe she would try to make me a match.

Yenta is a Bengal. She has checkered fur with shades of gray, white, and tabby, and her fore-chest is solid white. She stands with a majestic look. We got on the Brooklyn Bridge, and I noticed the sign that read "Welcome to Brooklyn. How sweet it is."

"So, how are the famous logic games going Alexandra?" Noah asked.

"They're fun, but I still struggle. Sometimes imagining the scenarios can be difficult. I write out the rules, the setup and all, but sometimes it just doesn't click, you know?"

"I totally understand. So … we're on our way to the vet. Imagine that the vet had to make rules about which animals can come on which days of the week. Dr. Lisa is only there Mondays and Thursdays. This could be a practical problem. They don't want to have cats and dogs on the same days, but they have to see both dogs and cats since they're the most common pets. They also can't have cats on the same day as hamsters or birds, but dogs can be seen on the same day as those two."

"So you're saying to think of the games as an actual real-life situation?"

"Exactly, Alexandra. I could even throw in some more rules. If there are no dogs on Monday, they can't be seen on the Thursday of the same week. Treat games during practice as real-life situations. They gain a certain degree of reality, and I believe that makes it easier to … how did you say it? Click?"

"I'll try that. My main problem is the timing, though. If I have enough time, I can get everything right. The problem is that enough time might mean 20 minutes, which is way too long."

"Oh, you actually reminded me of something, Alexandra. Do me a favor—open the glove compartment. There should be a brown case in there. It has my watch in it. Do you see it?"

It was a stainless steel watch, covered with a stainless steel oyster bracelet. The "glass" was sapphire crystal.

"Here it is. But the time is off. It reads 6:30, but right now it's 10:00."

"It's broken. I have to take it to my old friend, Leon. He's a watchmaker. Leon came from Ukraine to New York about 20 years ago. Nicest man you'll ever meet. And he's a wizard with watches. I don't trust anyone with this $12,000 watch except Leon."

"Twelve thousand dollars? For crying out loud, it shouldn't break if it's that expensive," I blurted.

"I hope the problem is the battery. I got it as a gift from my late wife's parents. They are lovely people. If you have time, we'll finish up with the vet and take a ride over to Bensonhurst to see Leon. I'm sure Leon will give you some good advice about timing. It'll be a fun day."

"Maybe we could stop at Coney Island and get one of those famous hot dogs?" I asked.

"Good idea."

"So I was thinking about how the logic games can relate to real life. For example, right now we're making a schedule for the day. We have three errands to run: stop at the vet, the watchmaker, and grab a bite to eat. Each place has its hours of operation, and of course, we have to follow a certain route, to get from place to place in a way that makes sense as far as their physical location. It might be a simple task, but I feel that it's a logic game in essence."

"You're right. It sounds like an ordering game, like, 'Which stop do we make first? Second? Third?' If there's traffic, then we don't go to Coney Island. That was a little if-then statement. So yeah, I think it's smart to think of this situation like a logic game. It will only make the LSAT's logic games look more familiar, and *friendlier*."

"Meet my best friend, the logic game," I said with a grin.

"Another thing I can tell you about logic games is that your performance has a lot to do with your hands' muscle memory. You develop muscle memory when you repeat certain movements, like playing the piano. In time, this repetition allows you to perform the specific task with little conscious thought and reduces the need for awareness.

"When you practice logic games, be as consistent as possible when diagramming rules. It usually doesn't matter which method of notation you use, as long as you understand it and it doesn't cross over to another type of rule. **Being consistent will build muscle memory and allow you to stay focused on the rules and the setup**. That will help you speed up the games."

For most of the way Yenta had been sleeping in the back, but somehow she *knew* we were at the vet's office. She woke up and looked alarmed.

We walked into the Bushwick neighborhood veterinarian and sat next to all the other pet owners who didn't look at all like their pets. There were all types of pets in the room, despite our hypothetical rules for the veterinarian logic game.

"How is Yenta?" Dr. Lisa asked, as we walked into the checkup room. Dr. Lisa was about my height, with short blond hair and strong blue eyes. You almost couldn't notice her small, frameless glasses.

"Purring and meowing, Doctor. I brought her in for her annual checkup. I still have this card you gave me last time that shows your findings from last year, but I bet you have all that on file. It shows today's date as Yenta's checkup day."

Dr. Lisa turned to me. "Noah loves his cat, you know, *love conquers all*. Nobody brings in their pet exactly twelve months after the last checkup."

The vet finished the checkup, wrote up her notes, and wrote the date of next year's checkup on the same card Noah brought in.

"So, Alexandra, what do you do?"

"I'll be going to law school next fall. Meanwhile I'm studying for the LSAT."

"And how is it going?"

"Noah here is helping me, but overall I'm not a big fan of the test. It's a tricky test."

Dr. Lisa nodded. "I mentioned this saying before, but I'll repeat it because it's so relevant. Love conquers all. If you can learn to love the LSAT you will have a much easier time. My daughter, who's about your age, was taking the MCAT for medical school. She hated it. I taught her this idea. She ended up acing the test. I believe she scored 40, and she got into a top medical program. When she was finally doing well on the exam she actually was loving it. Being a vet, my question was, 'Which came first, the chicken or the egg?' Did doing better on the exam cause her to love it, or did she start to love it, and did well as a result? My hunch is that it was the latter."

"That's amazing that your daughter was able to make such a big change," I said.

"Well that's not all," Dr. Lisa continued, "have you heard of Fielding Yost, the famous coach of the Michigan Wolverines?

"I don't think so."

"In the year 1900, the University of Michigan football team wasn't winning many games. They hired Fielding Yost as the new coach. As soon as he arrived on campus, he granted an interview to the local newspaper. Yost claimed that in his first season, his team would be undefeated and the combined scores of the opposing teams for the entire season would be 49 points or less. The team protested because they were concerned that Yost was setting them up for failure.

"Yost marched to the blackboard and wrote one word. He told the team that they would live up to the statements he made in the interview if they understood that one word and applied it to the game.

"That year Michigan went undefeated and ended the season with an 11 to 0 record. They outscored their opponents 550 to 0. It took their opponents more than five years to score more than 49 points. They were victorious at the first Tournament of Roses, and at three more national championships in the next three years. What do you suppose was the one word Yost wrote on the blackboard?"

"I have a pretty good guess," I said. "Love?"

"Precisely. If you start to like the LSAT, it will come easier to you and make; the changes it's supposed to make in your thinking will take place. This will make you smarter and a more logical thinker."

That was a new concept—to love the LSAT. "Thank you for that insight, Doctor. Good luck to your daughter in medical school."

"Thanks, doc," Noah added, "I hope we don't have to see each other too soon. For Yenta's sake."

We drove to Bensonhurst to see Leon. Yenta seemed more relaxed after leaving the vet. Noah asked me to take out the watch and have it ready for when we went inside. He also told me that Leon would have a lot to teach me. If he was Noah's friend, he was going to be an interesting conversationalist, one of the cadre. That seemed to be the pattern.

I heard a yell, in a thick Russian accent.

"Noah, how are you?"

"*Privet*, Leon, *kak dela*?" Noah demonstrated his limited, but accent-appropriate Russian language skills. Leon's clock store had an old-fashion look. The brick alley was reminiscent of an earlier time. The fresh blue paint gave the shop a robust fantasy motif as well, as if the watchmakers themselves were elves. As we walked into the store, I was taken aback by the many clocks all over the walls, each a different design and yet all doing the same thing; telling time. But upon closer inspection, the awe and wonder at the craftsmanship that was put into each piece was astounding; the Alice In Wonderland level artistry and engineering—playfully putting together pieces of fictional fanfare into the very meter and rhyme of the simple tick-tock of time.

"This is my friend Alexandra, and we came to get my watch fixed. You think you can handle that?"

"I'll take a look, Noah," he laughed. "If the price is right, I'm sure we can get something done." He took a quick look at the watch. "This old thing? Looks like it needs a new battery. That'll be $6, Noah."

Hard to believe that we traveled all the way from Bushwick to Bensonhurst for something that cost six dollars, but when you have a professional you trust (and an expensive watch) it's worth making the trip. Leon proceeded to change the battery and clean the inside of the watch. He held the watch next to his ear and listened for the tick tock sound. He held his breath.

"Ah, I love the sound of a high-quality watch. Everything sounds so perfect; like a symphony."

"Good job Leon. So, what can you tell us about timing? Alexandra is working on her timing for a big test she's preparing for."

"The main thing I can tell you about timing," Leon said, as he placed the watch on the table, "is that for your timing to be exact, everything has to work together, in harmony. There are three main parts of a watch, and three factors to exam time management. The watch has the mainspring, the balance wheel, and of course the escapement. When they work properly, the timing is perfect. If one of them goes out of whack, the watch won't work."

"What would be analogous to that in LSAT timing?" Noah asked me.

"First, I would say you have to **know what your task is**. Is the LSAT asking you to find an assumption, set up an in-and-out game, or look for the author's tone?"

"Right," Noah said. "Second, you have to **have a specific approach to each task**. And what would be the third thing?"

I was glad that Leon jumped in because I had no idea. "You have to be a *smart test-taker*. While I was helping my son to prepare for the math section on his SATs, I taught him how to **decide when to move on from a question that wasn't going well**. Sometimes you need to cut your losses and move on. Or if there is a certain type of question that you know is going to give you a hard time, it might be smart to skip it and come back to it later. As the Chinese proverb says 'He who fights and runs away, may live to fight another day.'"

"I think this would also mean to **know how to distribute your time wisely**," I said, "how much to spend on certain question types and the like."

"Well this has been a great use of our time Leon," Noah said, "no pun intended."

We stood up. "Thank you Leon," I said, as we headed out.

"Of course, anytime. Hey Noah, don't forget your watch."

We drove to Coney Island to get our hot dogs. Coney Island is such a beautiful place, so full of life, stores, attractions, and of course, hot dogs. We found a place next to the beach. The weather was still cold, so Noah was comfortable leaving Yenta in the car, with the window open a crack to let the fresh air circulate.

"Noah, we haven't spoken about the LSAT writing sample," I said, as we walked towards the hot dog stand.

"Sure, we can discuss that."

"I know it's not as important as the other sections."

"Well, in the legal profession, good writing is imperative. But that's something a good law school will teach you. Speaking of Professor Levine's spiel about law-school rankings, I'd rank a law school that has a strong legal research and writing (LWR) department a hundred spots higher than a school that doesn't have one."

"What do you mean by 'strong'?"

"A strong legal research and writing department will have professors who are practitioners, meaning practicing attorneys with a lot of current legal writing experience. It will have small LWR classes, a lot of help from teacher assistants, and an LWR class in your first semester with at least three credits – and graded, of course."

I added that to my iPhone notes.

"Legal research and writing are the most important skills for any new lawyer."

"What's the other one?" I asked, fingers on my iPhone keypad.

"Analytical skills. That's something you learn in your substantive law classes."

"You said those two skills are the most important for new lawyers."

"An attorney who's practiced for a few years should pick up other skills, mainly people skills and emotional intelligence, but that's a conversation for a different day."

"What were you saying about the LSAT essay?"

"The essay section, which isn't scored but sent to the law schools you apply to, is designed to test how well you can articulate a convincing argument in written form, using proper reasoning and the appropriate evidence, which is all given to you in the fact pattern. The first thing you need to know is there is no right or wrong choice. You can make a good argument for either side. Read the fact pattern, and see which side you are leaning towards. Start building a solid argument, as strong as you can make it, for that side. Be sure to stay on topic and follow the rules given. The best way to prepare for this section is to look at a few examples and practice writing full essays in response to the questions. I don't believe the writing sample is a huge factor in the admissions process, so while you want to do a good job, your study time would be more efficiently spent on the other three sections."

Noah ordered four hot dogs. One for me, two for him, and one for the cat. Noah smeared gobs of mustard and sauerkraut on his; I left mine plain. It's amazing how fast one can finish a hot dog, even two. We brought the last one back to the car for Yenta.

And I guess Yenta did teach me a lesson; *go for the ride, don't complain, and maybe there's a reward at the end.* She devoured it, just as fast as we did, and it was back to Manhattan.

Today I practiced reading comprehension. I used passages I had already practiced with, but I focused on the four incorrect answer choices. Many times, two or three of them would be wrong for obvious reasons. But there would be one really tempting answer, close to the correct answer but slightly different, just enough to make it wrong. Sometimes the differences are so darn close, and those are the ones I love to dissect. Understanding the small differences between a right and wrong answer can help develop one's analytical skills and ability to read closely. Latest practice exam: 154.

Chapter 21

The LSAT Café was crowded. Noah was already there, as usual. He had a pot of coffee ready for us.

"Good morning, Noah. I could sure use some of that coffee. It's only 8:30 but I've already studied more than three hours."

"Good morning to you, too. You know, I was sitting here with my coffee and adding sugar. And that's when it hit me, Alexandra."

Noah took a sip. I wasn't sure what hit him, so I asked.

"The spoon, Noah? You forgot the spoon in the cup and it hit your eye when you lifted it up?"

I thought that was clever. Noah didn't to notice.

"What hit me was the similarity between a good cup of sweet coffee and the LSAT. If you put in a small amount of sugar, the coffee will still be bitter. I personally don't like it when it's bitter. And if you put in too much sugar, it will be too sweet. So think about it—you need just the right amount of sugar to make the coffee good.

"As you know, the LSAT is full of arguments. The classic premise and conclusion. If the conclusion has too much or too little sugar, it doesn't follow logically from the premise."

"And if it doesn't follow logically, what happens?"

"By definition, a conclusion is something that follows logically from its premise. If I tell you that iced tea is liked more than hot tea, that would be a statement. But if I say that iced tea is liked better because a nationwide survey shows that more people buy iced tea than hot tea, then the statement is backed by the premise, so it becomes a conclusion. The assumption, of course, would be that the more something is sold, the more people like it. Do you see the difference?"

"So what happens if the premise doesn't provide sufficient evidence to support the conclusion? Is the conclusion automatically wrong?"

"Let's say that one person says he enjoys iced tea over hot tea, and therefore iced tea sells better than hot tea. That would be a bad argument because the conclusion doesn't follow. One person's opinion doesn't turn his statement into a universal truth. It might be that the conclusion is true—that iced tea does in fact sell better than hot tea—but the argument is still wrong."

"The LSAT then asks you to either strengthen or weaken that argument. I can see an easy way to weaken it, simply by stating, as you said, that one man's opinion doesn't make a statement universally true. But I'm not sure how to strengthen it."

"Just add sugar, Alexandra."

Just add sugar, heh? How would I add sugar to this argument? "I'm not sure, Noah. How would you strengthen that?"

"I could mention a nationwide survey that confirms that iced tea sells more than hot, for example."

"Yeah, but isn't that adding 'outside' information? The LSAT writers always exclude outside information, don't they?"

"You need to accept the answers as 'true'—meaning that if the answer is correct, would it strengthen the argument? By bringing in the nationwide survey, you add enough sugar to make the coffee sweet enough to drink. Does that answer your question?"

"Perfectly. Should we order some breakfast? I'm getting ravenous."

Noah ordered some eggs and I ordered some French toast. We had the same old waiter confidant.

"So, Noah," I said, as we were waiting for our food, "what else is on your list of the top LSAT tips?"

"Ah, yes. I was hoping you would ask."

Noah took his yellow notepad from his briefcase, and I took out my iPhone and opened the notes app.

Noah's Top LSAT Tips #4

"**Be organized.** I'm not talking about labeling your clothes with the days of the week and wearing them accordingly; I'm talking about organizing your thoughts. Start to notice when you're not feeling organized, and call attention to it. That way when you do not understand something you'll be able to differentiate between something you simply don't understand and something that just needs some organization."

"I see what you're saying. Sometimes my thoughts are all over the place, and I need to center myself, like they teach in yoga."

"What do you mean by 'center yourself'?"

"There are two main techniques I've learned. First, **regulate your breathing**. Make sure you inhale and exhale and breathe evenly. When we're under stress, our breathing suffers, causing a lack of fresh oxygenated blood to the brain.

"The second step in centering is to imagine the center of your body, somewhere around the middle of the chest, and by simply noticing that part, the rest of the body will align itself."

"Not getting anxious on the test will also help you stay centered and organized in your thoughts. So ... speaking of tips, where were we with your brain health tips?"

Brain Health Tip # 4: Relieve stress right away

"When something upsets you, reduce it as soon as possible. Go for a walk, breathe, meditate for a quick five minutes, whatever method you can use to calm down. Letting those feelings build up is not healthy for your body or your brain."

"That's an interesting idea. You're saying that not only should you release the tension, but you should do it sooner rather than later."

"Exactly."

I started eating my French toast, considering Noah's analogy about coffee. Putting in just the right amount of sugar was key.

"I think that the parallel questions have the same concept."

"The same concept as what?" asked Noah.

"Oh, sorry ... I'm going back to the analogy about coffee and the LSAT. When you're looking for an answer to a parallel question, you need to look for another cup of coffee that uses the same formula as your cup of coffee."

"Right," Noah elaborated, "For my coffee, I use the 1-2-3-4 rule."

"How does that work?" I had no idea Noah was using a formula this whole time.

"When you make instant coffee, you add one spoon of coffee, two spoons of sugar, three-fourths water, and a quarter milk. So if you're looking for a parallel to that, it doesn't have to be another cup of coffee, but maybe a cup of lemonade. Maybe something like one lemon, two spoons of sugar, three-fourths cup water, and a quarter of mint flavor. The structure needs to be similar, not the elements. It can be a different drink completely, but the structure needs to be parallel. Right?"

"Yes, that makes sense. I get mixed up when they use the contrapositives. That's annoying. How do you deal with that?"

"It's important to understand that the **contrapositive is exactly the same as the original statement**. If you get that, it shouldn't be a problem. Let's see … if you go to a baseball game, you will get popcorn. When you use an 'if-then' statement, the statement is accepted as absolutely true. So if you didn't get popcorn, then you didn't go to the game. Because if you had gone, you would for sure have gotten that popcorn. So if you think about it, it's exactly the same statement. Once you get that concept, the contrapositive and original statement become so interchangeable that it doesn't matter anymore, and that comes with practice."

Noah took a few bites of his eggs, and I poured some more maple syrup on my French toast. Noah took a sip of his coffee to clear his throat.

"It's also important to realize that some of the parallel questions are poor logic or bad arguments. They usually tell you when it's bad logic, but they don't have to. The trick with those questions is to understand that you need to find an answer whose argument uses not just bad logic, but the *same* bad logic. There are endless ways to write fallacious arguments—just watch the five o'clock news. Just find the bad logic or argument that is parallel to the one in the stimulus."

"Those bad arguments can be hard to define, though."

"That's true, but I wouldn't worry much about defining the exact name of the bad logic. It's too time-consuming. Sometimes you need to find one that has the same feeling to it. But don't forget that you can always narrow down the right answer by eliminating the wrong answers. Did we talk about that idea yet?"

"About eliminating the wrong answers first? No, we didn't talk about it, but I read about it somewhere online. Not too sure how I feel about that process. Do you recommend it?"

"Let's think about it from an everyday rational perspective. You sit down in a restaurant for lunch and look at the menu. You know that you're looking for a main course dish because you're starved. Dessert comes after the main course, and you have to get back to work, so wine is out of the question. So you've intuitively narrowed your options to the last two sections. The pastas and the meats, for example. It's hard to decide between the two, so you don't compare the two options; rather you compare each option to what you want. Am I in the mood for meat? Or do I want pasta? I had pasta yesterday, but meat might be too heavy. You remember that you're trying to cut down on carbs, so meat it is. That's how we naturally make choices, by eliminating a lot of the obviously wrong choices or answers, even if you don't do it consciously.

"On the LSAT, you need to use the same process. It's just the natural way we select things."

"I hear what you're saying, Noah. But I feel like it's almost cheating. I know that sounds crazy."

"It sounds crazy because it is."

Thanks a lot.

"I think the LSAT wants you to use that method, and I'll tell you why. Sorting out bad information is a skill that lawyers need. If I entertained every thought that goes through my head when I'm looking for a solution to a legal problem or issue, I would go nuts. When an awful solution comes into my head, I need to brush it away and move on to the next idea. Do you see the logic in that, Alexandra?"

"I do now. I can only imagine that using the natural way of doing something and gearing it towards the thing you need to accomplish can be beneficial, like in martial arts."

"How does that work? I never took martial arts."

"Simple, Noah." I was happy that I could explain something to Noah for a change. "Teachers of some martial arts, like the teacher I had a few years ago, teach you to use your own natural way of fighting or self-defense, and they simply tweak it. That way you aren't going against your body; you're going with it."

"That's the idea here as well. That's what they say—two heads are better than one, Alexandra."

Noah asked for the check, and I went to use the ladies' room. When I got back, Noah was on his cell phone. He gestured to wait a minute. He was listening to the person on the other side, but staring at me. He smiled and thanked the person, and said that we'd be there. What was that about? Noah hung up and said "Alexandra, I have a surprise. My good friend Leah is in town, and she wants to have dinner. She's a Doctor of Nursing. She works for a big government agency as the head nursing consultant. But I'm not taking you to see her for a checkup."

"And you're assuming that I have time to do this, Noah?"

"And you assume that what my friend has to teach you isn't important enough for you to clear your schedule? Besides, you already said you aren't busy today, so quit fooling around," Noah answered with a grin. "Leah has some awesome information to offer you, and it directly relates to the LSAT."

"Okay, if that's the case, I'll come," I said. "Where will we meet her?"

"At 'The View.' It is New York's only revolving restaurant. Where else?"

"Do you mind if I ask, why there?"

"Because Leah only comes to town once in a while, so when she does I make sure to take her to her favorite place. The restaurant has an amazing view of the city. We're meeting her at 7:30."

"I'd never been to a revolving restaurant," I said. "It sounds like it will be would be a spin."

Latest practice exam: 156.

Chapter 22

I took a practice exam that afternoon. It would be an ideal time because I was well rested and I had studied for two and a half hours in the morning after breakfast. Being alert is crucial for studying. I've had easy classes in college where even if I was tired I could still understand the professor and take notes. But the LSAT is like a triathlon. You need strength.

I got a 160. "Good for you!" I called out, raising my hands with glee, rewarding myself with a pat on the back, as I learned from Graham. I calculated that I'd studied about 80 hours since two practice tests ago, where I scored a 150. I'd been using a lot of the techniques Noah and his cadre experts taught me. I was practicing logic games in my head, without writing notes or diagrams. I usually didn't score high on those and they took me longer than usual, but they made the regular way of doing logic games much easier. I used Judge Brian's reading comprehension method, and I practiced the exercises he gave me. I also took to heart the Rabbi's message of taking in small bits, making sure I understood them, reviewing the material a few times, and only then moving on.

One thing Noah told me on the phone during those few weeks (when he was busy with his big case) was that the LSAT becomes harder and harder to improve on. That's because when you start off, there are so many concepts you don't know. As a result, everything you learn at that point enables you to get better and increase your score rapidly. But when you get into the higher numbers, each point is an uphill battle. So if it took me 80 hours to improve from a 150 to a 160, it would probably take me around 160 hours to improve from a 160 to a 165.

A Cadre of Experts

If I studied for four hours a day, it would take me almost six weeks. As Noah says, *oy*. But it's hella worth it.

"Alexandra, Noah tells me you're taking the LSAT in June," Leah said, as we sat at our table. "I remember when Noah was studying for that test, I could barely talk to him. He was so obnoxious," Leah said. It's never boring with Noah's friends.

"I'm trying my best to keep my sanity. Today I took another practice test. It's going well. I've improved about five points the last few weeks."

"I'm happy to hear that. Did Noah tell you what I do?"

"You're a nurse, I believe," I said, although I couldn't remember exactly what she did.

"I'm a nurse by training, but I work for a government agency that cares for people with developmental delays. I love my job. It's all about belief in the human race and doing the right thing. But what I love most about the job is celebrating the small victories. The people we care for all have goals and dreams. Most people only appreciate a victory when they achieve a great deal. When an athlete is training for weightlifting, they will only get excited when they go from lifting 100 pounds to lifting 120 pounds. But what happened to the other 19 pounds? What happened when they were able to lift 100 pounds and two ounces?

"I'm sure you've heard that quote about how a journey of a thousand miles begins with a single step. I add my own twist on that. I say that a journey of a thousand miles is made step by step. It's hard to imagine stopping after every step and celebrating, but if you're used to measuring your improvement every hundred miles, try being grateful for every 50 miles."

The waiter approached, just as the restaurant was turning to give me a view of the Empire State Building, but I was more interested in returning to our conversation.

"You improved by five points," Leah continued. "But every point is important. And when you're grateful for every point you get, you're more motivated to keep at it. Be happy and celebrate even a one-point gain.

"Even celebrate half-point increases in your score."

"I would, Leah, but there are no half-point increases. The LSAT is scored only with full numbers," I said.

"How sure are you of that, Alexandra?" Leah asked.

"I just am."

Noah smiled.

"Are you as sure of that as you're sure that the sky is blue?" Leah asked.

"Absolutely," I said. I wasn't sure where Leah was going with this.

"Alexandra," Noah said, "It's time you learned something called **'certainty with humility'**. Even if you're 100% sure about something, you could still be wrong."

"Am I wrong about the half-point increase?" I asked.

"Actually, yes," Noah said. "Let's say you take two practice exams every week. If your average score last week was 165, and the two exams you take today are 165 and 166, your average just went up to 165.5, and that's your half-point increase."

"Okay. I see what you're saying."

"The main lesson here isn't about the half-point increase. It's about having certainty with a sprinkle of humility."

The food arrived and we began to eat, but my mind was more focused on what Leah was telling me. Celebrate small victories. It started to sink in. We continued talking, about New York City, Noah's work, and Leah's recent research projects. When we were almost ready to leave, Leah had one more piece of advice, that would turn out to be a life changer.

"Besides appreciating every point or every five points, remember that you have you the brains and the ability to study. That itself is huge. You might take it for granted as many do. But so many people, like some of the beautiful individuals I work with, don't have the ability to study—and boy, they wish they could. **Just being able to get any decent score, to go to any law school and pass the bar, and to get any job as a lawyer is an enormous blessing, whether you realize that right now or not.**"

Now *that* was an incredible view, even better than the view of the city.

A Cadre of Experts

Practice exam. The full thing. 8:30 am. All five sections, and a 10-minute break between sections 3 and 4. The only difference between the real exam and my practice exams — besides the fact I'm not doing them in a test center — is that I allow myself only 30 minutes per section. That adds stress. It's an effort to simulate the real test, where you feel a lot more stress than you do in a practice exam. After the practice exam, I took a nice long break before I scored it: 163.

Chapter 23

Noah called his limo. We were close to the subway station, so I told him I would take the subway since my apartment was out of his way. There was only one train running at that station. I had my headphones on and was listening to my music as I walked down the stairs. The train arrived within a minute. What a town. The train smelled like urine. What a town.

When I'm on the subway, I love to observe people, or people watching as it's called. It's fascinating. Everyone is coming from and going to different places. Everyone has different jobs, different interests, different personal circumstances, and different likes. Everyone has different sexual preferences, different obsessions, hobbies, phobias, emotions. Different things made them mad, sad, happy, excited. And I was on the wrong train.

It took me five stops to realize that, and I knew the city and its transportation like the back of my hand. It had been about two or three minutes between each stop, so it wasn't a huge setback. But it made me wonder. It made me wonder how I could make such a simple mistake and not realize it until at least ten minutes had passed. I wasn't drinking that night or anything. Maybe I just wasn't thinking.

I met Noah for breakfast the next morning at the LSAT Café. He had his newspaper out and was mumbling to himself about an article he'd read. Something about what the mayor had said.

"Did you enjoy Leah's company?" Noah asked cheerfully.

"I did. She's wonderful." I poured myself a cup of coffee. "I had an

A Cadre of Experts

interesting ride back, though. I got on the right subway, but the one going the wrong direction. Did that ever happen to you?"

I knew that was a silly question because Noah hadn't taken the train in a while. Not since he'd gotten the limo, anyway.

"Sure, Alexandra, that's happened to me before, but not just on the subway. The truth is, I used to do that all the time on the LSAT."

"What do you mean?"

"People often can't distinguish between opposites. While you could remember clearly which train you needed, you got mixed up about the direction. The Q train has no opposite. The F train isn't the opposite of the Q; it's a different train.

"As I mentioned to you at our first breakfast, when we were talking about planning, pilots can get confused about whether they're flying up or down during high-speed maneuvers when the jet is twirling and spinning. Planes actually have a device installed in them that audibly tells pilots which way they're flying. A plane could be upside down and the pilot might not even realize it. The LSAT psychometricians know that, and they cleverly offer wrong answers that are simply complete opposites of the correct answer. I used to get those ones wrong all the time."

I took a sip of my coffee. "I know what you mean," I said, "I had a boss a few years ago who would schedule me to work and then frequently cancel. He did it so many times that I'd get mixed up and either come to work when I wasn't scheduled or not show up when I was scheduled. But I never went to work at the store next door."

"Exactly. So an answer choice that is completely out of scope is easy to eliminate. But an answer choice that has all the right words and concepts, but goes the opposite direction, can be trickier."

It made sense, but it was also incredibly annoying that the LSAT actually tries to trick you. What's the point of that? Noah sensed my feelings.

"I know it might seem like the LSAT is out to get you, but it's not. One of the most important jobs lawyers do is introduce logic and keep entrepreneurs on their best behavior—logically speaking, of course. People have so many worthy ideas, but because nobody challenges them, they might not be successful."

"How is that, Noah?"

"Let's say that you come up with a certain idea. There are probably many holes in the idea, not ones that completely destroy the idea, but holes that do need to be filled. Say you're planning a concert. Somebody asks you what you're planning to do about security. You didn't think about that. So you hire a security company. Another person who you share your idea with asks if you have sponsors, something else that didn't occur to you. So again, you fill that hole and find some sponsors.

"But if nobody is there to show you the holes, you may very well forget, or fail to address certain things. You may be thinking of the bigger picture and overlooking the small parts."

"So you're saying that the LSAT is there to show you the holes in your thinking?"

"Well put, actually. If the LSAT would pose a question and then offer you only one answer, you would accept it and move on. But they offer you the correct answer, plus another one or two very tricky answers, as if to say 'What about this one?' Tricky yes. But out to get you? *Au contraire.*"

"I had a friend who had to make a big decision about going to medical school. Her professor challenged her to go and observe the labs, you know, where they dissect human bodies."

"Oy."

"The professor wanted to show her a big hole in her plans, because a lot of people cannot handle the dissecting of bodies. If she could prevail at the challenge, at least she would know that she wouldn't have a problem with that part of the schooling."

"So what happened to her?" Noah asked.

"Happened to whom?" I said, from a daydream.

"To your friend who wanted to go to medical school. Seriously, Alexandra, I worry sometimes about your sanity." He was grinning, but maybe he was right; I was preoccupied.

"She got into medical school. She's in her second year, I believe. Dissecting bodies and everything. Must be lovely."

Noah asked for the bill and got up to go wash his hands. When he got back, I decided to tell him why I was preoccupied.

"So Noah, I don't want you to think that I haven't made up my mind

A Cadre of Experts

about going to law school, but I'm starting to get fed up with the LSAT. I know that the trickiness is for my benefit and all, but I have to admit it's annoying to be constantly shown the shortcomings in my thinking. Know what I mean?"

"I totally understand. When I'm in court, there is another attorney whose primary goal is to show how the arguments I'm making are not only illogical, but irrelevant, badgering, speculative, argumentative, calls for speculation, hearsay, leading, or just plain dumb."

"How does it make you feel?"

"I'm used to it by now. But it does make me work hard the weeks before the trial to make sure my arguments will be sound and logical. It's more of a motivator, Alexandra. But haven't you been seeing a lot of improvement in the last few weeks?"

"Yes, I have. In fact, on my last test, I scored 163. It's just starting to get to me."

"Why don't you take off for a few weeks? Go on vacation, maybe? My treat. My grandmother has an apartment in Florida she uses only a few times a year. How does that sound?"

"But my test is in a few months. A few weeks is a lot at this point."

"There is an ancient Talmudic saying, 'Revocation is its existence.' Sometimes you need to revoke something—in your case, to actually stop studying—and that will ensure its continued existence. Food for thought. Let me know what you decide."

Noah stood, gave me a quick kiss on the cheek, took his treasured thermal coffee mug and rushed to his meeting. I stayed a bit longer to think about Noah's idea. I sat with my hands in my lap and my head angled thoughtfully. A vacation, hmm? Where would I go? My friends were all busy so I wouldn't have anybody to go with. Maybe I'd take three days off and go stay in my Noah's grandmother's apartment.

I didn't want to miss time studying, but my body was telling me I should. I could study while I was on vacation, which would be stupid because the point of the vacation was to get away from the LSAT. If I went to Florida, I wouldn't take any books with me. That sounded like a plan.

I knew Noah was at a meeting, or at least on his way, so I sent him a text. "*Hey N, I tuk ur advice and wl b going 2 Flrida 4 3 dyz. C U whn I get bck.*" Noah responded promptly:

"*If I didn't know better, I would think you pay for your texts by the letter.*"

Chapter 24

I FOUND A DEAL on tickets, and before I knew it, I was in Miami. The cold in New York was horrible, so it was a great time to come to Florida. I got to the apartment and decided to relax religiously. I would sacrifice myself on the altar of relaxation. I would serve the idleness with love and passion, and in a few days return to being a relaxation atheist who believed in nothing less than 18-hour days. And of course the six hours spent sleeping were still a sin.

Relaxing and dozing off like Noah's Yenta was certainly refreshing. I started to understand what Noah meant about "revocation being its existence." It was true. I was again able to envision myself studying for a few hours a day without going nuts.

I flipped on the TV and came across my favorite show, Law & Order. I thought I'd love to work in the field of criminal law. Noah warned me that being a lawyer was not what was depicted on TV, and I supposed he was right. On the other hand, if that's not what lawyers did, maybe I wouldn't want to be a lawyer? I decided to call an old friend who went to law school a few years ago and was now working with a large law firm in New York.

I called Laura and started to pick her brain. I asked her what lawyers do, even though Noah had already given me an overview during the last few months. Laura turned out to be much less enthusiastic about being a lawyer in general, which proved to be helpful.

"Why would you want to be a lawyer, anyway?" Laura asked.

"Um, I want to be in a distinguished profession and make money," I said in Valspeak.

"Is that a question?"

"No, those are my reasons."

"Then you're in the wrong profession, Alexandra. Of course, you can make money, and compared to some professions, maybe being an attorney is a distinguished profession. But lawyers work hard, real hard, to make their money. Some people think that they graduate law school and automatically become a glitterati. It isn't so, at least most of the time."

"Well, okay."

"If you're not passionate about the law and law school, working as a lawyer will prove to be quite annoying, to say the least. It's really not for everyone."

"So what are you recommending? I know it's not the Law-&-Order type of lawyer that I had envisioned ... I guess I need to grow up."

"Alexandra, education empowers us to do incredible things throughout our lives. The problem is, we live in such an education-rich society that people are getting educated in the right ways but for the wrong reasons.

"The law is our covenant and our bond with society. It's what protects us and what binds us together. But, far too often, people go to law school to stroke their ego, or because their parents think it's a smart idea, or because they don't know what they want to be and law school is an easy step from college, since there are no prerequisites. These reasons are almost never the right reasons to go to law school.

"Nevertheless, there are still many compelling reasons to become an attorney. Helping people, brining justice to the world, and making a change to the system that governs what we can and cannot do are all valiant reasons to become an attorney. Let me give you **a test you can use to really start to understand your own intentions.**"

"That sounds exciting, I'm writing it down on my notes," I said, as I put in my headphones so that I could hear Laura and type at the same time.

"**Imagine,**" Laura said, "**you can go to law school only if you sign a contract that you can never tell any of your friends or family you're a lawyer. Would you still go to law school?**"

Wow.

"If your answer is an honest 'yes,'" Laura continued, "*go to law school.* That means you actually want to be a lawyer for its own sake.

Ask yourself whether you are going to law school for the real reasons, to help people, to bring justice to the world, or whether you're pursuing this path for the wrong reasons; like to show off or prove something to someone. Does that help?"

"Totally, Laura, and that's the advice I was hoping to get. Now that you've given me some insight into the legal profession, I can do the math and come up with my conclusion. From our brief conversation, I think I'm still interested. So thanks a million, Laura."

"Absolutely Alexandra. You know, I feel very passionate about this topic. More and more people are going to law school for the wrong reasons. Either because they have nothing else to do or because they think they'll make a ton of money. Unfortunately, that can cause people to become either uninterested in the profession, or greedy, which only gives attorneys a bad name. Whenever people talk to me about law school, I emphasize that they need to either go to law school for the right reasons, or not go at all."

"There are a variety of good reasons though," I said. "They all revolve around helping people, but in different ways, like policy work or public interest or public service, and many others."

"Very true, Alexandra."

"Thanks again for your time. I hope you're not billing me," I said jokingly, alluding to her reference of greedy lawyers.

"Anytime, Alexandra. Let me know how things turn out, and where to send the bill."

It's good to have friends to talk to so you can consider other people's perspectives. Noah had told me plenty about the legal profession, but hearing about it from another person put it in a totally different light.

I started to think about the question Laura asked me. If no one could know, would I still want to be a lawyer? Tough question. But what Laura really meant to ask was: do I want to become an attorney for everybody else, for my mom, for Noah, for the neighbors? Or do I want to become a lawyer the right reasons; for myself, and to help other people, to improve the world? Talk about food for thought.

I sat in Noah's grandma's old rocking chair and rocked myself back and forth until my thoughts were calm and my breathing became slow and quiet, I centered myself. I closed my eyes and repeated the question again and again. If no one could know, would I still want to be a lawyer? If no one would ever find out, would I still go to law school? Would I still be a lawyer? Would I?

The rocking slowed, as did my breath, allowing my thoughts to wander freely, until my subconscious was ready to surface the answers to my conscious. Deep down, my need for acknowledgment voted against the idea. It wanted everyone to know that I'm a lawyer. It couldn't fathom the idea that I wouldn't tattoo the word "Lawyer" on my forehead. Then my sincere desire to help people spoke, saying it didn't matter if my family and friends knew, as long as I was helping people. My ego spoke up, loud and clear, and said, no, if I couldn't tell my friends I was a lawyer there was simply no point.

From an even deeper place, maybe from my soul herself, I heard a meek voice whisper: "Getting through law school is an accomplishment in itself. When you start and finish a project, you become more whole, more confident, *more you*, like filling in pieces of a puzzle. Do it for yourself and for no one else. You're the only person who needs to know how smart, witty, well read, unique and genuine you are." There was a three-second pause. "And you are."

I woke up from what felt like a dream, with my eyes wide open, as if I were shown the other side of life. Maybe I had a glimpse. Maybe on the other side of life was knowledge of who we are, without judgment, and without worrying what other people think. True bliss.

I decided two things. One, yes, I was willing to go to law school, study long and hard, live on a starvation budget, get intellectually beat up by professors exercising the Socratic method, ace the exams, graduate top 3% of my class and pass the Bar, and not tell a single soul about it all. I decided that I would do it for the right reasons. And while, (of course), I wouldn't mind some positive attention, I would go to law school to be a lawyer with genuine motivation at heart—and not for the shtick.

Oh, and the second thing I decided, I don't give a *shit* about law school rankings.

Chapter 25

I ONCE HEARD ABOUT a soldier fighting in a war. At home, he had a sick mother and a newlywed wife he yearned for, but he loved his country, too, so he fought. As he struggled with his desire to return home and his need to stay and fight, he prayed, 'If I can go home tomorrow I will dedicate my life to helping the poor and hungry.' The soldier went to sleep, only to be woken up twenty minutes later by the blast of an enemy bomb. He quickly scattered to get his rifle and tried to shoot in the direction of the blast, but to no avail. His right-hand index finger was paralyzed by the blast. He could no longer fight —as he could no longer shoot—although he had no other injuries.

The army promptly released him, but asked him for a favor, to could carry out one final mission: to deliver some important documents to another base on the other side of the country. The train ride would take a few weeks, but he was so grateful to be absolved of his military duties that he agreed.

After that long journey, he returned home. But in the weeks between his promise to help the poor and hungry, and his return home, he began to lose interest. He had been inspired, motivated, at the *'go'* stage that comes after *'ready, set.'* But that few weeks' wait in between, extinguished his fire like a gallon of water poured on the candles of a five-year-old's birthday cake.

When you get inspired to do something, if you don't act immediately, you can easily lose momentum. I decided to return to New York, even at the cost of buying a new plane ticket for an earlier date.

I didn't want to be like that soldier. I didn't want to lose my second wind. I texted Noah:

"*On my wy bck 2 NY, gt mtivtd and dcded 2 come bck on the frst flgt out. C U 2mrrw?*"

Noah answered: "Glad to hear. Tomorrow, breakfast 8 o'clock?"

"*C U thn.*" Then came the announcement to turn off phones.

I woke up three hours later as the plane started to land. I could still feel the spring in my step, eager to get started. Not that the LSAT would be new to me, but in a way it felt like it would. I felt like I was starting fresh.

I got home and unpacked my bags, humming to a tune that I heard on the radio in the Uber ride from the airport. Was it Toni Braxton? I put my clothes away and sorted out my stuff, just as the door opened. Chelsea walked in, holding some envelopes.

"You've got mail," Chelsea said, reminding me of my Gmail. "How was your trip? Weren't you supposed to come back next week?"

"I went down to Florida to relax and think about my plans for law school and all that. I had a refreshing conversation with a lawyer friend and got my second wind. So here I am, all ready to continue." I sat on my bed as Chelsea handed me my mail. One envelope looked like a letter from my second oldest sister, Lorraine.

I opened it. Who sends letters these days? It had been something like 15 years since I'd gotten a letter in the mail. I was careful not to tear it.

Dear Alexandra, how are you? I know we haven't spoken in a while, but a little bird told me you're going to law school. I would advise you not to. Do you remember when we were kids and you wanted to build your own doghouse for the dog? You never finished that doghouse. You never finished anything. What makes you think you will finish law school? You'll just get yourself into debt and end up quitting in the middle, so what's the point? I know I sound harsh, but truthfully, I'm not. I am just trying to look out for my little sister.

I hope all is well, and I'm sure that you can find a better (maybe easier) path to embark on, and I'm sure you'll do fine with that. Love, Lorraine.

I started to cry. I'd just recaptured my excitement, and now this. Chelsea tried to calm me down, saying that she was probably jealous.

"That actually makes a lot of sense, Chelsea," I said. "My sister always wanted to be a lawyer. Then, she married young and had kids, and that was that for law school. But I don't understand why she would try to discourage me."

"Some people are sincerely happy when others succeed, and some just aren't," Chelsea said. "I don't know your sister and I don't want to say anything unkind-"

"No, no, go right ahead."

"Well, I assume she falls into the latter category."

"You're right, Chelsea. You're from the group of people who have a good eye and are happy when others succeed."

"Besides, you're probably much prettier than she is," Chelsea said. I sat up and wiped my eyes. Chelsea sat next to me.

"So what about that second wind?"

I gave Chelsea a hug. "My second wind is back, thanks to you. I'm starting again to study for the LSAT at full blast, from right now until the test."

"When's the test?" Chelsea asked.

"Whenever I'm ready, that's when," I answered. "But seriously, I should be ready by June."

"So do you have a plan?"

"I'm meeting Noah for breakfast tomorrow. He's going to help me come up with a solid plan for the next few months, and I'm going to blow the LSAT out of the water. You'll see."

"I can't wait. I'm so happy you're back in the game, Alexandra."

"Thanks to good friends."

Another practice exam, and another, and another. This is the key to improvement. More and more practice exams, and then some more. There are many individual skills and much knowledge needed to perform well on the LSAT, but **taking the full test is a skill in itself**. *It's like knowing the elements in the fire tetrahedron and how to extinguish a fire, and then actually entering a blazing building and putting out the fire. The theoretical knowledge is vital, but all the theoretical knowledge in the world isn't worth anything without experience. Latest practice exam: 166.*

Chapter 26

"Welcome back Alexandra, it's been so long," Noah said as I walked into the LSAT Café.

"Sometimes two days can be a long time, if you have accomplished a lot," I answered.

"That's true."

The waiter—good ol' waiter confidant—came over and took our orders.

"Noah, I wanted to talk to you about helping me plan for the next few months, you know, to use my time wisely. Any suggestions?"

"Why not just continue doing what you were doing?"

"I was improving, but after the last few tests I've felt stuck. Then I had my family-style meltdown, and that's when I went to Florida. So I'm looking to maybe change things up a bit. Start fresh."

"Okay."

"I'm debating whether to continue with practice exams or to hit the study guides again and pretend that it's all new information."

"If you're missing answers because you're in a rush or misread the question or answers, you should continue doing real questions and full-length tests.

"But if you're missing questions because you didn't understand what the flaw was, or because you didn't know how to set up a game, it would be smart to reopen the study guides. Maybe you missed something fundamentally important."

The waiter brought the food.

"Right now I'm struggling most with the logic games. Sometimes I just don't *see* the setup."

"Maybe I can help."

Noah grabbed the salt and pepper shaker, along with the maple syrup jar and a rolled up napkin.

"So here's the scenario. The waiter of this restaurant has to set the table here every morning. But his boss is a perfectionist, so he lays out rules for the waiter. The salt and pepper have to go first, in either order. If the salt is first, the napkin is last. Do I need to go any further?"

"No, I get the setup. But what's the point?"

"The point is to make the games real. Literally, **practice with real objects**, and either make up your own rules or take an actual LSAT logic game and apply it to real objects."

"Sounds a little unorthodox."

"Well, if the conventional way isn't working out, maybe it's time to try something new. I think that the logic games are so abstract that it's hard for many students to grasp them. I taught this method to students who were having a hard time. Some tried it and loved it, and some didn't try it. But it works."

I took the maple syrup from the lineup and poured some onto my pancakes.

"And now I'm eating a logic game variable," I said, as I jabbed the fork into the pancakes.

"And what does it taste like?" Noah asked.

"Not bad, Noah. Not bad at all."

Noah asked me about the next tip I had for brain health.

Brain Health Tip # 5: Get Enough Sleep

"During sleep, your mind strengthens memories of skills you've practiced during the day while you were awake. It's a process called 'consolidation.' You learn to a certain point with practice, but something happens while you sleep that makes you really understand it. If you're trying to learn something new, whether it's the LSAT anything else, you'll understand better after sleeping."

I went home after breakfast and studied for two hours. I went to the gym, ran on the treadmill for 45 minutes, did my regular stretches and lifted some light weights. When I went to grab the dumbbells from the neat stack of weights, I remembered what Noah had spoken about that morning, about looking at the logic games as real-life scenarios. With the weights, the rules seemed straight forward. Stack them according to their weight. But that was too simple. What happened if you added other rules? Even conditional ones, like "If the 5-lb weight is first, then the 10-lb weight is third."

I decided to start practicing with objects at home, like spices I have in my kitchen, and books. Maybe I'd even use some of my LSAT books.

I got home and went to work. I took out some seasonings I bought a while ago; pepper, salt, cumin, oregano, onion, and garlic powder, most of them unopened. I found a game that had six variables that had to be ordered and I applied those rules to the spices.

After about an hour, it hit me like a baseball bat. I felt the logic games becoming simpler, even alive. I was afraid I was getting too excited, so I decided to take out a logic game and time it. I finished in six minutes, answering all the answers correctly. But maybe that was an easy one. I opened another one. Again, I finished the game in record time. Record time for me, at least. Then I did a third and a fourth, and finally, a full logic game section.

I Uber'd straight to Noah's office. I'd never come there without calling, but I couldn't suppress my excitement. I was excited as the jets in a soothing spa. I got to the office and was greeted by Chris, Noah's assistant.

"Noah's in a meeting, but I'll let him know you're here."

"I'll just wait in the reception room until he's finished."

I sat on the leather seats in the waiting room, impatiently flipping through a magazine on the glass table. While browsing, I remembered the letter I had received from my sister Lorraine the day before. What had gotten into her? Maybe she was jealous, as Chelsea had pointed out, but there wasn't much I could do about that. I didn't understand what she was jealous about. She could go to law school now if she wanted. And what was she jealous about? Did she see the struggle and hard work I was putting into the LSAT? *It wasn't like it came naturally.* I'd been on an emotional rollercoaster ever since my LSAT endeavor started.

Just a few days ago, in Florida, I decided that even if no one knew

A Cadre of Experts

that I was a lawyer, I would still go to law school. I was doing this for me. I wasn't doing this to please anyone, and I definitely wasn't going to give up to please anyone.

Noah finished his meeting 30 minutes later. He was surprised to see me. I knew he'd be wondering what I was doing there.

"Noah, I came to thank you. The exercise you gave me for the logic games this morning was *incredible*. It made the logic games click. Until today, I was finishing games in about 9 minutes, but after practicing your method for about an hour, I did a bunch games in under 8 minutes each. Some were even 6 minutes. I hate to bother you at the office, but I was just too excited."

"That's awesome, Alexandra," Noah said, as we sat down at his desk. "And it's never a bother. Besides, you should get used to the office—I'm sure we'll find a job for you here after law school."

First the logic game breakthrough, and now this extremely early job offer. What a day.

"By the way, since I see the logic games are going so well, how's the reading comprehension?"

"I've been doing the exercise that Judge Brian gave me when we were in Texas. I still do the exercise for about ten minutes before every study session. The section is working out fabulously."

"Awesome. By the way, in the meeting I was in, we got a new high-profile case. It's going to bring a substantial amount of cash to the firm, not to mention media coverage and prestige."

"So how about dinner?" I suggested.

"That's what I was about to say. Pick you up at seven?"

"Seven it is. Meanwhile, I'll go home and do some more logic games. I'm feeling as optimistic as Superman."

I wasn't sure which restaurant we were going to, so I dressed somewhere between casual and formal. I had spent the afternoon doing logic games, so I was sure that my newfound superpower was indeed real.

"We started working on this big criminal case. It's going to be a lot of fun," Noah told me as I got into the limo.

"What's the case about?"

"A certain celebrity did something he wasn't supposed to do. But he'll be fine; he's got us in his corner. You could start reading about it in tomorrow's paper.

"So I'm happy that your LSAT studying is coming along."

"Me too," I answered immediately. "Where were we with your LSAT top seven tips?"

"Ah, yes," Noah said, as he took out his yellow pad from his briefcase.

Noah's Top LSAT Tips #5

"**Be strict with yourself**. For you to truly learn something, and to internalize it, you have to be strict with yourself. I've seen students repeatedly make some sort of mistake—like diagram rules incorrectly on a logic game, write out rules in a confusing way, or bubble in the answer in the wrong question number. And when I bring it to their attention, they say things like, 'Oh, I know that; it's just that this is practice. On the real test I'll be more careful.' The thing is, that doesn't work. **The way you practice is the way you will perform**."

The limo came to a sudden stop. "Sorry Noah," Sam said through the window, "a dog ran right in front of us."

"He must have been in a rush. No problem."

The driver closed the window.

"Be strict with yourself. **If you don't fully understand something, don't move on**. If you don't understand conditional logic or a certain type of logical fallacy, don't say to yourself that you'll get back to it later. Be strict. Does that make sense, Alexandra?"

"Would it also mean sticking to a study schedule?"

"While that's obviously important, I'm talking about being strict with your internal dialog. Don't cut yourself any slack, because the LSAT won't. Let me give you another example."

The driver told us we would be arriving in about two minutes.

"You get a question wrong, so you look up the correct answer. But even after knowing the correct answer, you don't get it. It doesn't register in your brain. Most students would just move on. Being strict with yourself means that you don't move on until you completely understand the question, why the right answer is right and why the wrong answers are wrong. Don't fall for that internal dialog that tells you to move on or that you'll figure it out later. Now does that make more sense?"

"Let me think about it first."

"That's the spirit."

We had arrived. It was a quaint French restaurant in the Upper West Side. The weather was cool, with a slight breeze. We went inside the restaurant and were greeted by the host, who swiftly seated us. There were other people in line, but the host knew Noah and probably had him on a VIP list.

The waitress brought us menus, glasses, napkins, and a wine menu. Noah ordered a house-made ricotta ravioli with herbs and tomato sauce, and I got Kasha pasta with veal meatballs. At this point, I'd learned not to look at the prices. Noah hardly looked at the check when he paid. Maybe just a glimpse to calculate a tip.

We ordered wine and enjoyed the lively environment of the restaurant.

"I came here with my late wife when we were law students, working as interns here in New York during our first-year summer," Noah said as he stared into his wine glass. "Sometimes I really miss her."

I felt awful for him. He had this appearance of a tough criminal lawyer, tall and rigid. But below all that he was vulnerable. I grabbed his hand and our eyes met; Noah knew I would be there for him.

The food arrived a few minutes later. I hoped we would talk about things besides the LSAT. Sure enough, Noah broached another subject, albeit still related to law school.

"When are you starting to write your personal statement, Alexandra?"

"I haven't thought about that. What should I write about?"

"Write about yourself."

"That I knew, but what about me? I've never spent a summer saving whales or curing cancer. I don't even know where to start. Any suggestions?"

"Start with one word. If you could tell the law schools one word, what would it be?"

Now I was completely lost. "I don't know, 'accept me'?"

"That's two words."

"Accept?"

"What I meant was, what single word would you use to describe yourself? Enthusiastic, smart, persistent, maybe kindhearted? You see what I'm getting at?"

"I would have to think about it. I'm not sure what one word I want to convey. Maybe another glass of wine will help."

Noah poured me another glass.

"'Wine,' should not be the one word of course," Noah remarked.

"Oh please, I rarely drink. I have noticed that lawyers like to though," I said, as Noah was pouring himself another glass. "What was your personal statement about, Noah?"

"Do you want the extended version or the one-word version?"

"Start with the one word."

"Tenacity," Noah responded.

"Why?" I asked.

"Tenacity means being persistent and getting things done. I was able to demonstrate through various events in my life that I lived up to that standard. I told them that I would continue to use that philosophy in law school; to study and practice the law with tenacity and integrity."

"That's a good place to start. I have to think a bit more about my word, though."

"I think that you'd want to tell them about your burning desire to become a lawyer, if you can back it up with facts and stories."

Noah took a few bites of food.

"Over the next few days, be open to ideas that pop into your head. One of them will be that one perfect word you want to share with the law schools."

"Is there really only one word that I want to tell the schools?"

Noah wiped his mouth with his napkin. "Even if there is more, let them know about them through your resume, letters of recommendation or your diversity statement."

"Don't other people write the letters of recommendation for you?"

"Yes, but you can ask them if they wouldn't mind writing about your specific qualities. The second point has to do with the 80/20 rule. Have you heard of it?"

"Sure. It's named after Pareto, the Italian economist. It's the idea that 80 percent of your results come from 20 percent of your actions."

"Exactly. Pareto observed that 80 percent of Italy's income came from 20 percent of the population. It applies to so many situations, and I think that you can apply it to your personal statement."

I laid down my fork. "Eighty percent of the effect that the statement will have on the law school will come from 20 percent of the document."

"Nice job, Alexandra. So the question is, how to wisely use that 20 percent, correct?" Noah asked, cross-examination style. "Most of the essay is fluff. Introductions, endings, examples, begging, you get the point. But that 20 percent is what's going to make the real impact. So in 20 percent of a two or three-page essay, you don't really have time for more than one idea. One encompassing, solid, stylish idea, but one idea, nevertheless."

"Got it."

"And even if you have more room to articulate another point somewhere ... say you have two intriguing ideas you'd like to convey. One of them is your number one best and relevant quality. You can't have two number one best qualities, right? Better to use more lines on the more powerful idea than divide the reader's attention."

Noah had a point. Drive one point home rather than half-driving two points. As we started to finish dinner, the waitress offered us a dessert menu. We declined.

"That's all I'll say for now. But after you finish the LSAT, I'll take you to an expert. Her name is Mary." Noah asked for the check and called his driver to tell him that we were coming out.

We climbed into the limo. I tried to organize some of Noah's papers that were just scattered all over. It's lucky his driver cleans the car every day.

"You know Noah, while I enjoy studying and all, I still wish there was one simple trick to the LSAT, one simple technique or tip that would just help me destroy the LSAT. I wonder if I could find something like that," I said, daydream like.

"There is a magic pill," Noah said. "In fact, I can take you to an expert who can give you one."

"Wait a minute," I said, "you mean to tell me that all this time there was such a thing and you never told me about it?"

"You never asked. If you're looking for the one magic pill to conquer the LSAT, my friend Fisch will tell you about it. We can go see him tomorrow after breakfast."

"I'm still surprised you never told me about it. I'm really curious about what it is."

"There's a little catch though, Alexandra."

"What would that be?"

"If Fisch gives you the magic pill, you basically have to get a 180 after that. You really won't have any excuses not to get a perfect score. I know students who were scoring low, and using Fisch's magic pill they got scores in the high 170s. So you might even have to promise Fisch that you'll get at least a 179 or 180. Can you do that?"

"I have no idea. My last practice exam was 166, so maybe I can."

"If you tell him that *maybe* you'll get a 180, he won't give you the magic pill."

"That's fair. I'll promise him that I will get whatever score he wants me to get. I'm up to it. When are we going?"

"Tomorrow morning, after breakfast?" Noah offered.

"How about before breakfast?"

"I'm not sure if Fisch is up that early. Let me text him."

The limo pulled up to my apartment building. Noah received a text from Fisch. We were set to see him 9:00 a.m. the next morning.

"We can still meet him before breakfast, Alexandra," Noah said, "as long as we eat breakfast after we see him."

"Sure. So when are you picking me up?"

"Fisch lives in Riverdale, in the Bronx, so we'll need about half an hour to get there. I'll be here at 8:30."

"Sounds awesome," I said, as I was getting out of the car. "Have a good night Noah. I hope I can sleep tonight."

Noah rolled down the window.

"Why is that?" he asked.

"I'm going to go nuts tonight. I'm so anxious to meet Fisch."

Chelsea was up, sitting on her bed, and combing her hair with a fancy hairbrush. She turned and smiled.

"How was it?" Chelsea asked in her upbeat fashion.

A Cadre of Experts

"Nice, okay. Interesting as usual, you know. How was your evening?"

"Well, I didn't go out with any flashy lawyer in his limo, but not bad. I got some homework done."

"Don't be jealous Chelsea. After the creeps I've dated, I deserve one normal guy."

"I'm not jealous, I just want you to appreciate what you have. You have to look at things in perspective. Sure, I'm positive Noah has faults, who doesn't? But you should be happy."

"I am happy. I just don't know if Noah is 'the one,' you know? He's successful and rich and handsome, but he can also be kind of bossy, and messy. We'll see. Anyway, I'm exhausted. Tomorrow we're going to meet a friend of Noah's, so I'd better turn in. Goodnight Chelsea, and thanks for the pep talk."

"Anytime," Chelsea answered, as she put away her hairbrush.

Chapter 27

"Good morning, Alexandra," Noah said from inside his limo through the open window.

"I'm glad you got here on time," I said, "I'm dying to meet Fisch."

"I'm sure Fisch will be happy we're on time as well. He's what we call a *yekke*. He's detail-oriented and likes things to start on time."

"How do you know Fisch? And how did he come across the magic LSAT pill?"

"He was my LSAT tutor. The man is a genius. And he came across the secret by teaching the LSAT to hundreds of students, well that and his background in chemistry."

Noah said that last part with a grin. I hoped he wasn't pulling my leg or anything.

"Did I mention that he scored 180 on his LSAT?"

"Not bad."

"Nine times," Noah added.

"Nine times what?"

"Nine times he got a 180. Maybe more, by now. But what's the difference between nine and ten times anyway? The bottom line is that the guy knows the LSAT inside and out."

"Did he give you the magic pill, Noah? Is that how you got your high score?"

"Yes, he did teach me the secret. And that was exactly how I got my score."

"Then why did you wait all this time to tell me it?"

"I didn't think you were ready for it."

"Is Fisch a nice guy?"

"Absolutely. Fisch is a fascinating guy. He just might tell you to your face that you should look for another profession if he feels that law school is not for you. I doubt he'll tell you that, though. But he has no problem telling people the cold truth, which is that not everyone should go to law school."

"Didn't you tell me that it's the hard work, not the smarts, that matters in law school?" I asked, surprised.

"There's still some part of the equation that has to do with one's raw talent and maturity. Would you tell an eight-year-old that he could succeed in law school if he puts in a lot of work and pulls all-nighters twice a week? There are still some minimum requirements. Did I ever tell you Professor Levine's story about his friend in law school?"

"No, I don't believe you did. What happened?"

"Professor Levine himself took the first LSAT in 1948. So he knew plenty of people at the time who went to law school based solely on their GPA and the other factors.

"A friend of his graduated *summa cum laude* from college with a major in history. Brilliant man, according to Professor Levine, and Professor Levine doesn't call everyone he meets brilliant. This history major went to law school, and he was about as successful in law school as you are at ancient Egyptian folk dancing. He failed the bar exam three times and gave up. Because stories like that the law schools decided that they needed a more concrete way to evaluate potential law students, hence the birth of the LSAT. And the LSAT has had an extremely high success rate."

"What do you mean by the LSAT having a high success rate?"

"The higher the LSAT score, the higher the chance that the student won't drop out."

We were approaching the Riverdale exit.

"The LSAT tests to see if you think in a certain way. The higher you score, the more you are in alignment with that way of thinking."

"Then how does studying help?" I asked. "If it's about the way you think, how can studying be effective?"

"Haven't you ever read something that altered the way you think from that point on? I read once about an error in human thinking. The error is when people think that just because they put effort or time or money into something, they should therefore not give it up or stop pursuing it.

"It's like when someone goes to a movie and realizes halfway through that it's the worst movie they've ever seen. They don't get up and leave because they figure that they've already spent the money and put in an hour or so watching the first dreadful half. But if you think about it, that's totally backward. Since reading that I've noticed when I do that and have corrected that type of thinking."

Fisch's house was made of stone; it was three stories high and was beautifully landscaped. The limo pulled into the driveway, which led to a three-car garage. I got out and glimpsed the inside of the house through the first-floor windows. White everything. White couch, white rug, white marble countertops. We walked to the front door, which was bright blue. It didn't fit with the rest of the house. The window shutters, too, were painted in this bright blue color. Perhaps it was designed to clash on purpose.

"As I was saying," Noah continued, "ever since I read that idea, it changed the way I think about that type of situation. A person can change the way they think. Studying for the LSAT, to answer your question, does exactly that. But if someone thinks in such a way that is so very different, it might be a losing battle for that person to change the way they think and go to law school."

Noah walked up to the door and gave it three consistent, quiet knocks. Five seconds later the door opened. An elderly lady stood there, holding an old-fashioned feather duster. She also had an apron tied around her waist. She had a soft, elegant voice.

"You must be the guests Fisch is waiting for. Please come in and have a seat in the living room, but first take off your shoes. Fisch will be down in a minute."

I wanted to sit on the coach, but it looked too expensive to actually sit on; when Noah sat down, I followed suit.

Noah continued quietly. "So do you get the idea, Alexandra, about the LSAT? About how studying for the LSAT will change your thinking, and that's how it raises your score?"

"Until now I thought that studying for the LSAT made you better at it, just like any other test."

A Cadre of Experts

"Now you know better," Noah said in his sage-like voice.

"I remember when I was a kid, I got my first computer. It was used, and huge, but it was magical. My Aunt Donna came over and, being an author, wanted to show me how to use the thesaurus. She taught me how to use the word processing program, WordPerfect. She wrote, and I quote, 'Today my Aunt Donna showed me how to use the thesaurus. Until now I thought that was a type of dinosaur, but now I know better.' What's funny is that a few years ago she pulled the same shtick when I showed her my new iPad."

"So you must be the girl Noah was telling me about," Fisch said, "Alexandra, right?"

Fisch was tall, probably 6'2 or 6'3, with brown hair and small brown eyes, and a pointy chin. He wore a white button-down shirt and black slacks. A handsome man, and I could tell he meant business. He was Noah's teacher, so he had to be smart. He also seemed to radiate kindness, so I felt comfortable right away.

"I've heard much about you."

"I hope only the positive things," Fisch said, looking at Noah. "Actually, I have a horrible memory for names, so if I remembered your name it must mean something. So, how can I help you guys today?"

I looked around the living room. There were pictures of Fisch with his wife and kids, and photos of some older people, probably his parents or in-laws. On a bookshelf was an old-looking jar. It was chipped and dusty and just had an odd look.

"Alexandra here is studying for the LSAT, and I told her about your magic pill that will help her absolutely destroy the LSAT, with a money-back guarantee. I didn't tell her what the secret is, just that you have such a thing."

"Ahh, the good old LSAT magic pill. I don't give it out that easily, you know," Fisch said. "What do I have to do to earn it?" I asked hopefully.

"How bad do you want to master the LSAT?" Fisch asked.

"Really, really badly. I'd do almost anything," I said.

"Why?" Noah asked. "Why do you want to get a perfect score so badly?"

"I just really, really want to. I can't explain it."

"Is it to show everyone else how smart you are?" Fisch inquired.

I pondered that question for a moment. Maybe it *was* to show people that I was smart. I wasn't exactly sure, to be honest.

"The reason I want to master the LSAT," I finally said, "**is to master the LSAT inside of me.**"

I could see that the guys thought I was nuts, so I continued.

"Studying for the LSAT is more than just a test. It's an intellectual pursuit; it's a mental fitness; it's a physical fitness; it's a stretch of your mind, and your body's ability to rise to the challenge and carry you through victorious. The knowledge ascertained in studying for the LSAT has greatly nourished and expanded my mind, and it has pushed my focus to new levels. My soul now reveals its higher purpose, given the tools to do so."

I think I had the guys in a trance.

"Take the reading comprehension, for example. By mastering it, I am learning a skill that is vital to everything I will ever do in law school and as an attorney. Or the logical reasoning—wouldn't it be smart to master my thinking and logical reasoning skills? And knowing what kind of flaws exist, I want to be careful not to make them and be able to call someone else out on them. I am improving my understanding of logic, how to make sound arguments, and how to better understand what I read and subsequently write. I can better understand what inferences can be made, how to appreciate an author's tone, how to summarize arguments, spot weak ones, strengthen them or make analogous arguments by paralleling the logic."

I took a breath. I could now see that the guys were looking at me with more respect. "I'm not too sure about the logic games, but I think I made my point about the other two sections."

"You certainly did, Alexandra," Fisch proclaimed. "I'm impressed, in fact. How about you, Noah? Do you think she's earned the magic pill?"

"I'm impressed too. That was a brilliant speech. And, truthfully, I never thought about the LSAT that way. While you're on the topic, let's think a bit about the logic games and why they're also necessary to master. They obviously help you get into law school, but on a personal level what incentive do we have to devote all our heart and soul to it?"

The room was quiet for a bit. Then Fisch spoke.

"Let's think about it for a minute, you guys," he said. "You're walking on the street one day and see a man dressed up as a king. Next to him is his wife, dressed up as a queen. Does that sound normal, Alexandra?"

"Maybe it's Halloween?"

"Exactly, so that would be okay. If what you see follows the rules, you're okay with it. You have to know the rules, of course. If someone who comes from a country that doesn't celebrate Halloween and has never heard of it sees that situation, he or she might call the cops."

I thought I knew what he was getting at. "So knowing the rules and how to apply them can help you understand life?" I asked.

"Exactly," Fisch said. "The Halloween example is a simple one, but it can illustrate that knowing the rules and how to apply them is a vital life skill. As a lawyer, you will be presented with many complex situations for which you will need to know the rules, or the laws, and how to apply them."

"I recently was sitting at a café studying for the LSAT, and they have this policy that you can sit only for 20 minutes at a time. I usually sit for much longer, but that's when the place isn't too busy, so it's not disturbing. Is that the sort of thing you're talking about, Fisch?"

"Sure. You know the rule that the sitting is limited to 20 minutes. But you also understand their rationale, that people won't hog tables and interfere with other customers. So you applied your own logic to the situation and allowed yourself to stay longer. That's awesome."

"It's not rocket science," I said. "But there are more complex logical situations like you said, a lawyer arguing a case."

"True," Noah said. "You can add that to your spiel next time someone asks you why you want so badly to master the LSAT."

"So, now do I get the magic pill?"

Fisch looked at Noah. They both looked at me. "Sure, take a seat," Fisch said.

I was already sitting, so I fixed my hair and sat up straighter instead.

"You know, Alexandra, "Fisch said, "I've taught hundreds of LSAT students over the years. I've interacted with all of them, and I've noticed some patterns. One pattern I noticed was among the students who were shooting for a 20-point increase. They were all looking for this magic pill, the one secret that would turn their LSAT studying into a piece of cake and cut the time needed to study by at least two-thirds. They wanted the one tip, one perfect technique, and no more, that would turn them into top LSAT scorers. So I invented one."

"I'm all ears," I said, eagerly.

"First, let me ask you this. Why do you think that this tendency to look for the Holy Grail of the LSAT was found, at least in my experience, among the students who had so much to improve on?"

"That's obvious," I said. "They're the students who need it the most."

"True, but what about the students who score in the top 160s or low 170s? Why aren't they looking for the magic pill? There certainly is a difference between a 169 and a 179, but the 169 students aren't looking for the LSAT secrets. How do you explain that?"

Noah chipped in. "Maybe they want to learn things the hard way. If they get to a 179 without any special help, they have more to brag about."

"That makes sense, Noah, but it's not quite the answer I'm looking for."

"Maybe because they already know the secret?" I suggested.

"Exactly," Fisch said excitedly, "but now the question is, how did they come across the magic pill?"

"I-I have no idea."

"They came across the magic pill on their own. And now let me tell you what that magic pill is."

Fisch stood up and went to the bookshelf. He grabbed that old-looking, chipped and dusty jar and sat back down on the couch.

The house phone rang. Fisch picked up. He looked up at Noah and me. His look told us that it was an important conversation, switched to his cordless phone and went upstairs with it. He said he would be right back.

"I told you you'd enjoy this guy, Alexandra."

"When did you say that?"

"Never mind."

Noah's phone rang; it was a video call from his sister. It was actually his sister's son, Eli, who was two and a half.

He was screaming, of course. "I want a choking hazard!"

What the heck was that about? Noah's sister came on. She explained that Eli had a favorite Lego set, but the small pieces were too small for him. When she took those pieces away, she told Eli that they were a choking hazard, so he now identified those pieces as 'choking hazards.' Finally, he relaxed a bit and his mom put him back on the phone to say goodbye to his uncle Noah.

Fisch returned. "Hey guys, I must apologize. I have to go help a friend right away. When can you guys come back?" He handed me his card.

"You're in a rush Fisch, so we'll be in touch," Noah said.

Noah and I thanked Fisch for his time and he promised that we'd get together again soon to continue our conversation.

Noah's limo had had plenty of room to park, so we didn't have to wait for the driver to appear from around the corner or down the street. We promptly got in and were soon on our way back to the city.

"I'm kind of disappointed that I didn't get the magic pill."

"I understand, Alexandra. But we got to hear that beautiful speech and we clarified what the benefits are of studying and practicing logic games. So it wasn't a waste of time. Besides, we can come back again, probably even this week."

"Okay. So, what're your plans for the day?"

"I have to get to the office, but we can stop for brunch if you want to hit the LSAT Café."

Truthfully I wasn't that hungry, but I'd come to cherish the time we spent in the LSAT Café. "Sounds good. But I'll make sure not to get their milkshake. Last time that gave me a stomachache."

"I don't want to bust your chops or anything, but I smell two logical fallacies in what you just said. But this time, I'm going to let you figure it out. Any ideas?"

"Fallacy of time?" I answered, almost immediately. "Just because something happened in the past, doesn't mean that it will happen again in the future."

"Yes, the second flaw was indeed the fallacy of time. But what was the first?"

"Hmm, causation?"

"Exactly. If you had a milkshake on Monday and a stomachache on Tuesday, that doesn't prove that the milkshake caused the indigestion. Good job spotting those."

"I'm still not getting the milkshake."

"Any more of those brain tips?" Noah asked, as we got on the highway.

"Sure."

Brain Health Tip # 6: Get More Sunshine

"Sunshine is important for many brain functions. For one, it prompts the body to create vitamin D. Scientists have found that the lower a person's vitamin D levels, the worse they perform mentally, such as on intelligence tests. Compared with people with optimal vitamin D levels, those with the lowest levels were much more likely to be cognitively weak.

"What's more, getting sunshine means being outside. Fresh air has cognitive benefits as well. There are indoor air toxins, not present outdoors. And lastly, the rays of sunshine go into our eyes are strengthen our brains as well, in my layman's terms. There are other reasons that sunshine is beneficial for your brain, but these were the easiest to explain."

Noah rolled down his window, maybe to get some sunshine. The ride back to Manhattan was smooth with very little traffic. I had almost said no to brunch, but it turned out that over brunch, Noah was going to pass on an important tip for LSAT mastery.

Chapter 28

My usual seat at the LSAT Café had almost taken the form of my butt from sitting there so much. I ordered a house-made pizza with pesto and jalapeño, a diet soda. Noah ordered salmon. After the waiter had taken our orders, Noah said he might order something else later and would like to hold on to the menu.

"Actually, Alexandra," Noah whispered, as the waiter walked away, "I probably won't order anything else; I just wanted to show you something you might find helpful."

What could he possibly show me on the menu that would be helpful to the LSAT? I was assuming, of course, that what he meant by helpful pertained to the LSAT.

"This I have to hear, Noah."

"The menu only shows the names of the dishes with minimal explanation. It doesn't tell us, or the waiter or chef for that matter, what the ingredients are."

"Okay."

"Why doesn't the menu show the full list of ingredients?"

"Probably because nobody cares about the particulars, about the small details."

"Maybe, but what about the chef? Why doesn't the menu show the chef the full recipe for each dish?"

"Because the chef already knows how to prepare the dish?"

"Precisely. When the waiter places the order with the chef for eggs or pancakes, or any other dish, that one word triggers in the chef's mind the entire recipe. The process, the variations that could be done, like well-done with meat, or spicy. But all the chef needs is that one trigger word.

"On the LSAT, you have many one or two-word phrases you need to know. Assumption questions, ordering games, main point, flaws, variables, linear, grouping and on and on. So, for practice, you would benefit immensely from creating a cheat sheet."

The waiter brought our food. I started to think how each dish had all these different ingredients and that the chef knew what to do after hearing just a few words. Noah squeezed a half lemon onto his salmon.

"Then, to review, you only have to read the one or two-word phrases that you wrote down, and that will trigger your brain to think about all that's included in that phrase, as long as you know exactly what those phrases mean."

"Sounds interesting," I said.

"When you have a chance, make a list of all the things you've learned. You can add a short description. Let's say you write down 'weakening questions.' You can add something like 'questions that ask you to weaken the argument.' Or if you write 'grouping games,' add 'games that ask you to place variables into two or more groups.'"

"What about adding details to that one, like 'sometimes all the variables are used and sometimes not, and sometimes there is a set number for each group and sometimes not'?"

"Make those detailed games their own entity and list them as separate games. Maybe 'full grouping games' and 'not full grouping games.' There is no perfect terminology, just find phrases that work for you and stay consistent."

"That's a phenomenal idea. I'll start working on that list today."

"Review the list periodically, to keep all the ideas at the top of your head. Every time you review the list, it will strengthen the associations in your brain. When you come across an assumption question for example, once the word 'assumption' pops into your head, you'll remember the prompt, find the gap between the stated premise and conclusion or however you phrase it. And that will shorten your response time, that is the time it takes you decide what your task is and how to go about it. Even a second or two faster will have quite a positive impact."

I started my pizza. The smell was as mouthwatering as the taste. I was thinking about Noah's idea of creating the cheat sheet. I started to

A Cadre of Experts

wonder when we could meet Fisch again. Without telling Noah, I texted Fisch in between bites.

Sorry to bother you, but I was wondering when could we get together the three of us and finish the LSAT talk. Thanks.

Fisch responded. *If you and Noah aren't busy tonight, I'll be in the city, and we can meet for dinner. Let me know.*

"So Noah, what are you doing for dinner tonight?" I asked, right as he put a bite of salmon in his mouth.

"We didn't even finish brunch, and you're already worried about dinner?"

"Well, Fisch wanted to meet for dinner tonight. I can meet him by myself if you are busy."

Noah looked at me with a hint of jealousy. "No, I can make it, Alexandra. Where and when?"

I texted Fisch and we arranged to meet at 8 o'clock, the three of us, at an Italian restaurant on the Upper West Side. I usually let Noah make the schedule, but I was eager to get the magic LSAT pill.

Noah might have been a bit annoyed about my making plans with his friend, but I wasn't going to let that bother me. Noah had a meeting to get to and I wanted to study for a few hours, so we headed out and planned to meet at 8 o'clock at the restaurant.

Chelsea was home when I got back, studying for an exam she had in a few days. I told her about Noah's idea of creating a cheat sheet. She seconded the idea.

"I do exactly the same thing with my schoolwork, and it can be quite handy."

I sat on my bed with my legs crossed, meditation style.

Chelsea clenched her bottom lip with her top teeth. "So how are things between the two of you?"

I looked down at my knees. "I don't know. Today I saw a side of him I didn't like."

"What side was that?"

"Jealousy."

"Jealousy? How did that come up? What was he jealous of even?"

I told Chelsea about the afternoon.

"I get it," she said. "So you think Noah is jealous of you texting his friend. Are you even interested in this friend?"

"No, I'm interested in what this guy has to tell me about the LSAT, that's all."

"Did you explain that to Noah?"

"I can't text someone without him getting all nervous? I'm not going to …"

"Alexandra, relax. All that means is Noah likes you. Don't take it the wrong way. So what is it that Noah's friend has to tell you that's so important?"

"His name is Fisch. What does he have to tell me? Only the secret to the LSAT. He has a magic pill that can make anyone score a perfect score on the LSAT. I'm not sure if it's some sort of advice or supplement or both, but I'm excited about it."

"A magic pill?"

"Yes."

"The secret to the LSAT?"

"Yes."

"*Anyone*?"

"Yes, what's with the sarcasm?"

"It sounds like a scam. How much is he charging you?"

"He's not charging me anything, and it's not a scam. This Fisch guy got like nine 180 scores. Besides, he's Noah's close friend."

"Okay, so it's not a scam, it's just that I've never heard of a 'secret' that will help you master a test that takes people months and months to study for."

Chelsea had a point. Whatever it was, it would be helpful, that was for sure. Noah wouldn't have taken me all the way to Riverdale for something useless.

"You know, Chelsea, not to be an annoying LSAT student or anything, but what you said implied a logical error."

"And what would that be?" Chelsea asked curiously.

"Lack of evidence doesn't prove lack of existence. Just because I've never seen a pink elephant doesn't prove that it doesn't exist. Just because you've never heard of such a secret to master a test, doesn't mean it doesn't exist."

"But if no one ever saw a pink elephant, wouldn't that prove that there's no such thing?"

"Logically it wouldn't prove anything. So the fact that you've never heard of the magic pill doesn't prove that it doesn't exist."

The LSAT has finally started to live inside of me.

"Actually, Alexandra, now that you've brought it up, I wanted to ask you something. I have this huge bill from an old credit card that I haven't even had in my purse for at least three years. Any advice?"

"You mean like, legal advice?"

"Yeah, if you have any ideas."

It's crazy how many people ask LSAT students legal questions. As if the LSAT was the bar exam.

"Sorry Chelsea, I haven't attended a day of law school."

"I know. But aren't you studying for the LSAT?"

I laughed. "I sure am, but you know what's not on the LSAT?"

"What's that?"

"Law!"

"Oh, I didn't realize that. Anyway, good luck with that magic pill that I wasn't able to prove doesn't exist."

"We're meeting Fisch for dinner tonight."

"Oh perfect, you probably have to take the pill with food anyway," Chelsea said sarcastically.

"I'll let you know when I get back. If you're here, that is."

"Yup, I'll be here, doing the same thing I'm supposed to be doing right now, studying for my exam."

"I have to study, too. Let's hit the books."

Today I tried something new. I read a reading comprehension passage and the questions, but before I read the answer choices, I wrote my own answers and compared them to the correct ones. This doesn't work with some question types, but with questions about the author's purpose, or main point, or in the comparative reading passages, it works well. At first, my answers were quite off, but after a few tries, they got closer and closer. After a few more, some of them were spot on. Then I compared my answers to the correct answer to see the differences and how my understanding of the passage correctly or incorrectly led me to my answers. Latest practice exam: 168.

I contemplated taking a practice exam that afternoon. On one hand, it had been almost two weeks since I'd checked my score. Last time I had gotten a 166 and I was hoping that my score had increased. On the other hand, taking a full exam made me tired, and I didn't want to be yawning during dinner with Fisch. On the other hand, I wanted to know what I was up to so I could compare my scores before and after meeting with Fisch.

I took out the next of the 20 tests I had designated for practice and sharpened my pencils. Every time I took a test, I felt like I was plunging underwater. I somehow got into this zone where I could see and hear no evil. When I was in that zone, I would get so submerged that I lost track of everything else. What was interesting though was that when I was scoring in the low 130s and 140s, I never felt I was entering that world. Only when I hit the 160s did I start feeling that way.

Of course, that's the old 'chicken and the egg' question. Did I become more focused and that was what improved my score, or did my understanding of the LSAT deepen and expand, and that, in turn, made me more focused? I'm not sure, but I do know that I have to get into that unique world to do my best.

It will come to me. That's what I started to tell myself whenever I didn't see the answer right away. If I don't understand a rule or how to diagram it, or if I don't spot an assumption or a flaw right away, it will come to me. Positive thoughts steer me in the right direction. And the answers usually do come after that. It will come to me.

A few hours later, I came back up for air. I'd learned by now not to check my score right away. After the practice exam I was too emotionally tired, and therefore vulnerable. If I scored lower than my past exams, I would take it badly, and if I improved, it would go to my head and turn me into an arrogant brat. As Noah's told me, arrogance is the source of all the other bad traits.

So I took a shower before checking my answers.

With my towel wrapped around my hair, I scored my practice test. I scored a hard-earned *171*.

Usually I would call or text Noah to tell him the news, but I figured

I'd see him in a few hours anyway. But I had to tell someone, so I knocked on Chelsea's door. Three knocks, and with each knock, I said a number. *Knock*, "One." *Knock*, "Seventy." *Knock*, "One." By now, Chelsea knew all about the LSAT scoring system. What score corresponded to what percentile of the LSAT world population, what it meant about my self-worth, which schools accepted which numbers, with which GPAs, and of course that the essay was not scored, but was supposedly read by the law schools you applied to. Since she knew all that, I didn't have to explain much. The numbers spoke for themselves.

Chelsea opened the door. She was crying.

"Chelsea, what happened?"

"My mother," she said between sobs. "My mother is in the hospital."

I didn't understand why she was home. Why wasn't she flying to Buffalo, where her parents lived? I gave her a hug, getting my shirt all wet from her tears, but I wasn't complaining.

"Chelsea, I'm sure everything will be okay. Are you going to fly home to see her?"

"I'd love to. But I don't have any money, and neither do my parents. Ever since my mom got sick two years ago, my dad has been staying home and taking care of her. My family is broke and so am I."

I wanted to help Chelsea, but I didn't have any money to spare. The rent was due, and my savings were scraping bottom. I couldn't afford to give her anything.

I phoned Noah.

"Noah, it's me," I said in a rush. "I told you about my roommate, Chelsea, right?" I didn't give him time to answer. "Her mom is very ill and she needs to fly to Buffalo, where her mom is in the hospital. If you can lend her the money, I'll pay—"

"Call my secretary, Chris," Noah said as quickly as I'd been talking, "Give him the details and he'll purchase the tickets. Tell him to send Chelsea my limo to take her to the airport."

I told Chelsea the news and she started packing right away. Within the hour Chelsea was packed and on her way to LaGuardia Airport. And I had to get ready for dinner.

Chapter 29

Something was bothering me. Chelsea's mom was in the hospital, but there was something else causing me to feel like autumn leaves.

Eight o'clock came quickly. Noah had to go straight from his office to the restaurant, so I would take the subway. I didn't mind, but I'd gotten used to driving around with Noah in his limo.

I swiped my Metro card and walked down the stairs to my train. I just missed the subway, but I had plenty of time to get there, and at that hour the train came every five minutes. I popped on my headphones. I sat down and noticed a $10 bill on the bench. I looked around to see if anyone was looking for it, but the station was almost entirely empty since the subway had just passed. A homeless guy halfway down the platform was the only other person in the station.

My mother always told me that if I found money, I should give it to charity. I picked up the $10 bill and walked over to the homeless man, who was sitting cross-legged on the floor. He looked up at me, probably in the hope that I could offer him some money or food. To answer his silent plea, I put the money in a little box that he'd placed in front of him. My mother also taught me to smile when you give someone charity; I did.

I felt I was looking into one of those mirrors that magnify and changes your face. When I smiled at the man, he returned a much bigger smile. When he saw the $10 bill, he lit up like fireworks on the Fourth of July. After wishing the man a good evening, I returned to my bench. I felt good about helping the fellow out. Maybe he'd even buy a full dinner with that money. Still, my previous uneasy feeling wouldn't go away. It was even stronger. Then, it hit me.

After seeing Chelsea upset about her mom and the fact that she had

A Cadre of Experts

no money to fly home, I started to realize that my "problems" were not really problems after all. I got agitated when I'd run out of ink for my printer, or if the soup I ordered at the LSAT Café wasn't warm enough.

Fifteen minutes later, I got off on the Upper West Side and walked a block and a half to the little Italian restaurant where we planned to meet. The host asked if I had a reservation and if we would prefer a table inside or out. I got to the restaurant before the guys, so I decided for the three of us that we would prefer to sit outside. The weather was perfect. The waiter brought over three menus and a jug of ice water.

I got a text from Noah telling me that he'd be ten minutes late. I poured myself a glass of water right as Fisch arrived.

"How did things work out this morning?" I asked Fisch.

"It worked out fine. Just some family issues, you know."

"I sure do, Fisch," I said, looking at my watch. "Just today my roommate and best friend got news that her mom fell sick and was hospitalized. Don't tell Noah I told you, but Noah bought her a ticket and sent his limo to take her to the airport."

Fisch shook his head. "Sorry about your friend's mom. And no, I won't mention anything to Noah. He does a lot of righteous deeds, and he's modest about them, so I can imagine he wouldn't want me to hear about it. Somehow telling others about good deeds you've done takes the *oomph* out of them. Where is the famous criminal lawyer, anyway?"

"He should be here in about five minutes."

"In that case, I'll make you a deal. I won't tell Noah what you told me if you don't tell him what I'm about to tell you."

I could feel the curiosity rising in my brain; I quickly accepted Fisch's deal, like when you press the "accept" button online without reading a word of the agreement.

"Well, I spoke to Noah a few days ago. Since his wife passed away, not only has he not dated anyone, he's had a hard time getting close to *anybody*. What he told me was that since he's met you, his whole world has changed for the better. He's not depressed anymore. To tell you the truth, I hardly could recognize him when you guys came to my house this morning."

"I don't know what to say, Fisch. I had no idea, thank you for telling me."

Before Fisch had a chance to answer, Noah showed up. He hurried in, shook Fisch's hand, and gave me a quick hug.

"Wow, Fisch," Noah said, "It's been hours since I've seen you."

"So let's order some food already."

We ordered wine and main courses. Fisch ordered eggplant parmesan, Noah and I ordered steaks. The food and wines arrived 15 minutes later. My order looked awesome. Roasted tomatoes on the vine that had shriveled up slightly. They had the perfect acid to sweet ration. Green beans to the side. They looked plain, almost raw. The steak was a thing of beauty: deep, dark crosshatched sear lines on the outside, pink-to-red on the inside. It sliced like hot butter on the plate and was seasoned simply with salt and pepper. The first bite of the steak was buttery with a splash of zest. This chef knew what he was doing.

"All right," I said between bites, "I won't let you get away without giving me the LSAT secret, or magic pill or whatever you want to call it. But I wanted to share a little insight into life that I had today, if you don't mind."

"I'll drink to that," Noah said, raising his wine glass. I raised my glass only halfway, not sure what there was to drink to yet. Noah didn't seem to care, though, and made a toast anyway.

"Our lives are *so* incredible, and we must be grateful for all that we have. I was waiting for the subway on the way here, and I found a $10 bill. My mother told me that when you find money in the street you should give it to charity, so I gave it to a homeless man at the station.

"So while the LSAT and law school are important, I suddenly felt that life itself is the most important thing. We need to have gratitude for being alive, every day. I know my little insight may not be the biggest revelation, but it hit me hard today, especially after what happened to Chelsea. So that's my spiel for tonight."

"And that's a superb spiel, Alexandra," Noah said.

"I concur," Fisch added.

The street was fairly quiet, with some foot traffic and an occasional car passing by. It was a cozy environment. We each took a few more bites of our food. Fisch stood and excused himself to the bathroom, mumbling something about how eggplant Parmesan always goes right through him.

A Cadre of Experts

"So you told Fisch what happened with Chelsea?" Noah asked me.

"How did you know that?"

"Simple," Noah responded, "when you said that your revelation hit you hard, especially after what happened to Chelsea. Fisch didn't ask you what had happened."

"Aha, I see," I said. "Well, you'd almost be right, except for the fact that you've just committed a logical fallacy."

"Oh?" Noah said, with a playful look. "And what would that flaw be?"

"Don't ask me for the Latin term or anything, but you've treated a plausible explanation as if it's the only explanation. It's lucky you're not taking the LSAT anytime soon."

"When you're right, you're right, Alexandra. One you, zero me."

Fisch came back to the table. That's it, I told myself. I was going to get this magic LSAT pill from him if I had to pay for the whole dinner myself. But maybe not for the wine.

"Okay, Fisch," I said, "Where's my magic LSAT pill? I've been waiting patiently until now," I said with a smile, since it wasn't in my nature to be stern.

Fisch looked at Noah, and Noah looked at Fisch. They both looked at me, and I looked at my plate. The waiter came to ask if we needed anything, I told him we were good.

"Alexandra, my dear," said Fisch, clearing his throat, "here you are, the famous LSAT magic pill I've invented. I'm sure Noah has told you about my many 180s. Not to brag or anything, I just mean it as a way to bolster the magic pill's credibility. So without further ado, here is the secret."

The waiter came and asked if we wanted our bill, and whether we wanted to split it. Arg. Fisch said he was paying to make up for kicking us out that morning.

"The secret sauce, the magic pill, the LSAT Holy Grail ... is that ... *there is no such thing*. There is no secret sauce, there is no magic pill, and there is no holy grail of LSAT study, prep or mastery. That's the secret."

I stared at Fisch as if he had grown a third eye.

Then it hit me.

There is no secret. *You just have to study.*

"So you simply need to study and put in the work?" I asked, without waiting for an answer. "You know, that does make sense, Fisch, although I can't say I'm not surprised. Honestly, I figured the secret might be some incredible guessing system or meditating for a week on the top of the Empire State Building. But this makes more sense."

"I hope you're not disappointed, Alexandra," Noah said.

"One question, though, Fisch. You said this morning that students who score in the mid or high 160s aren't the ones looking for the magic pill, but the students who score lower are. Why is that?"

"There are two answers. When a student is scoring much lower than where he or she wants to be, it's natural to look for something that will help. Second, after a student hits the high 150s or mid 160s, they kind of 'get it.' They realize that the LSAT tests their ability to think, reason, and read well. The only way to get better at those things is to practice, study, and commit oneself to the test's logic and to apply that logic in everyday situations until it becomes so second-nature that a high score is basically inevitable."

"In a way, it's actually a relief that there's no such thing as a magic pill. I can stop looking for one and focus my time and energy on legit studying."

"I'm happy you get the idea."

"So what was your last score?" Noah asked.

"It was 171. I understand that it came from hard work and that I deserved it. It wasn't because I had a lucky day."

"I'm proud of you, Alexandra," Noah said.

"Well, a lot of my success was a result of your tips."

"You should learn to take compliments, Alexandra, especially where they're due. Speaking of my LSAT tips, I wanted to share my next LSAT tip with both of you."

Before he did, Noah told Fisch about his top LSAT tips, and about how he'd shared them with me one at a time. Fisch thought that relaying them slowly—and giving me time to absorb and apply them—was smart. I showed Fisch my iPhone notes app with the other tips Noah had shared with me. Fisch read them and looked impressed. Noah took out his yellow legal pad. I took my iPhone back.

A Cadre of Experts

Noah's Top LSAT Tips #6

"Your score is not equal to your IQ. **Your score is the number of hours you've studied, and the number of practice tests you took.**"

Noah took a minute to let me write it down, and maybe to digest what he'd said, before he put his legal pad back into the briefcase. I think I understood him, but I wanted more clarification.

"Most people look at their score and think it shows where they are percentile-wise, or how smart they are compared to other LSAT students. That can be counterproductive because it makes people feel inferior or unintelligent, as if success is out of their hands. But the truth is, it only shows how many hours they've studied."

"But what about when someone takes their first diagnostic test?"

"Some people have a background in computer science or logic, which helps them initially score higher than other students. So maybe their score does represent how many hours they put into LSAT-related topics, knowingly or not. And of course, everyone has put in time reading. But the main idea is that **any increase in score reflects an increase in study time and practice tests**.

"For some people, every point is equivalent to 20 or 30 hours. For others, it's more, or less, and of course, it can change along the way, depending on where the student is scoring. The number doesn't matter. You shouldn't actually spend time calculating how many hours you'll need to raise your score to this score or that score."

The waiter brought the bill and gave it to Noah, even though Fisch was paying. Maybe because Noah was the best-dressed.

"Do you see my point, Alexandra?"

"I think it's a profound tip, especially after hearing about Fisch's magic pill," making quotation marks in the air when I said *magic pill*.

Noah offered to pay for his and my plate, but Fisch refused. He pulled out his credit card and the waiter took it without saying a word.

"You're right, Alexandra," Noah continued. "It is a profound insight. There's really no way of getting around it. You study, you succeed. The more you study, the more you succeed."

"Noah," Fisch said, "before I leave why don't you share your next tip with me? I'm just really curious."

"Well I like to spread them apart, but maybe in honor of Alexandra receiving the magic pill I'll make an exception. Let me get out my ol' legal pad again."

His yellow legal pad reminded me of Santa Claus's big red bag. There was somehow room for an endless amount of gifts. The legal pad never seemed to run out of pages.

"Ah, here we go. Last but not least, tip number 7."

Noah's Top LSAT Tips #7

"**Don't think, do.** In Latin, they say *acta non verba, deeds, not words*. Perhaps *the* most common question that LSAT tutors get from their students has to do with how to study. Students ask: '*How* do I study? Should I repeat questions I got wrong until I get everyone right? Should I practice with every LSAT ever published, or only stick to the more recent ones? Should I only do timed practice?'"

"But didn't we speak about making plans, and how important that is?" I asked.

"True, Alexandra. But the point of this tip is to not overdo it. It *is* important to plan and to figure out the best possible methods of attack. But at the end of the day, an hour spent planning could be spent more wisely on actual studying. Students tend to over-obsess about this issue. **As long as you're sitting and studying, with your phone turned off and other distractions put away, you're fine.** As long as you're practicing logic games, logical reasoning, and reading and dissecting reading comprehension passages and their answers, you'll be okay."

"So what *I* need to do is *study*. What I want everyone else to do is to *talk* about studying."

"Um, yes," Noah said, "a bit sardonic, but that's the idea."

"Alexandra," Fisch said, swirling his wine glass, "well put!"

Chapter 30

The next morning, I got a call from Chelsea. Her mom was okay, turned out it was a false alarm. Yes, her mom was sick, but her trip to the hospital wasn't her last. Chelsea would be home soon. Meanwhile, I had a new outlook on life. Yes, the LSAT was important, and yes, law school and being a lawyer was important. But I had put things in perspective, and that took a lot of the pressure off.

I'd heard about test-takers who threw up in the test center's bathroom before taking the LSAT. If you're a lawyer defending a client who is at risk of getting sent to death row, and you're extremely nervous, I get that. But tossing your cookies for the LSAT?

I remembered Professor Levine's words about it not mattering which law school you go to. It was true. Since meeting Professor Levine in Berkeley a few months ago, I'd met and heard about successful lawyers who'd gone to all kinds of third and fourth-tier schools. What mattered was the student, how much she prepared for classes, how much work she did, and her overall attitude and talents.

Not to diminish the importance of the LSAT. Not at all. Studying for the LSAT, like my conversation at Fisch's house yesterday, was an important element in preparing for law school and had implications for life in general. That said, it was still just a test.

I went to the gym and exercised for 45 minutes on the elliptical, and another 25 minutes on the Stairmaster. After a sauna and shower, I was on my way home. When I got to the building, Chelsea was just going in. We shared the elevator up to our apartment.

Chelsea was so happy that her mother was well, and she kept thanking me and saying she didn't know how to repay me.

"It wasn't me, it was Noah, but you're welcome."

"Sure, but you were the one who asked him, so I feel like I owe you a favor. In fact, I already have something for you."

I gave Chelsea a hug. "Chelsea you're the best, but you shouldn't have ... Where is it?"

"Oh, it's not something that I have with me. It's an appointment I booked for you with my incredible friend, Michelle."

"Appointment?"

"Michelle is a hypnotherapist. She teaches people something called 'affirmations' to help them succeed in whatever they're trying to do. Michelle and I grew up in Buffalo. She was a few years older than me, and moved out here about three years ago. She finished her degree in hypnotherapy. She even wrote a book about affirmations."

The elevator door opened. I helped Chelsea carry her stuff into the apartment.

"I told Michelle what you did, and she offered to meet with you for coffee and give you some tips for the LSAT. I know you got a 171 the other day, but I figured a bit of extra help wouldn't hurt."

"That's amazing, Chelsea. Thank you from the bottom of my heart."

"Call her and make a time to meet. She's a friendly person, to say the least," Chelsea said, handing me Michelle's card.

"Michelle speaking. Who is this?"

"Um, my name is Alexandra. I'm a friend of ..."

"Alexandra, hello darling," she said, rolling her Rs. "Yes, yes. Chelsea told me all about you this morning. We can meet at the café below my office at seven if that works for you."

"Sure," I said, without checking my calendar. "Give me the address and I'll ..."

"The address is on the business card that I'm sure Chelsea gave you. So see you then, dear."

"Chelsea," I yelled so that she could hear me behind her closed door. "I'm meeting her at seven. Want to come?"

Chelsea emerged from her room. "That was fast. You talked for about 30 seconds."

I looked at my iPhone. "Actually, 27 seconds. So you're coming with me, right?"

"I don't know. You might want time with her by yourself, you know, to tell her your feelings and see how she can help you with the LSAT. But if you want, I can come."

We arrived at the café below Michelle's office at exactly 7:00 p.m. We took a table and ordered tea.

"Chelsea, I'm so happy your mother is well. I have to say that it put a lot into perspective. I was worrying about the smallest things and getting anxious over nothing. You don't realize what's important until your best friend's mother gets sick."

Chelsea nodded. Her eyebrows took a leap north, and her smile widened as she saw Michelle.

"Hello Michelle," Chelsea said in a voice that everyone in the tiny café could hear. Michelle walked just as fast as she'd talked on the phone. Surprisingly, once she sat, her speaking slowed down a bit.

"Okay, so let's get to work. What is it about the LSAT, mentally speaking, that you could use help with?"

"I've been focusing on the analytical and reading skills, not so much on the mental attitude."

"Okay-okay-okay," Michelle said, reverting to her speed talking. "Everything is mental. Everything. Haven't you ever seen Dumbo?"

"Maybe, when I young. But I don't remember all the details."

"In a nutshell, Dumbo is an elephant who learns to fly when some crows give him a magic feather. As you may guess, the feather has no magic powers, but the elephant believes in the magic feather and, as a result, is able to fly.

"So, as you can see, when we believe in something, it becomes true. Of course, this belief is based in psychology, not the movie, but Dumbo does do a good job of showcasing the concept. What I teach is something called affirmations. They are positive statements you make about what you want to believe or have happen. I'll get into it a bit more, but first let me tell you how and why I got into affirmations."

The waitress brought us more tea.

"When I was a kid, my dad would take me to the skating rink. I wasn't so talented at skating, so I started playing the air hockey they had at the rink. I played against my dad, and at age seven my dad let me win every time. Next time, when I went there with my mom, she let me win, too. I remember thinking how nobody could beat me at this game.

"Today, 30 years later, when I play air hockey, I still win every time, even though my opponent isn't letting me like my dad did. I'm not much of an athlete, nor is there any reason I can think of that would make me so skilled at that game. I can only attribute it to my belief. Now, we don't have to be tricked into believing something, like with the air hockey. We can simply talk ourselves into a new or better belief.

"Everything we do, I believe, results from our believing that we can do it. If you train for years to play the piano, you can play the instrument because you've practice, and, therefore you believe you can, but studies show that one can forget years of piano playing after twenty minutes under hypnosis. Once the pianist stops thinking that he or she can play, it manifests into actual forgetting that they can play, and they can no longer play a note."

"I hope they hypnotized them back," I said.

"I'm sure they did," Chelsea said.

"So how do you do these affirmations?"

"We'll get to that in a few moments. First, it's important that you understand the meaning behind it. Henry Ford said 'Whether you think you can or think you can't, you're right,' whatever you believe in will in fact happen.

"I once dated a guy who drove a PT Cruiser. Before dating him, I could have sworn that there were no PT Cruisers on the streets of Manhattan. But all of a sudden I started noticing them.

"When we are prompted to notice something, such as by declaring that something is true—like, 'I am really great at the LSAT'—our minds start to pick up on small differences in our study habits, for example, and make sure we utilize those practices. The other reason it works is because of the tension it creates. If I declare 'I am at a healthy weight' when I am 20 pounds overweight, it creates tension in the subconscious because the mind hears the statement but sees the body and realizes that the statement is not true. So I would either have to stop saying the affirmation 'I am at a healthy weight' or my subconscious will have to prompt me to avoid sugar and carbs, and to walk more, in order to lose weight and ease the tension. So, you asked how I do these affirmations."

Michelle took a sip from her tea.

"Quite simple, actually. You create some positive statements and read them to yourself every night before you go to bed. You also make sure that whenever a contradictory idea pops into your head during the day, you counter the thought by stating the opposite. Give me some ideas about the LSAT and what it would mean to you to succeed at it."

I told Michelle about the three sections of the test, about the timing issues and how I could sometimes forget what I'd just read. I also told her about the need to be persistent when studying, and the need to remember things I studied, such as the different flaws and game types and their setups. Michelle took out her notebook. It was raspberry flavor I think.

After a few minutes, she looked up from her writing and showed me the following list of affirmations she'd created.

"I put this together based on the things you've told me. You can, and probably should make it more personal by adding or subtracting from the list to make the affirmations resonate with you."

Michelle showed me her list.

I Approach Every LSAT Question with a Calm Mind
I Always Know the Right Answer to the Questions
My Subconscious Mind is My Partner in Success
My Intuition Always Helps Me Anticipate the Correct Answer
I Always Understand the Question after the First Reading
I Get Every Question Right
I Am Great at Taking Timed Tests
I Am Persistent in My Studying
I Am Thorough and Calm When Studying
The Skills and Facts I Learn When I'm Studying I Remember Always
I Think Quickly and Accurately
I Am a Genius

"Wow, if only all this were true," I said.

"It can be true, Alexandra, if you believe in it. Repetition is the key. Read these to yourself every night before you go to bed. Repeat them two or three times. You can also read them every time you sit down to study or repeat them randomly throughout the day. Eventually, usually within two weeks or so, the messages will start to sink in, and you'll see results. Believe in the process, like Dumbo did, and you too will be able to fly."

Chapter 31

Over the next few days and weeks, I used the affirmations. *I am great at taking timed tests. I get every question right.*

I hadn't forgotten what Fisch had told me. **There's no substitute for studying**. *But you also have to eat and sleep.* You need to balance things out. I figured that the affirmations fall under the same category as sleep. You needed them to succeed—not the affirmations themselves per se, but the mental attitudes and beliefs they yield. Reading the full list took less than a minute, so the benefit to time ratio seemed appropriate.

The test was coming up in a few weeks, and my anxiety levels were skyrocketing. I remembered what Donna taught me: *Trust your training.* I also started doing some of Coach Graham's exercises, practicing a logic game in the slowest possible manner and again as fast as possible, and found myself doing some of those mini memory exercises Josh taught me at the most random moments. I always set my intentions before studying, as I learned from Professor Levine. I felt that it was all coming together.

The test was scheduled for Saturday, October 7th at a college here in the city. I let Noah know it was scheduled. We planned to meet the next morning at the LSAT Café.

It was getting nerve-racking close to the test, so I figured that whatever I was scoring would be close to what I'd score on test day. I'd heard of students who improved a few points in the weeks leading up to the exam, maybe it was from the pressure, or maybe from letting everything they'd learned settle in the brain and consolidate.

I decided to take another practice test. It was the first time since I'd met Michelle that I'd taken an exam. I was curious to see the results. I'd studied for about 60 hours since our meeting. The last test I scored

A Cadre of Experts

a 171. I was eager to see whether anything had changed. As Noah had said many times, and as Leah had pointed out, each point was a victory. When you were scoring in the 130s, simply learning how to set up one type of logic game correctly would improve your score by a few points. Then you learned a few flaws, and you'd start to get the easy questions right. Another few points. But after you hit the 160s, each point only came after hours and hours of practice.

Today, I focused on focus. Whenever I thought about anything unrelated to my task at hand – whether it was unrelated to the LSAT, or about a section I had already completed – I brushed it away. But first, and most importantly, **I immediately noticed that the thought came up, rather than letting it take me on its ping-pong journey.** *I'm hungry – when did I last eat? It's crazy how much food we eat in a lifetime. Am I crazy? How would I know if I was? If I think I'm crazy, does that mean I'm not? That's a catch-22. I never read that book. I haven't read any books in a while. I wonder if there's a library near my apartment. Did I leave the stove on?*

I finished the test and right away noticed something interesting. I might have noticed it during the test, but being in the zone didn't allow me to fully and consciously think about it. What I noticed was that the affirmations that I had been saying over the last few weeks had started to play in my head automatically. When I was doing the logical reasoning section, I heard, "My logical reasoning is perfect." When I was looking at my analog watch, I heard "I am great at taking timed tests."

I started checking my answers. It may sound funny, but as I saw how many I was getting right, I heard, "I get every question right," in the back of my head. And I did get most questions right—I ended up with a 174. I was ready for the test on the 7th.

"So this is it, Alexandra. You're almost there. How's the feeling?" Noah asked, pouring his second cup of coffee.

"I'm ecstatic about my recent score. On the other hand, I am absolutely freaking out about the test. I may look calm right now, but my nerves are having a party like their parents are out of town."

"In that case, let's talk about test day. Where are you taking the test?"

"At Pace University, Saturday at 8:30 am."

"Okay, I have an idea. Why don't you schedule the test at a test center in a hotel? You can check in the night before and wake up at the test center. You won't have to worry about driving directions, parking, and the like. You can work out at the hotel's gym, get a massage and eat a nice dinner at the hotel's restaurant."

"That's a fantastic idea. What about the morning of the test?"

"I recommend you get to the hotel early, so you have time for exercising and relaxing. Maybe watch a funny movie. Go to bed and wake up early, about 6:00 am. You could go a for a 20-minute jog, shower, and eat breakfast. Even then you'll still have some time before 8:30 to relax. You can sit and enjoy watching the other students nervously rushing in."

"That doesn't sound very nice."

"You don't have to laugh out loud at them, but one of the best ways to overcome something is by laughing at it, as they say in Latin, *castigat ridendo mores,* meaning, once corrects morals by laughing at them. I had a friend in law school who was terribly arrogant. It got to the point where he couldn't date because every girl he dated gave up on him after the first date. He even had a girl walk out on him in the middle of a date. His professors never called on him in class. Even though a lot of law students would pay for that kind of treatment, he hated it. He knew they weren't calling on him because of his arrogant answers."

"What did he do?"

"He found a therapist who taught him to laugh at himself. By laughing at his own foibles, he was able to see how arrogant he really was. After that, he'd come over to his friends and say in a British accent 'Do you reeeealize just how important I think I am?' We all got a kick out of that."

"So what happened to him after that?"

"He got better. All I'm saying is if you still feel anxiety right before the test, try to laugh it off."

"That makes sense."

"You should give yourself enough time to relax before the test. For breakfast, eat something like eggs, which will keep you full, and have some fruit. And since I know you love coffee as much as I do, I'd say to drink a cup, but go low on the sugar. If someone never drinks coffee or eats eggs, they wouldn't want to try it for the first time right before the LSAT."

"I don't drink my coffee with sugar anymore, Noah. You know that."

"Oh, and don't forget to have a snack with you to eat during the break. Some dark chocolate would be a smart idea. The cocoa is good for your brain and the sugar will give you a little energy boost."

"How long do you have exactly until the test?"

"Two weeks. Fourteen days." I took out my iPhone under the table and opened the calculator app. "That would be 336 hours, or ... give me a second ... 20,160 minutes, to be exact."

"So, what are your plans for the next two weeks?"

"I haven't really thought about that. I'll do a few more practice exams. I also have some reading comprehension passages and logic games that I had missed two or more questions on that I want to review."

"That's an excellent idea. **Narrow down exactly what issues you were having a problem with and review those issues**—that will definitely give you a boost."

"Then that's what I'll do."

"And do some speed training. Do the games and logical reasoning and reading passages in a third of the time allotted for each, like Graham taught us."

"I've done that, but I just get a lot of them wrong."

"Well here's how I understand it. When you are a runner in training, there are two objectives. Speed and endurance. To gain endurance, you run uphill. That builds muscle and strength. To gain speed, you run downhill. You're not fighting gravity like when you run uphill, so your feet get accustomed to running faster.

"For the LSAT, you also need both. You build endurance by breaking up arguments and dissecting them to gain a deep level of understanding. By turning logic games into non-abstract experiences—just what you've been doing—you increase your grasp of the logic. Of course, that increases your speed as well. The better you know something, the faster you can perform.

"But for intense speed training, you need to run downhill. Force yourself to do questions in a fraction of the time. Even if you don't get everything right, **the process will speed you up**. Then, when you give yourself the full amount of time, it feels like a luxury."

"It sounds like it works off the principle of comparison."

"That too. There's an old story about the guy who had ten children. He couldn't stand the noise his kids made, so he went to the wise man for advice. The wise man told him to bring his cow from the barn into the house. After a week, the man went back to the wise man and told him that the noise was even worse, not to mention the smell. The wise man advised him to bring in the goat, as well as the sheep. After two weeks of torture, the wise man told the man to remove the three animals from the house. After that, the noise from the ten kids didn't seem bad at all.

"But on top of that, the speed exercises make your hands work faster. Many students are slowed down simply because the speed at which their hands write and diagram rules correctly and neatly. It's like typing. We can think much faster than we can type, but our hands slow us down."

"Okay, Noah, that's what I'll do. I'll do some more practice tests, speed exercises, brush up on a few last questions I had answered incorrectly. And I'll go over the cheat sheets."

"It's a plan."

Studying is like a workout. Every time I complete one, I feel just a bit better at two things – at the LSAT, and at studying. I used to think that I absolutely had to find the perfect spot to study, like a dog sniffing for the right spot to do its business. The problem is, that doesn't always work. I have specific spots in the city I like to study at, but sometimes they're full, or I'm full and don't want to buy anything to eat or drink. I've learned to be more flexible. When it's time to study, which is every day, if I haven't found that perfect location, I'll start studying at the first place I can find. With or without a cup of coffee, whether I'm in a great mood or not, I start studying. And it never seems to matter whether I had found that perfect spot, I still get a great study-workout.

The next two weeks passed quickly, with many hours of studying, resting, meditating, repeating affirmations and more studying. And more studying, *and then some more*. I took a practice test the Saturday before the real test and *scored 176.* I was happy with that, to say the least, considering that I'd started off with a 134.

Of course, I appreciated the enormous jump in my score, but what I appreciated even more was **the person I'd become.** Now, when I heard ads or watched the news, I could call them out for their erroneous logic. For example, one day I looked into a pre-law-school course. They showed statistics that their students had better grade averages in law school than students who didn't take the course. The problem was we didn't know anything else about these students. Were they extra motivated to get better grades? They probably were, because after all, they took a pre-law-school course. So was it the course that got them better grades or their motivation?

Thanks to my LSAT prep, I'd become a much more critical reader and thinker. I felt more confident talking to people. My self-esteem has grown. No test, or anything else for that matter, had ever changed my life, not to this extent, or even close. The LSAT wasn't simply a test. **It was a life-changer, a transformative tool.** Thank you, LSAT.

On the day before the test, I arrived at the hotel and checked in. I brought one change of clothes and my running shoes, copies of seven logic games, twelve logical reasoning questions, and four reading comprehension passages. Noah told me that although I could take the test cold and still do totally fine, I would probably benefit from going over the main seven types of logic games, the twelve main types of the logical reasoning and the four types of the reading comprehension passages, plus a comparative reading passage. These were all questions I'd done before, so it wouldn't take too much brain power, and it would be good to do a quick review of them the night before and the morning of, even if just to calm my nerves. I also brought my list of affirmations, and my favorite mantra; *trust your training.*

The hotel was stunning, and I loved the view from my room. The road sloped downhill and curved like a snake, with scattered houses along its twists and turns. Two and three-story homes, all with well-kept gardens and trees. Green was the dominant color. The sky was clear and looked like an ocean above this forest. The sun shined down and cast shadows on all of the houses, the trees, the mailboxes, and the ant-size people.

I unpacked, put on my running shoes and headed for the hotel's gym. I passed the auditorium and saw that it was set up for the LSAT the next morning. I walked in, dressed in my activewear, and sat at one of the tables.

So this is where I'll be tomorrow morning. I'm going to do great, just like any other practice test. No difference. There will be a few hundred nervous test-takers scribbling with their pencils, but compared to the noise in my local Starbucks, it won't seem that loud. I took a few breaths and shouted, "I can do this!" I stood and continued to the gym.

After a half-hour run on the treadmill, I returned to my room, showered and got into bed. I turned on the TV and looked for a perfect movie to rent, and I found it: "Legally Blonde."

One hour and thirty-six minutes later, and minus $14.95 from my bank account, I turned off the TV and headed for the restaurants downstairs. It would feel weird eating alone at a restaurant, but my thoughts quickly drifted to the next morning's events. Would I be tired, cranky, or alert? Would all the hard work pay off? Would I do okay?

Can I get you any water? What?

It was the waitress.

"I'm Sara, your waitress. Can I get you some water?"

"Oh sure," I responded. "With ice, please."

I looked at the menu, but all I saw were words from the LSAT. "Maine lobster" looked like "Main Point." "White Wine" looked like "Weakener." "Mixed Green Salad" looked like a logic game. I started imagining that the chef had had to follow salad-making rules. The lettuce could only be added in second or third, the tomatoes had to be either first or last, and the onions couldn't be next to the peppers. But what would happen if the chef put the onions next to the peppers, and added the onions first so the peppers came second and the lettuce last? Would he be fired? I was sure he'd find another job; there were lots of hotels in the area. But if the other hotels heard that he'd added onions next to the peppers, would they still hire him? Probably not. He'd broken the rules ...

The waitress came back with the water and asked if I was ready

A Cadre of Experts

to order. I asked for another few minutes. The waitress reminded me of the waiter in the LSAT Café, which reminded me of Noah and all the conversations we had there. That reminded me of our visits to his friends, which reminded me that I'd be taking the LSAT tomorrow morning.

The waitress came again. I explained that I was taking the LSAT the next morning, which was why I was so preoccupied.

"Oh, I'm planning on taking the LSAT, too," the waitress said, "I want to be a lawyer. But I'm sure you guessed that already."

"Best of luck. It's a journey, but it's worth it." I realized how fortunate I was to have had a mentor to accompany and help me on my journey.

"I'd better get back to work," the waitress said, "or they'll probably fire me. That's what happened to the last waiter here. He was talking too much on shift, and they fired him."

"Are you assuming that past events guarantee future ones?" Listen to me. "That would be called the fallacy of time. The fact that something happened in the past doesn't prove it will happen in the future. You'll need to know that for the LSAT."

She laughed. "Thanks for that tip. I better get started studying for the LSAT. I want to do well on it. Is it hard?"

Wasn't that the question of the year?

"It's difficult, but learnable. I started out scoring quite low, but with the help of some tutors and many, many hours of study, I'm doing much better. It's mostly a matter of willpower and putting in the long hours of study. But I don't want you to get fired, how about you take my phone number and call me anytime after tomorrow?"

"That sounds awesome."

"Actually, before you go, let me give you one tip. This is something I learned from Professor Levine, who is my mentor's mentor. It's about setting intentions."

"Is this an LSAT thing?" Sara asked.

"Not specifically. But it can be extremely helpful, and I highly recommend it."

"Well you're the expert," Sara said.

"Hardly, but I know what was helpful for me, and I learned things from some really smart people."

"I'm all ears."

"You need to anchor a specific goal or outcome in your mind. For example: 'Today, I am going to recall everything I read,' or 'I am going to practice noticing details so that it becomes a habit,' or 'I will get over test anxiety and do extremely well on the LSAT,' or, 'I will start reading faster today on the reading comprehension section.' Do you notice how specific those were? You get the best results when your intentions are detailed and specific.

"When you fill your intention with specific scenarios, you'll find yourself automatically doing things that demonstrate your commitment to that intention.

"For instance, if you've set an intention to go to the gym, your subconscious will work twice as hard to overcome emotions like laziness that might stop you from seeing it through. To start out with, try setting intentions for outcomes that you have a good chance of accomplishing. An hour at the gym, for instance, is doable. So is practicing a few logic games. But you can't fulfill an intention to run a marathon in one day. It's important that you build up your self-belief by turning your intentions into reality. Once you get the hang of this, you'll find yourself accomplishing virtually anything you set an intention for. Start studying for the LSAT using these or other intentions."

We exchanged phone numbers. Then I ordered a main point, I mean, a Maine lobster, with butter sauce and a side of the mixed salad logic game.

Chapter 32

I woke up at 6:00 a.m. I went for a jog outside in the fresh morning air, took a shower and relaxed in the armchair in the corner of my room for a twenty-minute meditation. I hurried down to eat breakfast and to practice a bit.

On the way to the restaurant, I noticed free coffee in the lobby, but I was going to order breakfast so I would get a cup there. I ordered eggs and fruit, as Noah had advised, and a cup of coffee. While I was waiting for the food, I called Noah.

"Good morning, Alexandra," Noah's voiced boomed over the phone. "How are you?"

"How am I? How are you, is the question."

"I had a relaxing afternoon and evening. I did a 'morning of' LSAT practice last night and got a restful night's sleep. I'm waiting for breakfast, and after that, I'll sit and watch everyone pour in, all nervous and wondering if they're in the right place."

"*Are you trusting your training?*"

"I absolutely trust my training. Your training, that is."

"The credit goes to you, Alexandra. You were the one who studied for hours and hours and weeks and months. Maybe I steered you in the right direction, but you're responsible for the outstanding score you're about to pull off."

"Thanks, Noah. I also wanted to tell you something. I never properly thanked you for everything. I don't know if I can ever thank you. Even if I had hired a tutor, it wouldn't have been the same. Nobody would have cared as much as you. So, to make it short, thanks."

"I love you, Alexandra."

"I love you, too."

The waiter brought the bill. I noticed that they'd charged me $4.99 for my coffee. I couldn't believe it, since the coffee in the lobby, which was right next to the restaurant, was free. I motioned for the waiter.

"Just curious ... I didn't know that you charge for coffee. Isn't it free, just a few feet from us?"

"Yes, but here we charge for it."

"I understand, but if I'd known that I would have brought a cup from over there myself. How about I go over there and bring back two cups, one for me and one for you, so you can take off the $4.99 for my cup and add an additional credit to my check for another $4.99?"

"Well, here we charge for it. You see ..."

"I see that I paid $280 for a room," I said in a confident, steady, clear tone of voice, "and now you're going to charge me double the price that Starbucks charges for a cup of coffee. How about you go back over to your station and bring back a new bill, hmm? Thanks."

The waiter mumbled something and came back a minute later with a bill that did not include the coffee.

The tests were handed out. The proctor began the instructions. He said, *inter alia*, that he would give us a five-minute warning before the end of each section.

I looked around the room and noticed the familiar rows of tables and chairs. I started to breathe and focus my breath and thoughts, focus on centering myself, trying to get into that zone where I could access my peak performance. I mentally rehearsed some of my affirmations—"I get every question right; my subconscious mind is my partner in success." I got the same feeling I had every time I entered the zone.

The test began. I got nervous. Even after all my practice tests, I still felt the anxiety building up. I remembered that I needed to trust my training. I also remembered a tip that I heard about test anxiety. The tip was to simply wait for 20 seconds after the proctor said to start, and to just breathe and relax. The collective anxiety in the test room only fueled your own personal anxiety, waiting those 20 seconds would cause you to start the test after the anxiety has been eroded a bit.

I waited a solid 15 seconds to begin, gazing around the room in silent thought. The chairs and desks were meticulously arranged in rows of eight—in columns that stretched from the very front of the room all the way back and around to the point where you'd have to round your neck through its whole circle of motion just to see them all. Every desk had a student—each in their own attire, feet on the soft gray carpet and pencils to the page of an examination. You could practically hear their thoughts racing back in forth as they diligently read, calculated, analyzed, and pressed their minds through the hoops of the test, all hoping to find their singular excellence in a room of many. The room was framed in such a way that it could have held the test today and a wrestling match the next. Perhaps that was, in part, happening right at the moment.

The first section was logic games. I had a game where I had to order Dead Sea products on a shelf. The salts couldn't go next to muds, and the wraps had to be first or last. At this point, after all my practice, I was truly able to see the products on a shelf and feel that it was a real assignment. It wasn't abstract at all. It felt real.

The second game in that section was a grouping game. I had to put three types of jewelry in each of three groups. The pearls had to be in either group one or two. But the diamonds couldn't go next to the pearls, which meant that the pearls had to go into group one, and the diamonds into group three.

The second section was a reading comprehension section. I followed Judge Brian's method, allowing the images to rise up in my head as I read them. By now that was happening naturally.

Then came a logical reasoning section, the first one of two. I focused on each question as if it were the only question I had to do. After I had finished each question, I forgot about it and left my brain open to the next question. I finished the first ten questions in ten minutes, and then slowed down. I had a bit of trouble with questions 19 through 22, but I bubbled in an answer anyway even though I wasn't sure, to not to get mixed up. The last four questions were easier than I'd expected, and as the proctor issued the five-minute warning, I went back to finish four questions I was having trouble with.

During the break, I ate a few pieces of dark chocolate. I sat quietly on a couch outside the testing room, refocusing my brain and breathing.

At the end of the ten minutes they called us all back into the testing room and rechecked our IDs. They handed out the tests again, and within a few minutes I started the next section. Another logic games section.

That meant that either the first section of logic games was the experimental one, or that this one was, even though they both felt like a regular logic games section. I was told not to put any thought into that, *so I didn't*.

This logic game section threw me a few curveballs. For one, there was no linear game, which I was good at. There were two in-and-out games, which are generally less common.

The last section was the second logical reasoning section, full of flaw and assumption questions. I was glad I'd reviewed all the flaws. Again and again, over and over.

Finally, there was the essay. I decided that the flower shop should hire the younger, more ambitious marketer. He didn't have as many clients or as much experience as the senior marketer, but he knew the flower business; his family was in the flower business.

I finished my essay five minutes before the deadline and sat quietly in my chair soaking in the idea that I'd finished the LSAT. I didn't have my score, but I felt confident about my performance and was pleased that I'd finally finished. The proctor called time.

For the first time that day I started to think about how I would get back to the city. I figured I'd Uber it to the train station, and take the train into the city.

I joined the exodus. There was little talk, just a common feeling that we were all LSAT survivors, exhausted but happy to have finished the test. People were nodding to each other in solidarity, as if to say, "I was there." I walked out of the room, and lo and behold, Noah was standing there, dressed casually in light blue jeans and a dark gray, untucked button-down shirt, and a light black blazer. I had no idea why he was there.

Noah had a big smile on his face. He also had something in his hand. He approached me, his tall presence pushing people to the side. He pulled his hand from the behind his back and *dropped on his right knee.*

"Alexandra, will you marry me?"

I started to cry. Not because I was overwhelmed (though I was), and not because I was tired and emotionally fragile after the test (I was that, too). I started to cry because I didn't know what to say.

Meanwhile, people near us quieted down and stood in an informal circle around Noah and me, waiting for my response. Some were filming us with their phones, which had magically appeared from their pockets after leaving a test room where cell phones weren't allowed.

"I-I-I don't know Noah," I sobbed. I remembered what his Aunt Donna had told me, how hard it was for him to open up, and what Fisch had mentioned about how since he'd met me, Noah was a different man.

I also thought about the times when I couldn't stand his arrogance sometimes. He was materialistic, and always had to win.

"Maybe we could continue our conversation in my room, Noah?"

Noah seemed calm, in spite of being disappointed in front of all those people, but I was still shaken. I sat on my bed. Noah sat in the armchair, where I had done my morning meditation.

"All right," Noah said. "Now we can continue our conversation. I don't want to pressure you or anything, but I want to be with you, you know, for the rest of our lives. Don't you feel the same way?"

"It's not that I don't love you or anything. I just finished the LSAT and my mind is racing at a million miles per hour. I have the whole law school application process ahead of me, and I don't think I can make a clear judgment call right now."

"I understand. How about this? Let's get through the law school application process. I promise not to bring up the M word until after you finish the applications. How does that sound?"

"Deal. How does some lunch sound?"

Chapter 33

We had a late lunch at a beautiful Korean restaurant on Long Island. The waitress wore a traditional Korean hanbok, and the walls were painted with trees, white flowers, and red leaves. Our waitress translated the Korean words written on the walls: "Welcome guests, enjoy your food."

I ordered the stuffed mushroom appetizer and Jap Chae (noodles with beef). Noah ordered the Gam Ja Jeon and bulgogi-jun-gol (vegetables with beef).

"So how was the LSAT?" Noah finally asked.

"I think it went smoothly. No big surprises, just the same old stuff I was practicing. You know what was fun?" I asked Noah, as was returning an email on his phone.

"Do tell."

"How everything I've been doing for the LSAT all came together."

Noah smiled. "That's awesome. I want you to relax and enjoy your meal, of course, but what I wanted to ask you about your personal statement? Have you put any more thought into?"

"I thought about it a bit, but I'm not sure how to get my point across. Like you said, to put everything into one word and tie everything back to that point. I want to tell them about my struggle in life and how I overcame obstacles, but I'm not sure if that's even a point that would make me a better candidate."

The waitress returned with the only American food we ordered: Diet Coke.

"Always remember this, when writing: show, don't tell. I'm sure you've heard that idea." Noah said.

"Yes, vaguely."

A Cadre of Experts

"I took some writing classes in college, I always dreamt of writing for the movies.

"The first thing they teach in writing is, 'show, don't tell.' I can tell you that Mr. Smith is a nice guy, or I can show you that Mr. Smith spends his Saturdays and Sundays collecting and handing out food for the homeless. That way, I don't have to tell you that he is a nice guy. You can make that conclusion by yourself. So on the personal statement, don't tell them that you are this or that. Illustrate it using stories and examples from your life, without actually saying it."

The waitress placed appetizers in front of us, but did it so quietly that we hardly noticed until the food was on the table.

"What topics are you thinking of writing about?" Noah asked.

"I think what makes me special is the way I overcame certain problems and obstacles in life. Yet here I am, applying to law school. The thing is I don't feel special because of that. Lots of people overcome problems in life."

"True, but it doesn't mean the trials and tribulations you dealt with weren't unique. You don't have to save whales or discover a cure for chickenpox. Write down what you've done in life and let the law school decide what they want to do with it."

"I'll write a first draft tonight and give it to you for feedback. What about the letters of recommendation and the other things—like a resume and a diversity statement? And the addendum?"

"Let me take you to a friend of mine who's a real expert in the field. She's a whiz at all this stuff."

We finished our late lunch and Noah paid the bill, saying that it was my gift for finishing the LSAT. We thanked the quiet waitress and left. After getting into Noah's limo, Noah asked his driver to take us to Darien, Connecticut, to visit his law school colleague, Mary.

"I heard that the law schools use the essays to evaluate your writing skills. Is that true?" I asked Noah after we hit the highway.

"I'm not exactly sure, but that would be a question for Mary."

"How do you know Mary, by the way?"

"We went to law school together. We dated briefly in our first year, but that didn't work out. We stayed friends, and she actually introduced me to my late wife."

"It's always wise to part as friends from any relationship. You never know down the road when your paths might cross."

"That's true. So ... be honest," Noah grinned, "did you sit and laugh at the other students coming in all nervous and anxious?"

"Actually, I did. What they don't know can't hurt them I guess. And I did like your idea of laughing at something as a way to overcome it. I found that to be helpful."

"When my grandfather's parents came to New York from Hungary, they were orthodox Jews and didn't work on Saturday. My grandfather told me how his father would find a job at a bakery or a meat market, and then Friday afternoon would come and he would tell the boss that he had to go home for the Sabbath. The boss would usually tell him that if he left and didn't come to work the next morning, he shouldn't come back at all. So every Sunday he would look for a new job.

"On his way out Sunday morning to look for a new job, his wife would wave goodbye and say, 'don't worry dear, things can only get better.' They laughed, and that was their way of getting through hard times, by keeping things light and funny."

"That must have been hard on the family."

"No doubt. But it taught them the values of determination and integrity. No matter what happens, you don't give up on your beliefs and way of life, and *you get things done*. Later he became an insurance salesman and did quite alright."

Darian had a lot of charm, a real busy small town feel. The sidewalks were inlaid with brick, making them extra wide for lots of foot traffic to come and go. We passed many happy looking people. Children walked around with ice cream from the local shop. Adults strolled around with shopping bags in their hands as they stared down at their phones. The shops were modernized in a way that made them feel quaint and old-fashioned. Still, the faux-brick exteriors, the tin letter signs, and the retro interior designs imparted a reasonable facsimile of "old."

Mary was a delightful person. Her upbeat personality was fun, and she was funny. Noah and Mary hugged, and for the first time Noah introduced me as his girlfriend.

"I hear so many good things about you, Alexandra," Mary said.

"Likewise," I said, "excuse me if I look a bit tired. I took the LSAT this morning."

"This morning?" Mary asked, "And you're still on your feet? I slept for the rest of the week after my LSAT. Good for you. So how can I help you?"

"Alexandra needs to work on her application."

"I see. How did you do on the LSAT?"

"I haven't gotten my scores back yet."

"Alexandra scored consistently in the mid-170s, so I'm betting her score is somewhere north of a 173," Noah said.

"We can go with that," Mary said. "But the truth is plenty of students score a full ten points less on their real test than they got on their practice exams, not to get you worried."

"How does that happen?" I asked, worried indeed.

"For a number of reasons. For one, students get nervous on the real test, but also because—and probably the main reason this happens—is that when students take the practice exams, they let themselves cheat. They take an extra-long break between sections three and four, or only do four sections, or even use a stopwatch so they can track their time precisely, down to the seconds. When they see a minute twenty on the stopwatch, they move on to the next logical reasoning question. Of course, you can't use a stopwatch on the real test."

"What would you recommend that students do, Mary?" Noah asked.

"They need to tighten their practice exams, so they're as close as possible to the real thing. The main thing they can do is to practice exams with only 30-minute sections. That's the best way to imitate the feeling on test day. When you have five minutes less, you are automatically more anxious, and that helps match the feel of the real thing."

"I always did only 30-minute sections," I said.

"Oh perfect. In that case, can I get you two some tea? My mother is from England, you know, we drink a lot of tea."

Mary brought out the tea and set it on the table. She went to her desk and grabbed a yellow notebook. She picked up a quill pen and an inkwell.

"I do my most creative work with my feather pen, a family heirloom I received from my great grandfather. He was an attorney, too. He worked on Constitutional issues during the Second World War. And for friends of mine, I only want to do my finest work, so, let's get started."

Mary began scribbling something in her notebook. I loved the combination of antique pen and modern legal pad.

"So you see here, Alexandra, I drew a pie. You can make as many slices as you want, and they don't have to be equal. Let's start by making a list of traits, stories, ideas, philosophies and the like, that you want to let the law schools know about you."

"Alexandra is kindhearted and persistent, and she never gives up," Noah offered.

"Alright, we got those three, what else?"

"I had to overcome some hardships in life. Does that help?" I asked.

"Sure. I'll write down 'Tenacity.' What else?"

"She's smart," Noah added.

I couldn't remember the last time someone called me smart, but it felt good.

"Okay, so we'll start with this list. You can refine it later, either add a few ideas or replace them, but let me show you my method and how it works, and you can apply it to your application."

I took a few sips of tea.

"First, you have to prioritize; you have to decide what the most important thing is that you want the law schools to know. As an example, I would list either persistence or tenacity at the top of my list; second I would list intelligence, and lastly, kindness. In real life, I would rather be surrounded by friends whose kindness is their number one trait. For law school, it's important, but not as important as being smart and having the tenacity to get things done.

"The next thing is to list stories that illustrate each of these things. Let's say you have a story where you jumped off a boat without hesitation to save someone who was drowning. That story would fall under the kind-hearted idea, or maybe tenacity. Do the same for the other ideas as well, by finding a story or two for each one."

"Is it important to not sound too arrogant?" Noah asked.

"Absolutely. At the end of your personal statement, you might write something like 'During my years volunteering in Africa I learned what hard work is and I will apply it in my law school studies, and therefore I will be the best law student ever.' That sounds arrogant and not an attractive way to end your essay. But you could easily tweak that by saying 'I know what hard work is from my experience volunteering in Africa and I will apply the same level of effort toward law school in the hope that it will make me the best law student and lawyer that I can be.' See how that has a different feeling?"

"I like that," Noah said.

"The thing that students would most likely come off as arrogant about is their intelligence. Regardless of your LSAT score, I wouldn't say anything about yourself that implies you are smart. It just sounds too desperate. Besides, the admissions committees like to decide for themselves who's smart, they don't need you telling them that. It's like if you tell them that you are a great candidate for their school; they want to make that decision. How's the tea?"

"Great," Noah said.

"Awesome. The next step is deciding which document will tell which story. You have up to seven documents that you must submit to the law schools. Two or three letters of recommendation and your personal statement are requirements of basically every school. But don't take my word for it. Check the school's website first.

"Then you have a diversity statement. Most law schools will give you an opportunity to submit one. You have your resume, and you can write an addendum.

"You need to choose the number-one quality you want to convey to the law schools and address that in your personal statement. You can highlight your other qualities in your resume, such as the fact you are a kind-hearted person."

"I told Alexandra about not *saying* these things, rather *displaying* them with stories."

"Exactly," Mary said.

"But aren't the letters of recommendation written by other people?" I asked. "You can't insert information in those."

"Of course. The letters come from the people writing them, but it's you who decides who writes the letters for you. If you want to highlight something specific, find a person who thinks you embody that particular quality. If you want to showcase your persistence, ask someone who knows that you organized and participated in a marathon, for example."

Mary stood and went into the kitchen to take out some freshly baked cookies. She brought them back along with some homemade chocolate.

"I love making chocolate. It would have been neat to be Willie Wonka's legal advisor."

"These cookies are delicious, Mary. I didn't know you cook," Noah said.

"I *bake*, dear. Cookies you bake, not cook."

"What's the difference between baking and cooking?" Noah asked.

Mary and I laughed, but Noah looked funny. He's not used to being wrong or not knowing something, but you can't be an expert on everything.

"Next you have your diversity statement. Many students feel they are obligated to write one, but that's not true. If there is nothing substantial that makes you diverse, don't bother writing one. First of all, anything *that is about somebody else* doesn't make you diverse. If your sister or brother or best friend is an endangered species, that doesn't make you one."

"What qualifies as diversity?" I asked.

"It's widely interpreted, Alexandra. If something really makes you feel different, or diverse, write about it. Law schools care a lot about diversity because having a diverse classroom contributes to the legal education. People have different perspectives and experiences. If something is different about you, or if you had an experience that makes you look at the world in a different way, tell them.

"For some things in life, we say that if it doesn't help, it can't hurt. In the application process, that idea doesn't apply. If you write a diversity statement that talks about something unimportant or insignificant, you'll come off as desperate, which is not a quality schools are looking for."

"On first thought, I don't have anything that makes me feel diverse."

"Well then that's your answer," Mary said. "If you have something that actually makes you diverse from others, you would think of it right away. Okay, so the resume."

Noah's phone rang, but he didn't pick up. He was pretty interested in our conversation, despite the fact that he graduated law school a while ago.

"The most common mistake on the résumé is that students just rehash the stories and qualities already present in the other documents. An excellent way to use the résumé is to explain gaps in education for example. If you graduated high school and enrolled a few years later in college, the resume should show what you did during those years. Even if those years you weren't in school but you were working, you can show what you learned from those jobs. Another use is to list interests or accomplishments that are not listed anywhere else. If you wrote a book or trained as an acrobat, or wrote a book about how to train as an acrobat, list those in the resume. You wouldn't want to write your whole personal statement about your acrobatics, but it would be interesting for the school to know about, to see that you are a dynamic individual."

"That leaves us with the addenda," Noah said.

"Here I have to point out something crucial. The point of the addenda is to explain anything that might raise questions. If there was a gap in your undergrad education, and nothing to show for it in the résumé, or if you got an F in some classes, or if you were suspended from school, for example, explain it in the addenda.

"The two main things to remember with the addenda are the need to write the addenda in a mature manner, and to describe what you learned from the experience.

"When students write about something that they are not proud about, such as if they got a DUI, a common theme in these types of addenda is to blame someone else, a friend, the bartender, the cops, basically anyone and everyone else but themselves. That doesn't show maturity. Take responsibility, know that everyone makes mistakes, and show what you learned from the experience. That way, you can use the wrong thing you did to your advantage."

"How can you use something like that to your advantage?" I asked.

"Remember my great-grandfather, the one who gave me this quill pen? Well, his son, my grandfather, is also an attorney, and a businessperson.

When he was younger, he would meet his clients at the airport, help them with their bags and give them a lift to their hotels. He would get their business and sell them some property for millions of dollars. When he got older, he would tell his clients that true, they could hire a young attorney who could come and pick them up at the airport, and offer his or her amateur advice. Or they could hire my grandfather. So while he wasn't a strapping young lad who could pick them up from the airport and carry their bags, he could offer them sixty years of hard-earned legal and business experience. The lesson is that you need to use every circumstance to your advantage.

"If you were on academic probation, for whatever reason, show the school how that situation made you a better student, a more responsible, mature student."

"Mary," Noah said, "I might be smart, but you're a genius."

"Thank you, Noah, and you're right. I am smarter than you."

The three of us laughed.

"One last thing, Alexandra," Mary said after taking a sip of tea. "You should look at the big picture of your application. When the school's admission committee finishes reading your file, they're not going to call you if they have any questions. If they have issues with your application, chances are they will reject you. After everything's in place, print everything out on paper and go to Starbucks with all the documents, and a pen. Read everything you have, word for word. Do your best to look at everything as an outsider, somebody who has never met you. Read carefully and make sure everything matches. All the details on your résumé and personal statement should match as far as the timeline and your general persona. If you have boxing on your résumé as your favorite pastime, don't claim in your personal statement that you're a simple soul who couldn't hurt a fly.

"Now, I'm not saying that somebody can't be a boxer and a gentle person at the same time, but you have to admit that those two ideas sound incongruous. Unless the person on the admissions committee knows you personally, he or she might think that you're not telling the truth.

"If you can, hire a professional editor who doesn't know you, to read the entire application and **look for discrepancies** and make sure that you come across in the way that you're trying to."

"That's a lot of info to process all in one day," I said, "but I took notes on my iPhone, I'll review everything you said tonight."

"That's great, Alexandra. I see you have a lot of ambition, I'm sure you'll do well with your applications and in law school. My last piece of advice is to do exactly the opposite of whatever Noah tells you to do."

"Hey ..." Noah protested.

"You know that Noah was in the top three percent of our class, Alexandra?"

"Top two percent, actually."

"And he was so modest about it."

"I'm sure he was," I said, half asleep. I was actually holding up quite well, considering my long LSAT morning.

Chapter 34

In the following few weeks, I was busy preparing my law school application. I contacted some professors and a few bosses to ask them for letters of recommendation. I worked hard on writing my resume and an addendum about a few F's I got. I couldn't come up with a strong personal statement.

Meanwhile, exactly three weeks after I sat for the LSAT, I got my official score. I opened the email and couldn't look, scared as to what I might see. But I looked anyway.

It was 175, I got a 175! I couldn't believe it. I rushed to call Noah, my mom, Chelsea, and a bunch of other people. I sincerely can't remember being happier about anything. In fact, if I would bundle all the happiness I'd ever experienced into one moment, it still wouldn't add up to this one experience.

But you know what? *I deserved it*. Every one hundred and seventy-five points. I'd put much time and effort into the LSAT, and I'd earned it.

I decided to use all this excitement and happiness and channel it into a personal statement. Using those intense feelings, I wrote the first draft of my personal statement, with the key word being "determination":

I am writing this essay because I followed my ambitions. I wanted to be a lawyer and was told that I'm not smart enough, or that I don't have the "lawyer personality," whatever that is supposed to mean. Despite the naysayers, I am here.

And maybe I am not that smart, maybe I don't have any unique traits that would make someone look at me and say "You should be a lawyer." But I do have determination. That's how I went from a 134 LSAT score to my official 175 LSAT score in less than a year. That's how I came from a broken family and got myself through college. That's how I am the first in my family to go to college and apply to law school. That's how I am writing this essay.

I want to go to law school to become a lawyer. I know that might sound simple or obvious, but I am going to law school for the sake of being a lawyer and not to impress anybody. This was a psychological barrier I had to get over when I had an LSAT breakdown and decided to stop studying for the LSAT. I had to come to the conclusion that I am doing this for myself, for the positive change I can accomplish as an attorney and not for anyone or anything else. I learned that when you do something for an external reason and that reason disappears, so does your desire to carry out the goal. But if you do something for its own sake, no matter what happens, you can still go for your dreams.

I want to be a lawyer so I can help others on a larger scale than I can today. I was witness to many injustices and stood helplessly on the side, wanting but not being able to help.

I was arrested for driving a car that was wrongfully reported stolen. I spent some time at the precinct, and while it was only a few hours, it got me thinking about people who are convicted of crimes and sent away for thirty years when in fact they hadn't done anything wrong. If a few hours were as hard as they were, I can't imagine thirty years.

I want to dedicate my professional work as an attorney to helping wrongfully convicted people, a.k.a. victims, obtain the justice they deserve. I want to reduce suffering in the world. That drive has been with me ever since that night at the precinct, and it is the same drive that will get me through law school—maybe not as the brightest student in the class—but no doubt as one of the most driven.

Within the next week, I got my personal statement fixed up, I sent my letters of recommendation to the LSAC, and got the rest of my documents in order. I had saved about a thousand dollars for the applications, so after checking and rechecking everything at Starbucks, I sent out all my applications, all at once, in one night.

And the waiting began.

Chapter 35

After I finished the applications, Sara, the girl I met at the hotel restaurant, sent me a text. She asked if we could meet, and I happily agreed to meet her at the LSAT Café. We sat in the same seats where Noah and I always sat. Sara was eager to hear about the LSAT.

"Let's talk about some reading comprehension strategies, Sara."

"Great."

"First of all, let me explain what an antithesis passage is, which is the most common type of reading comprehension passage. An antithesis passage is where the passage has two opposing or divergent viewpoints. First, you need a clear understanding of both sides of the argument. Then you must understand what the author's opinion is, which could be siding with one of the sides, or combining the two, or criticizing either or both sides, including the side the author appears to agree with."

"Is there anything that can help me understand where the author is going?"

"There definitely are some keywords, such as 'however,' which indicate a change. My favorite phrase is 'While some legal scholars maintain that ...' which means that the author is about to disagree with those legal scholars. Or, similarly, something along the lines of 'Although many scientists agree that ...' will probably end up as 'modern science suggests otherwise.' See how that works?"

"Yeah, that sounds like a fun way to start a passage."

The waiter brought our coffees.

"Then, of course, some authors are silent about their own opinion and don't offer clues about which side of an argument they might agree with."

Sara started adding sugar to her coffee. I made a mental note to send her my brain health tips.

"You also need to notice the main point of the passage, as that will be tested almost always. If you understand all the details, but not the main point, that doesn't show good comprehension. The main point will be a combination of both viewpoints, and if the author advocates for one side, the main point will include her opinion.

"Another common question is about the 'Primary Purpose' of the passage. If the author has advocated for side A, the primary purpose of the passage will be 'to advocate for side A of the argument.' If the author hasn't taken a side, the primary purpose will be to inform or present the two or three sides of the topic. Which reminds me: there can be two, three or even four sides to an argument in the same reading comprehension passage."

"That makes sense, Alexandra. I'm taking notes on my phone."

"That reminds me of a very smart person I know," I said with a grin.

The waiter brought some warm croissants.

"The last point involves the author's attitude. There are many types of keywords or phrases that help you understand what it is."

"What kind of phrases?" Sara asked.

"I can't give you an exhaustive list because there are so many, but here are a few. 'Scientists have done humanity a great service by discovering the X element.' Doesn't that sound like the author is happy with the discovery? Or 'Historians have misled the world in many circumstances, and haven't improved their accuracy with the report about XYZ.'

"The best way to learn this is to read passages and practice finding the author's attitude. The same goes for the main point, the primary purpose, or anything else."

I took a few sips of coffee and let Sara write her notes. I took the time to mentally express gratitude for my achievements, and thought about how I got to where I am today, and where I started from.

"Wow, this is great stuff, Alexandra. How did you learn so much?"

"I learned this stuff from reading LSAT practice guides and by practicing a lot, and I had a great mentor. Too many people attribute their success or failure to their raw intelligence. The truth is that raw intelligence is just one factor, and not even the most important one.

Hard work, diligence, and putting in the time are what really determine success."

Sara nodded. She was a good listener.

"And that reminds me of another point about reading comprehension. While reading the passage, you might simply scan the words—what's called 'passive reading'—but not really understand what you're reading—not internalizing the material. The flip side of that is 'active reading.' That is where you truly pay attention to what you're reading and re-read something if you give in to passive reading. A great way to notice whether you're reading passively is to summarize as you read. You should **summarize each paragraph after reading it, and then the whole passage**. You also need to make sure you spend enough time on the passage. An extra 30 or 60 seconds on the passage will save you at least double that time answering the questions."

"I hate to take so much of your time," Sara said.

"No worries, I'm glad to help. I do need to leave soon, so let's just talk about one more thing, logical reasoning. First, you need to learn about the different types of logical reasoning questions. There are different ways to group the questions. Use your LSAT study guides to understand all the specific groups or families of questions. Then, after you understand how a certain question type works, practice only those questions. There are many old LSATs available, so you have the luxury of practicing each question type individually, to really understand the question types."

"How many questions of each type should I do?"

"Maybe 50 to 100. A common way of categorizing the questions puts them into 13 different groups, so 50 to 100 of each of the 13 types would be good."

"That makes sense. Should I try any questions before learning the methods?"

"It's much better if you don't. You might start to develop bad habits. The study guides are good at explaining exactly how to attack each type of question."

"I guess that the next step is to mix up the types."

"Exactly. And for that, all you need is some real LSATs. Just take the logical reasoning sections and complete them in 30 minutes each.

Although you have 35 minutes on the actual exam, the best way to train is by completing sections in only 30 minutes, because the stress this creates is similar to the anxiety you'll feel on the real LSAT.

"You should also practice 100 logical reasoning questions in 30 seconds each, in one sitting. That will take 50 minutes. Use a timer, and commit to not going over 30 seconds. You can just circle your answer—you don't have to use the answer sheet. This will speed up your reading and your thinking. Do this exercise five times, a week or so apart. You will probably miss a lot of questions, but it's not about complete accuracy. Like I said, it will speed up your reading and thinking."

"That does sound like an excellent exercise. Thank you so much for your time Alexandra."

"Just pay it forward, and if you'd like you can pay for the coffee too."

Chapter 36

The next morning, I met Noah at the LSAT Café. I was more than ready for the cup of coffee Noah had prepared.

"How many law schools are you applying to, Alexandra?"

"You mean how many did I already apply to? Ten."

"But didn't you finish your personal statement last night?"

"I finished it at about 5:00 p.m., and by 8:00 p.m. I had applied to all ten law schools."

"That must be a record. If you'd asked me, I would have said to apply in the morning, when you're rested and less likely to make mistakes. But I'm sure you did everything correctly."

"I was eager to submit my applications; I'll know for next time."

The waiter brought Noah some eggs and he brought me a menu. I ordered waffles. I got my waffles and ate them thoughtfully, thinking about how my applications were now sitting on the tables at the different law school admissions offices, waiting to be read. They do everything online these days, but the metaphor put my mind at ease.

"Now that it's all over, what do you say about us, Alexandra?"

"What do you mean?"

"Well, until now we always met to discuss LSAT matters or to talk about law schools. Now that you're all set, are we still going to meet as often?"

"Sure, we just have to find something else to talk about. How about I teach you how to cook? First I'd show you the difference between cooking and baking."

"You're right; we can talk about a million different things. It's just weird now that you're done with the LSAT. I know—we can talk about law school."

A Cadre of Experts

"That sounds like fun."

I was surprised that Noah didn't bring up the marriage question. If he wasn't going to, neither was I.

"How long do you think I'll have to wait to hear back from the schools?"

"It depends on a lot of things. Sometimes a school will see somebody they like and get back to them fairly quickly, other times it can take much longer. I know students who got accepted into Yale the day before the first day of class. Be patient and try to focus on other things. Don't go crazy."

"Maybe I'll take up a hobby, like shopping."

"Perfect, if you don't want to have any money left for law school."

"That's true. But don't they give you loans to cover everything?"

"They give you the loans that cover the basics, like rent, food, personal expenses. But they don't give that much for any category, and don't forget that you're paying interest on everything. Try to minimize the amount you need to borrow. As the old adage goes, 'Live like a lawyer in law school, and you'll live like a law student after you graduate.'"

I started to hear back from law schools. It started off badly. I got three rejection letters in a row. Harvard, Yale, and Virginia all told me that I have a lot of potential, and that they were sorry to let me go at the same time. I was waitlisted at Stanford, Chicago, and Duke, but on the same day, I got my first acceptance letter. Boalt sent me an upbeat letter, with a congratulations and everything.

I was about to make the down payment when I remembered what Noah had told me. I had plenty of time to submit the deposit, there was no rush. I still hadn't heard back from three schools.

The next morning I'd already started to have doubts. On one hand, Boalt was where Noah alma mater, but on the other hand, Noah was in New York and I wanted to at least continue dating him during school. Of course, if I didn't get into any school in New York, I'd go to Berkeley.

Then I got an email from Columbia. *I got in.* They were even offering me a small scholarship. I almost fainted. It felt like a dream. Just like after getting my LSAT score, I made a round of phone calls to half the contacts on my phone.

I called everyone I knew, except for Noah. I wanted to tell him in person.

Chelsea was happy, too. She called me when I was at the gym, and told me excitedly that there were letters from NYU and Cornell. I ran home with my gym clothes on, knowing that I'd have to run back afterward to get my stuff from the locker room. They cleared out all the lockers every night, and the ones with locks, they would actually pry open.

I got home and ripped open both letters.

I couldn't believe it—two acceptance letters. Ironically, I actually felt more anxious after getting into four schools than when I hadn't been accepted by any school. Maybe it was because I now had to choose between them, and that sounded dreadful. My mother said we should all have such problems, but when you're in your own little world, these types of problems *seem* big. I was meeting with Noah the next morning, so I decided to bring it up with him.

I met Noah at the LSAT Café. I had printed out the emails from Columbia and Berkeley, and grabbed the letters from NYU and Cornell and brought them with me; it seemed more official on paper. Noah was already there once again, and he could tell that I had some news.

"Good morning, Alexandra. You seem happy. Is it that you're glad to see me?"

"That, too, Noah. But I have something to show you." Still standing, I laid the documents on the table in front of him. About three seconds later, Noah looked up with a huge smile.

"Wow, congrats, Alexandra," Noah said, clapping ever so lightly. "This is amazing. And I'll tell you something. Law schools rarely make mistakes accepting people, (although they do make mistakes rejecting people). If they accept you, that means you're smart enough to succeed. And I'm glad to see that the schools were smart enough to accept you."

I finally sat. I was too excited to eat, so I ordered coffee. Noah had some eggs or something. I was too jumpy to notice. He looked at me and with his know-it-all wit.

"Now you have to make some decisions. That's going to be fun.

A Cadre of Experts

But I might be able to help. I have this friend, Daniel. He's an old war veteran and a lawyer."

Once again, I wasn't sure how this expert had anything to do with choosing law schools, but I'd learned that Noah knew the right people.

"Where does Daniel live?"

"North."

"North, huh? Would that be North Manhattan or like the North Pole?"

"Actually, somewhat in the middle. Daniel is from here, but after retiring from the army, he moved to Ontario, Canada. What are you doing tomorrow afternoon?"

"As of now, I'm going to be busy deciding between schools, but my gut tells me that we'll be on a plane to Ontario."

Noah called Chris and asked him to book two tickets to Canada. My gut was right.

"All set," Noah said. "Daniel is an army veteran. During his service, he was able to complete his Ph.D. in psychology, and he actually wrote his dissertation on decision making. He based it on his military experience, I believe. And after all that he went to law school. He's our guy. He'll be our expert witness."

"Sounds interesting, Noah. I've always had trouble making decisions. I could certainly use some decision-making techniques. What time is the flight?"

"It's 4:00 p.m. Bring a coat. It's cold up there in Canada."

"You like the cold, right?"

"I love cold weather. There's nothing like cold, rainy weather outside with a hot cup of tea indoors. Anyway, I got to run; I'll see you tomorrow. Don't forget your passport."

It was true. I wasn't thinking about my passport. I thought of Canada as part of the U.S. With that, Noah stood, paid the bill, and gave me a kiss on the cheek.

"Where were we with those brain health tips, Alexandra?" Noah asked as we sat down in our first-class seats.

"Number 7, but I've somewhat forgotten about them after I finished the LSAT."

"If you think that the end of the LSAT means you don't have to worry about brain health or your mental performance, you're wrong, to put it bluntly. In fact, it's just starting. Law school will make the LSAT look like a newborn kitten up against a lion that works out regularly. What is number seven?"

I got Noah's point. I took out my iPhone.

Brain Health Tip #7: Learn new skills

"When you acquire new skills, your brain becomes challenged and thus develops. It also boosts your self-confidence, which in turn helps with performance. Also, since the brain is connected in many ways, learning new skills in one area can affect and contribute to other parts of the brain. It can also improve your creativity."

"Wow," Noah said while making a pouting frown. "I should look into that. What new skills would you recommend?"

"It seems that almost any new skill can offer the benefits I mentioned. Learning to type, learning a new language, how to build a phone app or a website, stuff like that. Even learning how things work, like the science behind humor or how certain medications work, will help your brain stay active and alert. For example, I'm going to learn how to make smarter decisions as soon as we land in Ontario."

"I like that tip, by the way. It makes a lot of sense. I'm thinking of making a list of ten things I want to learn by this time next year. What do you think I should learn, Alexandra?"

"I'll Google it. Luckily this plane has Wi-Fi, even though it costs what I pay for Internet service in my house for a month."

The flight attendant arrived with drinks. Noah got water and I got a diet Coke. Meanwhile, my Google search gave me a few ideas.

"How about learning CPR, how to build a fire using a flint, or how to drive a stick shift car?"

"All excellent ideas, Alexandra. Especially the fire building—that'll come in handy for an urban lawyer," Noah deadpanned. "I'll sleep on it, literally, because I'm going to take a nap. I had a late night preparing for court on Friday. I'll see you in a bit."

A Cadre of Experts

Noah drifted off to sleep.

I took out a book to help me think. Holding onto a book makes me think better. Don't know why.

I wondered what Daniel would teach us about decision making. I always had a difficult time with that. NYU was a great law school, but Cornell was upstate in a quiet small town. I adored that environment, and spending time there learning law might be a more pleasurable experience overall. On the other hand, I'd be far from Noah. But maybe I'd be less distracted. And of course Columbia and Berkeley each had their strengths. We'd see what this guy in Ontario had to say, and I'd make my decision there.

Noah woke up about an hour later.

"Are we there yet?" he asked, the same way I used to ask my mother on long car trips when I was a kid.

"Almost," I said.

On our way out from the airport, I got a text from Sara, asking if we could meet again. I told her that I was in Canada, but that we could talk over the phone.

"When it comes to logic games," I told Sara, hoping this call wasn't costing me a fortune, "my advice is similar to what I said about logical reasoning. Learn the methods first, practice game types together, and then mix it up. Practice sections for only 30 minutes rather than 35, and do 12 games in four minutes each once a week.

"One important thing about the games is making sure your setup, or diagramming, is clear and consistent. Also, remember that there can be new rules on the LSAT that you haven't come across, so be ready to come up with simple ways to diagram new rules."

"How can I prepare for that?"

"Well, I can't give you a specific exercise for that because by definition, a new rule is a rule you've never seen. Keep an open mind and be flexible. Many times, your initial thought about something will determine your outcome. If you see a new rule and right away think it's a disaster, you'll struggle with it. If your first thought is '*I'll just figure it out*' you're more likely to."

"Wow, Alexandra. You're really smart."

I was beginning to hear that more often. I guessed I should get used to it.

"Thanks, Sara. For saying so, let me give you a wonderful technique I learned from this guy named Graham, who's the Oakland A's coach. The technique is to make the practice harder than the real thing. With games, you can make the practice harder by practicing games without diagramming anything. You can do this using the full eight minutes and 45 seconds, but you can only use your head. That technique helped me a lot."

"How many times did you do this?"

"About twice a week. It can be tough. It's like lifting weights with your brain."

"This is great stuff," Sara said, as she wrote notes into her phone. "Enjoy your time in Canada."

"I will," I replied, not knowing that that would turn out to be quite the understatement.

Daniel was about 5'10" with brown hair, a scruffy beard, and a huge smile.

"Wow, I'm thrilled to see you Noah," Daniel said as we walked into his house, his eyebrows raised. "How have you been?"

"Pretty good. How about you, Daniel?"

"The air is fresh, the people are friendly, and it's quiet at night, so you could say that I'm miserable. You know me, I'm used to smoke and smog, rude people and noisy streets, but hopefully I'll get used to it here before I die. If I live that long."

"Daniel, this is my girlfriend, Alexandra. She's going to law school next year."

"That's why we came to you, Daniel," I said. "Noah tells me you're an expert decision-maker."

"I'll decide that," Daniel said, cleverly. "Exactly what decision do you need to make?"

"I got into a few law schools, and I need to decide which one to go to."

"It doesn't matter."

"What do you mean?"

"Law schools, they're all the same. I've known lawyers from so many different schools. They were all great lawyers. Lawyers tell me that once you get a job, nobody cares which law school you went to. Do you agree Noah?"

"I have to say I do. I've lost cases to lawyers who went to fourth tier law schools. But what Alexandra needs to decide is which law school to attend, based on the locations, and scholarship money, not by the golden-calf rankings, heaven forbid. So there is still need to make a decision."

"Either way, you're going to law school. It's not like you have to decide which side of a war you'll be on."

"Yeah, but I still want to learn how to make the decision—especially if I can use your techniques in future decisions."

"Of course. And sure, you can use my process in any situation. But first, understand that your subconscious already has all the answers you need. You just need to figure out a way to surface them to your conscious. How was the ride here from the airport, by the way?"

"I watched the scenery, the people, you know. It basically looks like the U.S., but different enough to know I'm not in New York."

"What else did you notice?"

"I saw this fabulous piano store as we were stopped at a red light. They just had the most beautiful display of pianos."

"Interesting, because I live here, but have no idea what piano store you're talking about."

"I think I saw it too Daniel," Noah said.

"Oh I believe you, and that's exactly my point. You see when you're in a new place, your senses are heightened. You notice things that people who live there their whole lives wouldn't see on a daily basis. It's a survival technique. You're familiar with the local saber tooth tigers, but when you venture to another place you don't know what to expect, so you're on high alert.

"Now that you know that, you can **channel your high alertness towards creativity or decision-making**. That's the first step. Even walking a few blocks away to somewhere you aren't really familiar with will do the trick. Find a café you've never visited and sit down with a notebook and pen. Draw two columns, one side for pros, and the other for cons. Write down as many pros and cons, however minute, for the decision you want to make."

Daniel stood and went to the kitchen to bring some cookies his wife had made. She was out of town for the week at a podiatrists' convention in Orlando. He came back with the cookies and cups of milk.

"Here's the trick. You have to place a time limit on your decision-making. Once you've written down your pros and cons, set a timer for no more than two minutes. Scan the advantages and disadvantages of each side and let them all sink in. Your subconscious will make up its mind and let you know its decision. Or, *your* decision."

"Is that all there is to it?" Noah asked.

"Pretty much," Daniel answered.

"I was expecting something a bit more complex, to tell you the truth," Noah said. "But if it works, it works."

"Simplicity," Daniel said, "is the ultimate sophistication. Do you know who said that?"

"Leonardo Di Vinci," I answered.

"Alexandra gets ten points for that," Daniel said. "And it's true. The most sophisticated ideas are usually the simplest. It is actually quite profound, the whole idea that the subconscious mind knows how to arrange everything together and deliver a well thought-out answer. Our side of the process doesn't have to be complicated.

"In fact, if you take longer than two minutes, you're actually doing yourself a disfavor. Your subconscious has already come up with the answer. Waiting longer will just cloud your judgment."

"You know," Noah said as he finished one of the cookies Daniel had brought out, "looking back at the some of the important decisions I've made in my life, I did reach my conclusions within a few minutes of deciding that I needed to make a decision, and they were good decisions."

"It's something we do intuitively," Daniel said. "Our conscious mind sometimes gets in the way. But it should be easier now that you have a process. Can I offer you guys anything else? Or would you like to check out the neighborhood?"

"That sounds like fun," I said, "In fact, you could drop me off in the

A Cadre of Experts

middle of nowhere, and I'll make my decision using your process. Why wait longer? Four schools have accepted me; I might as well make my decision today. What do you think?"

"Sure," Daniel said. "Go for it."

Noah sat quietly. "I thought you might wait a bit longer, but you're probably right. Do you have a notebook?"

"I have a few on my desk, Alexandra," Daniel offered. "If you go to my desk, look in the bottom drawer."

We got into Daniel's SUV and drove into the city. On the way there, Daniel pointed out landmarks, and I noticed that indeed my senses were heightened. I tried not to think about the pros and cons of each school on the way there, to keep the process as simple as possible.

About twenty minutes later we drove up to a café, right near Niagara Falls. They dropped me off, and Noah told me to call him as soon as I was ready. They wouldn't be far away.

Sara called me again. This time, she wanted to ask me briefly about law school rankings. Oy. I actually had put a lot of thought into it. Sure, my LSAT scores got me into Columbia and Boalt, but most students don't end up going to top ten schools, I mean it's math. As Professor Levine had said, the whole idea of rankings jeopardizes student's mental health, besides the fact that it's just not important. And if not by chance, Daniel had just confirmed. So, I gave it to Sara straight:

"While I know that many students may think otherwise, I am highly skeptical about the entire enterprise of law school rankings. A single number cannot represent everything a law school is. Does it capture the extraordinary quality and commitment of students, illustrated not just by their work in the classroom but by their pro bono work, moot court and trial team, and editorial work on law journals? Does it capture faculty members' commitment to teaching and mentoring, or their scholarship, published in top law journals and university presses all over the country? And does it even come close to recognizing the school's alumni who are leaders of the bench and bar? No one number could capture all that a law school is."

Jacob Erez

I ordered a cappuccino and a cornbread muffin. I sat with my notebook and pens at a table in the corner of the entrance, facing out. I drank some of the coffee and watched the people passing. I could see and even hear the falls. I tried to notice details, making my mind relatively alert and proceeded to write down all the pros and cons of each of my four schools. Some items were both pros and cons. I had more scholarship money from Cornell, but I had some family in the Bay Area. Columbia has some famous professors, but NYU's campus was more appealing. Noah was a Berkeley alum, and I knew one of the professors there, Professor Levine. Cornell was a quiet, scenic town, but hard to get to. NYU offered me a generous scholarship and an easy way to maintain it.

It took me half an hour to get everything on paper. I kept adding more pros and cons to each of my options to delay setting the timer. I remembered what Daniel had told me about how **I was incredibly lucky to have this type of decision to make,** something Leah told me as well, as we were spinning around in the restaurant. I wasn't choosing between four different ways to die or be tortured, but between four amazing places to learn the law.

I finally got everything on paper. I set my iPhone timer for two minutes and began scanning everything I'd written. The timer beeped, and I knew I had to make my decision.

Columbia. I'm going to Columbia Law School!

Chapter 37

I called Noah and let him know the wonderful news. I'd made my decision. I sent emails to all four law schools. I happily accepted Columbia's offer, and politely declined the other three.

Noah and Daniel came to pick me up. Noah looked cool driving in the sleek SUV. I'd never seen him drive in anything but his limo. Not that he actually *drove* his limo.

Noah got out and gave me a bear hug. "I'm so proud of you, Alexandra. You're a totally amazing person, and I love you."

"I love you too, Noah."

Looking around at the majesty of nature, my mind filled with wonder. As each tiny molecule and atom that comprises the infinite, unfathomable pool of molecules and atoms slowly sifts through the watery abyss of time. Here is an endless expanse—a universe in its own right. What is now cool water was once fire and magma—and yet, billions of miles away, and towards other stars, this colossal feat of nature is all but a tiny spec—hardly noticeable amongst the cosmos. Ah, but the beauty of it all, and the endless cycles of water, just like life.

Then, standing beside Niagara Falls, amid the chatter of the tourists and the roar of the water, Noah got down on his knees. He pulled out something small from his blazer pocket, and opened it up, revealing the most gorgeous ring I had ever seen. All around us, people watched, smiled, pointed, and posted on Facebook. I realized I was wearing the same toasty coat that I was wearing the first time I met Noah, on that fateful, rainy Tuesday morning.

"Alexandra," Noah said with a sniffle, "*will you marry me?*"

My eyes watered up. "Noah, you're the nicest person I've ever met. You're handsome, kind, smart and educated, but you're also arrogant and messy. You helped me through the hardest time of my life, mentored me and taught me so much. I'm only where I am today, a soon to be law student who is happy and content, because of you. It would be comfortable to have a home of my own during law school, but it would also be stressful being married as a first-year law student. I've been thinking about it since you proposed last time. So, after much thought, my answer is yes!"

THE END

Appendix

How to Choose a Law School

Choosing a law school can be a daunting task. There are many variables, some I will point out here. Because of the first impression of the complexity of choosing a law school, the "ease" that the US News Rankings gives students is easy to fall for. Rather than figuring out the whole thing myself, one might think, let me consult the magazine. Don't. Doing your own research will yield much more benefit. You are the only one who can take into account your personal situation. What I've listed here is hardly an exhaustive list, but it is a good place to start.

So, how does one choose a law school? It really depends on #1, where the person wants to live, and #2, where they hope to practice, and, how certain they are about #1 and #2.

You also need to evaluate the real price of the education, including tuition, the cost of living, and wages for new lawyers in the school's range.

So, for example, BC (Boston College) is a law school that tends to place people very well in the Boston area, but not in other areas. But it's expensive. So someone who goes to BC but then moves to, say, Texas, may find that BC does not open as many doors as a UT degree might; the inverse is true too; some regional state schools are affordable because they are still heavily subsidized by the state and they tend to have a strong regional alumni network.

As you can see, the factors need to be weighed and evaluated. No ranking system can do that. As the protagonist of this book pointed out, Cornell may have been a good decision because of the area's tranquility. This might be a reason for someone else not to go there. She also took into consideration the fact that she has family in the Bay Area when considering Boalt. This too might be a reason for someone not to go to a particular law school.

The old saying was "Harvard teaches lawyers, Yale teaches judges." Whether that is accurate I don't know, but that brings us to two more factors to include in your analysis: #3, what kind of law does the student want to practice, and #4, which schools are the best for that specialty.

For example, Boalt and Hastings are both University of California law schools in the Bay Area. Boalt is well known for job placement in large firms and Hastings is well known for litigation.

Other factors to consider:

Accessibility of professors

Competition among students

Practical skills and opportunities (such as clinics, externships, etc.)

A strong legal writing and research program

A hard working career services

Do some more research

It's true that Alexandra doesn't follow this deep analysis, and for two reasons. One, her personal situation wouldn't match anybody else's and thus not helpful to the reader, and two, I wanted her (and you!) to learn about that amazing technique for decision making when the factors aren't so apparent, or if they're equal.

Good luck on your law school journey!

Thank you for reading "A Cadre of Experts." I hope you enjoyed this book and took away some of the lessons and mindsets that will help you succeed on the LSAT and in life. I would love to hear from you! If you have any feedback or would just like to say hello, you can contact me directly at my website:

www.cadreofexperts.com

Good luck on the LSAT and in law school!

Always,
Jacob Erez

Made in the USA
Charleston, SC
04 June 2016